Aboriginal Frontiers and Boundaries in Australia

Aboriginal Frontiers and Boundaries in Australia

S. L. Davis and J. R. V. Prescott

MELBOURNE UNIVERSITY PRESS
1992

First published 1992

Designed by Lauren Statham
Printed in Malaysia by
SRM Production Services Shd Bhd for
Melbourne University Press, Carlton, Victoria 3053
U.S.A. and Canada: International Specialized Book Services, Inc.,
5602 N.E. Hassalo Street, Portland, Oregon 97213-3640
United Kingdom and Europe: University College London Press,
Gower Street, London WC1E 6BT, UK

This book is copyright. Apart from any fair dealing for the purposes of private study, research, criticism or review, as permitted under the Copyright Act, no part may be reproduced by any process without written permission. Enquiries should be made to the publisher

© Stephen L. Davis and John Robert Victor Prescott 1992

National Library of Australia Cataloguing-in-Publication data

Davis, Stephen, 1951– .
  Aboriginal frontiers and boundaries in Australia.
  Bibliography.
  Includes index.
  ISBN 0 522 84483 9.
  [1.] Aborigines, Australian—Land tenure. 2. Australia—Boundaries. 3. Australia—History—To 1788. I. Prescott, J. R. V. (John Robert Victor), 1931– . II. Title.

333.2

This book is dedicated to all those senior custodians who have maintained in their oral traditions the territorial knowledge of their people.

Contents

Preface   xi
Acknowledgements   xiii

1 Territorial Limits of Aboriginal Peoples   1

Limits of Aboriginal Territories in Other Continents   3
Cartographic Evidence for the Existence of Aboriginal Boundaries   16
Study of Boundaries in Political Geography   20
Research Methods   25
Plan of the Book   26

2 Tropical Coast   28

Environment   30
Seasonal Use of Resources   33
The People   35
Non Aboriginal Contact   37
Clan Territories   38
Evolution of Boundaries   44
Boundary Definition of Territories   45
Changes in Boundary Location   50
Succession to Territory   51
Rights of Access and Permission   53
Conclusion   58

3 Southwest Arnhem Land   60

    Environment   61
    Exploration and Non-Aboriginal Settlement   64
    Claims and Elaboration   70
    Boundaries in the Modern Period   78
    Conclusion   79

4 Central Australia   83

    Environment   84
    Exploration and Pastoral Settlement   86
    Effects Upon Territoriality   94
    Movement North of the Amadeus Frontier   95
    Boundaries of the Watarrka Sub-Territory   99
    Traditional Proofs of Territorial Rights   102
    The Luritja Frontier   109
    Conclusion   113

5 Torres Strait   114

    Environment   114
    European Contact and Exploration   115
    Maluigal Territory   119
    Clan Boundaries   124
    Territorial Rights   127
    Conclusion   129

6 Conclusions   131

    Traditional Aboriginal Boundaries   131
    Administrative Aboriginal Boundaries   135
    Aboriginal Boundaries in the 1990s   142

Glossary of Aboriginal Words   148
References   149
Index   159

Illustrations

Maps

1 The Territory of the Seri Indians   8
2 Named Localities on Balmawuy Sub-Territory   44
3 Boundary between Gamalangga and Balmawuy Territories   47
4 Area Held in Common by Munupula and Wilrangkuwila Clans   56
5 Aboriginal and Pastoral Interest in the Katherine and South Alligator River Area   62–3
6 Mineral Activity in the Alligator Rivers–Pine Creek Area   66–7
7 Land Claims in the Katherine and South Alligator River Area   74–5
8 Aboriginal Groups in the South Alligator River Area   80–1
9 The Lake Amadeus, Luritja Land Claim Area   85
10 Major Pastoral Stations and Settlements, Northern Territory, 1870–1896   88
11 Kuningga Native Cat Track   95
12 Watarrka Sub-Territory, Lake Amadeus, Luritja Land Claim   101
13 Lake Amadeus Land Claim Boundaries and Frontier   110
14 Torres Strait   116
15 Territories and Localities on Mabuiag Island   118
16 Territories and Localities in Western Torres Strait   120–1
17 Boundaries of Regions and Zones Created by the *Aboriginal and Torres Strait Islander Commission Act* 1989   137

Figures

1 Seasonal Change and Resource Availability in Yolngu Territory   34

Tables

1 Aboriginal Land by Area in mid-1987   141

Preface

This book has been written to make two contributions. The first is to political geography. In the 95 years since Ratzel's seminal *Politische Geografie* [Political Geography] was published the main contributions to the systematic study of political boundaries have been by geographers. This claim does not deny the brilliance of some lawyers such as Lapradelle or historians such as Lamb in their respective studies of boundaries and the law and the McMahon Line between China and India. But no other discipline has matched the comprehensive study of political boundaries provided by geography.

In Australia geographers, with occasional assistance from others, have extensively studied and written about the boundaries of States and Territories, local government authorities, electorates, maritime zones and claims to Antarctica. Boundaries related to the political organisation of Aborigines in contrast have attracted little attention from geographers or anthropologists. We hope that this book will remedy this neglect and round out the study of Australia's boundaries by looking at the continent's oldest political units.

Aboriginal boundaries are not only Australia's oldest political limits; they also bid fair to become very controversial during the next decade. This decade has been designated a period of Aboriginal reconciliation by bipartisan agreement of the federal parliament. We believe that this process will result in increased demands for rights related to land by Aboriginal communities throughout Australia and expect that some of those demands will be treated sympathetically.

It is our hope that the dispassionate analysis in this book will contribute to the decade of reconciliation. That hope will be achieved if we can show that traditional Aboriginal boundaries were precisely defined in most of Australia, except in some remote, harsh deserts where frontiers existed, and that knowledge about those precise definitions still exists in some communities. Unfortunately every year the knowledge about the boundaries of some groups literally dies out.

The corollary of this statement is that over most of Australia, especially south of the Tropic of Capricorn, much of the precise knowledge about boundaries has been lost forever. It seems to us that where the knowledge is intact land claims should be decided on the basis of that knowledge when the proofs are provided. Where the knowledge about the precise extent of traditional territories has been lost mechanisms must be devised to make land grants or compensation without the charade of re-inventing knowledge or elaborating traditions that are imperfectly known or found in the records of anthropologists who did their work decades ago.

Acknowledgements

We are most pleased to acknowledge the efforts of the many people who have assisted in this work. In particular we wish to mention Nahassan Ungkwanaka (deceased, Matutjara tribe), Helmut Parerultja (deceased, Western Arranda), Eric Panangka (Anmatjerre), Felix Holmes (Limilngan), Raphael Apuatimi (deceased, Tiwi), Old Elsey (deceased, Yangman), Buthugurrulil (deceased, Gamalangga), Liyadarri (Gupapuyngu), Niburrurru (deceased, Mudburra), Mamakun (Birrkili), Makani (deceased, Mildjingi), Cliff McCormack (deceased, Tiwi), Yithirri (Gupapuyngu), Danyala (Liyagawumirr), John Baptist (Tiwi), Mick Wagu (Ngalia), Gideon Jack (Pintubi), Demaga Warria (Maluigal), Kami Pai Pai (Maluigal), Gib Gaulai (Maluigal), Sandy Barraway (Jawoyn), Andy Andrews (Jawoyn), Peter Jatpula (Jawoyn) and Nipper Brown (Jawoyn). Gary Stoll (Fink River Mission) has one of the most profound outsider's understandings of Aboriginal culture in Central Australia and gave freely of his knowledge. Michael Maurice, Q.C. whilst Aboriginal Land Commissioner afforded us access to much of the archives of the Northern Territory land rights cases. The manuscript has been typed and refined through the very efficient word processing of Catherine Haensel whilst Eric Ireland has skilfully interpreted our every requirement in constructing the maps.

Finally, funding for a significant part of the research on which this book is based was generously provided by the Australian Mining Industry Council without whose assistance this information may not have reached the public domain.

1

Territorial Limits of Aboriginal Peoples

With the exception of a motion passed by the national convention of the Young Liberals in early 1991 political parties in Australia generally see merit in the concept of land rights for Aborigines. The Young Liberals were persuaded that Aborigines in 1788 had no concept of private ownership, did not attempt to convert the land into private property through development, exploitation or settlement and so no property was taken from them or their descendants. This view was rejected by the parliamentary Liberal Party.

The widespread acceptance of the concept of land rights for Aborigines has not produced uniform legislation to provide for such rights throughout Australia, but it is based on the judgement that throughout history Aborigines have had a special relationship with the land. That relationship is based on two prime strands. The material relationship involved using the food resources of the land in a life-style based on hunting and gathering. These activities were carried out most successfully when the Aborigines developed a detailed knowledge of the location of food supplies and the seasons when those supplies were in their best condition (Davis 1989).

The spiritual relationship centred on the belief that ancestral beings created the form of the land and the people. The spatial coincidence of these activities established the identity of clans and the limits of their territories. Evidence of the unity of the group and their affiliation and responsibilities for that territory is found in ritual emblems and paraphernalia made, carved and painted by traditional elders. The unity and traditional knowledge is preserved and passed on to initiates by the performance of ceremonies.

During the creative epoch the ancestral being travelled over the territory and performed all the activities which Aborigines performed on a daily basis for the continuance of life. He hunted, built shelters, sang songs and slept and so the territory is composed of hunting and gathering areas, camp sites, ceremonial sites and sites where resources are available for making spears or obtaining pigments for body and bark paintings. Each site where the ancestral being performed some activity was then named and the sum of all named localities constitutes a description of the entire territory. The place names are usually recited or sung in the order they were visited, and the language in which they are publicly uttered confirms the identity of the group that holds primary rights in the territory. Around the coast of northern Australia these discrete territories extended into and included coastal waters. Reefs, rocks, sand-banks, channels and tidal races were often named localities and some were of special cultural significance.

The general acceptance of the appropriateness of land claims by Aborigines has not been matched by acknowledgment that their traditional territories used to be marked by precise boundaries in most cases and by frontiers in the others. Although the terms 'boundary' and 'frontier' are used as synonyms by journalists and some academics, they refer to separate features and that distinction is preserved in this analysis. A boundary is a line and a frontier is a zone.

The reluctance or refusal of some to endorse the precise definition of traditional territories of Aborigines can be illustrated by three examples. First, neither the Northern Land Council nor the Central Land Council has ever produced a map showing the extent of Aboriginal territories in the Northern Territory. These Councils would appear to have the resources, contacts and influence to have established the extent of traditional territories in the regions for which they are responsible. It is possible that such maps have not been produced because it is deemed more sensible to negotiate claims without any self-imposed limits.

Second, in November 1988 Aborigines on Groote Eylandt and Bickerton Island in the Gulf of Carpentaria and on the adjoining mainland in the vicinity of the Roper River asked the Federal Minister for Aboriginal Affairs to create a separate Land Council for them. The Minister then was Mr Gerry Hand and he agreed that he would set in train procedures to establish that a substantial majority of adult Aborigines favoured this change. The first step was to establish the exact boundaries within which any referendum would be held. According to press reports it was thought that it would take an anthropologist three months to make this determination. Sources close to the secessionist group were quoted as saying, 'just another bloody delaying tactic'.

The reasons for such an allegation can be understood. The Northern Land Council should have known where the limits of the disaffected clans were located. But even if, for strategic reasons, the Northern Land Council had avoided identification of specific boundaries the groups seeking the new Land Council might have expected the Department of Aboriginal Affairs to know where the proper limits were. Minister Hand, when outlining the proposed structure of the Aboriginal and Torres Strait Islander Commission in April 1988, noted that the limits of the electoral regions reflected historical, cultural, linguistic and other important factors. In short, these were limits of which the Aborigines approved and they were determined over a period of two years.

Third, the unwillingness of some to accept the concept of precise definition of traditional territories was revealed in the final report on the Kakadu Conservation Zone by the Resource Assessment Commission. In one section dealing with Jawoyn territoriality it is noted that the Commission's anthropological consultants disagree with Davis and claim no clan can be identified exclusively with any tract of land (Resource Assessment Commission 1991, vol. 2, p. 296). This view persuaded the Inquiry that Davis's boundary maps provided only very general indications of the location of Aboriginal groups (Resource Assessment Commission 1991, vol. 2, p. 297). Similar views have sometimes been expressed by lawyers involved in land rights cases.

It is curious that people who are convinced that Aborigines in Australia, before and after 1788, had a very special relationship with the land, also believe Aborigines didn't know the exact limits of the territory in which they had primary rights. It seems strange that people who knew in great detail where food could be found and when those foods were in the best possible condition and who could survive in apparently hostile environments, were unaware of where their territorial rights ended and those of an adjacent clan started. It is odd that the concept of boundaries of traditional territories should be rejected when there are plenty of examples of such boundaries in aboriginal societies in North and South America and Africa.

Limits of Aboriginal Territories in Other Continents

Forde (1952, p. 371) has noted that the hunters and gatherers are the cultural ancestors of all mankind. The cultivators and pastoralists were successors and in Australia they came from Europe. This discussion focuses on aboriginal hunting and gathering communities in other continents so that the comparison with traditional lifestyles of Aborigines in Australia is direct. Forde (p. 373) again sets the theme for this discussion of limits of aboriginal territories:

> The food gatherers are not homeless wanderers. Even among the least organised and the poorest in equipment the unit groups of families each occupy an inherited and adequately delimited territory.

He goes on to note that the boundaries of their territories would probably change in some way over the course of a number of generations, but asserts that at any one time the lands of adjacent groups are in relative equilibrium. That would certainly fit in with the observed changes in the limits of traditional territories in Australia in accordance with known processes of succession. The following examples will demonstrate that in other continents aboriginal food gatherers lived within defined territories just as they once did throughout Australia.

In eleven months of fieldwork Isabel Kelly mapped the distribution of the Southern Paiute and Chemehuevi as it existed in the 1850s. These groups lived in the Great Basin that lies in the dry lee of the Sierra Nevada in the west of the United States between the Colorado and Columbia rivers and near the junction of Arizona, Nevada and Utah. This is an arid area consisting of plains bearing hardy grasses and sage brush with intervening scattered plateaus where pines and junipers might be found. The highest plateaus rising to 2150 metres support dense coniferous forests.

Before this region was overrun by the American settlement frontier, the main food supplies were small mammals, insects (especially locusts), grass seeds, berries, wild onions and the bulbs of tiger lily and spike rush. In favoured locations the groups diverted streams during the Spring, when they were flowing, to encourage the growth of these wild plants. However, no tilling of the soil was involved in this activity.

Kelly (1934) identified fifteen 'bands' as the sub-groups of tribes were called. The fieldwork was done by questioning the descendants of the bands and recording the extent of territories on the largest scale topographic maps available. In some cases such maps were not available and the boundaries are marked as 'Probable Band Boundary' on the published map that has a scale of 1:2.5 million. Kelly was also careful to seek definition of each boundary from both sides and she is able to make the following statement (p. 556):

> In the majority of cases boundary evidence from adjacent bands is well in agreement; and the precision with which informants are able to delimit their territory certainly does much to dispel the long-standing impression of weak localisation which attaches to Great Basin tribes.

Most of the boundaries coincided with topographic features as the following selection of examples shows (pp. 551–2):

> ... the lateral boundaries followed the crests of the bordering plateaus. The western boundary is definitive: Whitmore wash [dry stream bed] and the prominent scarp of Hurricane cliffs. The northern and southern limits of the St George group were respectively the Vermilion cliffs and the scarp of Shivwits Plateau.

There were two occasions when Kelly failed to secure the information needed. In the first there were no informants and the second concerned the great Escalante Desert which was unoccupied but might have been claimed. In the first case Kelly identified the location of this deceased territory by defining the limits of adjacent bands. Only once was Kelly fairly sure that she had been provided with wrong information. It concerned the crest of the Colorado–Great Basin divide which was not claimed by the flanking bands even though the well-marked crest might have seemed an obvious limit. Apparently this area was associated with the Mountain Meadow massacre of 1857 and 75 years later Indians were still reluctant to assume responsibility for the area.

In the area of northern New England there used to live hunting and gathering peoples generally called the Algonquian. One of the subdivisions of the Algonquian was called the Wabanaki and this group was studied by Snow (1968). He was making a contribution to a debate that had raged or spluttered along for about forty years. At issue was whether the Algonquian hunting ground system was aboriginal or a product of the development of the fur trade. Cooper (1939) had written the most detailed defence of the concept that the precise definition of hunting grounds for families could be traced to the aboriginal period. Jenness (1935) was one of the strongest proponents that the practice of dividing up group territories into precise family areas for hunting was only two or three hundred years old, dating from the advent of the fur trade. Snow makes a good case that the division of group territory existed amongst the aboriginal Wabanaki and then makes this important point (p. 1149):

> The advent of fur trading allowed the Penobscot and other Wabanaki groups to formalise their methods of exploiting the environment by way of the institution of family territories in tributary drainage basins. This, however, need not have involved a drastic change in the previous pattern ... A shift to a slightly more formalised system might not have been even perceptible to an observer, had one been present.

The Wabanaki calendar was divided into two main seasons. In winter the groups hunted beaver and other mammals throughout the headwaters of their territory. They operated in small bands during this season. In the summer they moved down to the mouths of the rivers or to the coast and fished and collected shellfish. The enormous middens that still survive in considerable numbers testify to this prehistoric pattern. The main effect of the fur trade on this pattern was to allow the establishment of large, permanent settlement on the rivers, some distance from the mouth or the coast.

It is Snow's belief that the boundaries of the Wabanaki territories were not as precisely defined as those of the northern Algonquian. He attributes this to the fact that the Wabanaki occupied an entirely riverine habitat based on clear defined valleys and drainage systems. The northern Algonquian occupied zones where the drainage pattern was more confused and there were many more lakes. The territories of these bands were not restricted to a single catchment but sometimes included sections of a number of adjacent catchments. In such cases it was necessary to mark the boundaries more precisely by rivers, ridges, lakes and clumps of cedars or pines (Speck 1915, p. 4). Snow refers to such limits as terrestrial rather than riverine. Although Snow notes that the Wabanaki sometimes blazed trees to mark their bounds near watersheds, they were largely unworried if those lines were crossed by neighbours. What was important was that the neighbour should not approach the rivers and streams without permission. If you held the waterways securely that was all that mattered for these hunters of beaver. Snow emphasises that archaeological investigation of aboriginal sites in the area occupied by the Wabanaki shows that, before the fur trade started, the beaver and other sedentary fauna formed an important resource for food, clothing and implements made from bones.

Turning now to the people inhabiting arctic North America, variously called Eskimo, Aleut and Inuit, there are different views about the presence or absence of boundaries in the aboriginal period. Parker (1989, p. 19) asserts that in Alaska these people did not claim defined territories. Ray (1967) appears to take a different view and holds that there were some exclusive hunting and fishing grounds. Steenhoven (1962, p. 57) reports Inuits as denying claims to exclusive hunting and fishing territories. Lester (1981) in weighing the evidence on this question gives prominence to the work of Correll (1976).

Correll was concerned with language and location in traditional Inuit societies and discovered that the whole of the territory used by any group was named, as were features in its landscape. Correll wrote about the Paatlirmiut in terms evocative of the practices of traditional Australian Aborigines (p. 174):

1 Territorial Limits of Aboriginal Peoples

... [The Paatlirmiut] consider themselves to have unique rights to a certain territory. This is also true of other Caribou Eskimo demes. The locales can be identified and located on the basis of the use of place names by members and non-members. Fundamental criteria for the alignment of deme with physical space can be discovered in the use of such names.

The limits of claimed territory can be identified by the way in which any individual speaks the place names. Those of the individual's territory will be spoken directly in the individual's own dialect. When pronouncing the names of locales beyond the individual's territory, speech will be indirect and the dialect will be that of the area in which the places are located.

Parker (1989, pp. 17–18) refers to about 500 small tribes occupying California in aboriginal times. These small groups occupied distinct territories and their limits were recognised by neighbours. The boundaries were guarded against trespass, but permission was readily granted to visitors to gather food when there was a clear need. In some cases individual families within some small tribes, such as the Shasta, the Northern Yanas and Coast Miwok, had exclusive use of oak groves, fishing areas and clam beds.

McGee (1898) has provided a detailed account of the Seri Indians whose aboriginal habitat on the eastern coast of the Golfo de California was defined by natural limits. This very fierce group centred their organisation on the island called Tiburon. It has an area of 1300 square kilometres and has two ranges up to 1220 metres in height trending north–south. The group also controlled an area of the adjacent mainland amounting to 3900 square kilometres. This mainland section McGee (p. 42) describes as 'at once a dependency, an alternative refuge and a circumvallation'. The eastern limit of this dependency was a frontier set in the Desierto Encinas which in aboriginal times was practically impassable (Map 1).

The island and mainland are separated by the strait called Estrecho Infiernillo and a southern bay called Bahia Kunkaak. These waters also have an area of about 3900 square kilometres, mainly in the bay. In one sense the strait might be considered as a second line of defence to supplement the desert but in a more important sense it was at the core of the Seri's territory.

McGee (1898, p. 45) puts it nicely when he states that the 'seas washing Seriland are notably troubled by tides and winds'. The shape of the Golfo de California produces tides of 7.6 metres at its head. This rising tide, as it surges through Bahia Kunkaak and through the narrow gap east

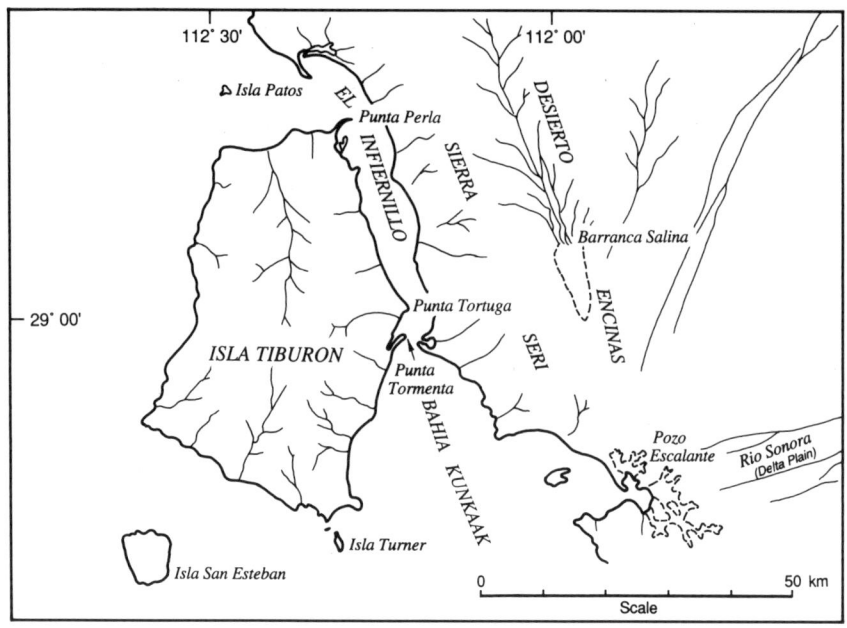

Map 1   The Territory of the Seri Indians

of Punta Tormenta, becomes a tidal race. Before this race reached the northern exit near Punta Perla the main rising tide passing west of Tiburon is entering the strait from the north. McGee calculates that the waters in the strait are doubled every neap tide and tripled every spring tide twice every 24 hours. Thus this well-named strait is a raceway for nearly continuous tidal rips.

These amazing tidal floods have created wave-built gravel projections along the coast of Tiburon such as Punta Tormenta, Punta Tortuga and Punta Perla. These are the preferred settlement sites, and the crude shelters of the Seri were constructed at the landward edge of these points. Seafood was unlimited for the fish and green turtle were abundant and near at hand. Turtle shells were used to reinforce brush walls of the shelters. In the sheltered area in the lee of the point, boats could be launched safely and on the associated lagoons waterfowl were plentiful and the lagoons were bordered by bushes that provided cover for hunters. Water was scarce throughout Seri territory and settlements were not built at the few permanent waterholes but at some distance from them, perhaps to discourage wasteful use or to conceal them from invaders.

Although the *Sailing Directions* for these waters announce that they are unsafe for the smallest vessels the Seri were masters of the seas in craft called balsa. These vessels were 9 metres long, 1.1 metre wide and had a freeboard of less than 0.5 metre. They were made of three bundles of canes lashed together and the Seri sailed them confidently in the strait and bay. As McGee explains, the Seri were canny navigators who hugged the shore in bad weather and were prepared to wait for hours or days until they had the right combination of tide and wind for the passage.

The Seri edge of the frontier in the desert was marked by two outposts called Pozo Escalante in the south and Barranca Salina in the centre. From these points tracks ran westwards into Seri country and not eastwards into the frontier. There are a few small islands around Tiburon and these were visited to capture ducks or secure mineral pigments used in painting faces for ceremonies.

A Seri presence survived with complete independence from 1539, when Ulloa, one of Cortes's captains found the island, until 1700, when the first Spanish invasion of the country was launched, and then with a declining measure of autonomy until 1844 when the last major Seri forces were defeated. So the Seri provide an example of territory lying within physical limits. The desert to the east and the sea to the west. The territory was unattractive to settlement by groups with more developed systems because of the shortage of water and the dangerous nature of the waters between the island and the mainland. The early attraction of this area for the Spaniards was the opportunity to save the souls of the Seri through the activities of Jesuit missionaries. Later there was the commercial interest in pearls and the need to end the raids into settled areas by fierce warriors.

At the southern tip of South America there were other groups with maritime skills. The Yaghan occupy part of the archipelago formed by the drowned southern tip of the Andes Range. The Yaghan belonged to the Feugian peoples. Cooper (1963) records that members of one of the five divisions of Yaghan were chary of trespassing into a neighbouring district unless there was a serious shortage of food or a whale had stranded itself. Each group had its defined territory but the definition was clearest at the coast for that was where the Yaghan found their food and other resources. So Cooper could note that the Ushuaia occupied 20 miles (32 kilometres) of coast on the Beagle Channel. Lowie (1963, p. 351) observed that because the Yaghan spent most of their time near or on the sea they were less vigilant in protecting their landward boundaries than some aboriginal groups. In contrast the Ona, who occupied the main island Tierra del Fuego, had few marine skills. Their fishing consisted of spearing and netting fish in the shallows. According to Lowie they guarded jealously separate well-defined territories held by mythological sanctions. Each territory was bounded by topographical boundaries and exploitative trespass on another's territory was one of three main causes of feuds or war. The other causes were murder and witchcraft (Cooper 1963a).

Lowie has summarised information about territoriality and the use of defined areas contained in the detailed studies in *The Handbook of South American Indians* (1963) edited by Steward. Proceeding northwards from the land of the Ona, the Tehuelche occupied the semi-arid areas of Patagonia. This group lived mainly by hunting guanaco and ostrich and gathering wild parsnips, spinach and grass seeds. They had clearly defined territories and regarded trespass as a fighting matter (Lowie 1963, p. 352). The Botocudo lived in the dry tropical forest north of Rio de Janeiro and were mainly gatherers of fruits, nuts and the shoots of palms. Large animals were scarce and larvae and honey were important items of diet. These groups posted sentries at strategic points along their boundaries to warn of danger.

In the tropical rain forest of the Jurua–Purus rivers southeast of Manaus the Cashinawa had a defined territory on the Embira River. The men hunted agouti and other large mammals, drugged fish with the sap from creepers and the women gathered fruits and roots. This group eventually developed the ability to cultivate sweet manioc. Their territory was demarcated by placing cleft sticks holding tufts of agouti hair along the boundary (Lowie, p. 352). It is not clear whether the territory was demarcated before or after the cultivation of sweet manioc.

In the Ilanos of Colombia and Venezuela there were many aboriginal groups. In this habitat of extensive areas of tall grasses divided by rivers flowing through gallery forests some groups concentrated their activities along the rivers. The Yaruro, who had specific territories, were one group that specialised in fishing and hunting riverine animals. They hunted crocodiles and turtles and caught fish. They were skilled canoemen in contrast to neighbouring tribes based mainly in the grasslands who occasionally used crude rafts.

No examples can be provided of the territorial arrangements of aboriginal groups on the west coast. Some were changed beyond recognition by the chiefdoms and civilisations in the period from AD 600 to 900 and the remainder disappeared through incorporation in the Inca Empire in the 15th and 16th centuries. Rowe (1963, p. 185) noted that at the time of the Inca conquest there were many small political territories and a wide diversity of languages. This diversity was simplified by the imposition of the language called Quechua and the arbitrary grouping of small territories into large and medium provinces. Rowe attempted without complete success to reconstruct the aboriginal territorial boundaries in this area. His comments (pp. 786–9) reveal the problem:

> Six linguistic groups occupied this area [highlands], but their territorial limits are not well known. As the tribal units long since disappeared, their identity and habitat must be reconstructed from the fragmentary information of chronicles, inadequately studied land grants and the fairly well known aboriginal toponymy . . .
> Aboriginal groups on the coast varied in cultural complexity and linguistic affiliation. Their boundaries are even more uncertain than those of the Highland Indians . . .
> The boundaries of inland [between highlands and coast] groups are even more tentative.

Moving offshore to the islands of the Pacific Ocean, aboriginal boundaries have been identified on larger islands. Burrows (1939) identified defined aboriginal territories in New Zealand and the Marquesas. Of the Maori he notes (p. 6) that 'Each tribe had a recognised territory, however shifted by migration or war'. In the Marquesas some major groups occupied a whole river valley. These valleys had a distinctive quality noted by Buck and endorsed by Burrows (p. 21):

> The tribal territories there, most of them at least, were valleys separated by precipitous ridges. These natural barriers discouraged communication and may well have reduced intermarriage and adoption between tribes. They also acted as fortifications, making conquest harder than in more accessible terrain, and tending to prevent permanent subjugation of one tribe by another.

Dening (1980, pp. 45, 64) makes the same point in a more lyrical fashion:

> All the islands of Te Henua [Marquesas] are without coastal plains, their shores fall to the sea in giant cliffs which are broken by the deep rifts of valleys, sometimes narrow, sometimes broad and curved, rarely stretching back more than a mile or two to the central mountain core. The valley walls are ribs and spines of rocks. They stand sheer along the valley's sides and backs. Access by land is difficult. Paths wind up cliffs or through saddles in the mountains, or they fade away into rock faces. The line of the mountain tops is jagged and disordered but clean, unmarked by men. A man standing against the sky is always startling. He will whistle or shout if he is coming as a visitor; he will raise his fan and staff if he comes as a messenger with an invitation to a feast; he will gesture his threats and goads if he comes to fight. At night no one comes save the enemy . . .

The ridges between the valleys, as everywhere in Te Henua, marked with fair precision the limits of social obligations and bonds.

Parker (1989) has provided a useful description of boundaries in Hawaii. By the time Europe discovered these islands in 1778 the aboriginal population had developed levels of state administration that could no longer be described as aboriginal. However it does seem that the limits of the *ahupua'a* (an administrative land unit) correspond to the limits in the Marquesas, although the topography of Hawaii is less dramatic than that of the Marquesas (pp. 13–14):

> The ideal ahupua'a existed as a self-sustaining pie-shaped wedge with its base reaching from the coast to its apex at the centre of the mountaintop . . . Some ahupua'a extended into the sea to include deep-sea fisheries . . . If breakers existed the ahupua'a stretched to them, and if not it extended 1.5 miles into the sea . . .
>
> Each of the ahupua'a had specific names and boundaries. Certain individuals within the community were trained to know the boundary lines and were called upon to settle any disputes. Distinctive geographical characteristics such as a ridge, depression, stream, the line of growth of a specific tree, grasses or herbs, or the location of a rock or a certain bird's habitat marked the boundaries of the ahupua'a. Altars erected for the purpose of collecting tribute during the Makahiki festival also delimited the borders of the ahupua'a on the seacoast.

By the time that Cook visited the islands for the first time the Hawaiians had passed beyond the hunter and gatherer stage and were skilled cultivators. They had also established seawater ponds within coral and basalt walls where they could rely on regular catches of mullet and milkfish. These ponds varied in extent from 1 to 500 acres (Parker, p. 15).

It is convenient at this point to introduce the concept of sea rights as a logical extension of land rights. Section 12(1) of the *Aboriginal Land Act 1978* permits Aborigines in the Northern Territory to claim the closure of seas within 2 kilometres of Aboriginal land (Bergin 1991). The closure applies to any persons other than Aborigines who are entitled by Aboriginal tradition to enter and use those seas. Up to 1991 there had been two successful applications to close seas in the area of Milingimbi, the Crocodile Islands and Glyde River and the area of Howard Island and Castlereagh Bay.

Davis (1984 and 1991) has reported on the existence of precise boundaries that separate the marine areas of adjacent territories of coastal clans. Such boundaries extend seawards to enclose marine sections of the Hawaiian ahupua'a and others have been recorded in additional Pacific

Islands. E. Hviding (personal communication 1991) has made a detailed analysis of current indigenous maritime limits in Morovo Lagoon. This lagoon lies between the adjoining coasts of New Georgia and Vangunu Islands in the Solomons. Seawards the lagoon is bounded by a chain of reefs and islets extending for a distance of 40 miles (64 kilometres). Hviding found that marine boundaries between the territories of adjoining groups, called *butubutu*, usually coincide with channels and reefs. The limits extend through navigable gaps in the inner reef to the outer reef. Rights to navigation through these channels are held by both adjacent groups. When mining and timber industries in catchments draining into the lagoon have threatened the lagoon's ecology the coastal people have sought help from the peoples inhabiting those catchments. These peoples have traditionally been given access to marine resources in the lagoon and appeals to them have resulted in some mining and forestry industries being stopped.

N. A. Sims (personal communication 1991) identified the existence of marine boundaries between traditional territories on Manahiki Atoll in the Cook Islands. These patterns of traditional marine tenure were destroyed after the 1920s during the period of administration by New Zealand. When authority over marine matters reverted to the authorities on Manahiki in the 1980s the islanders declined to return to the traditional system. They preferred to deal as a single group with the multinational pearling companies for the sale of rights to cultured black pearls.

M. C. Falanruw (personal communication 1991) has reported on the continued existence of marine boundaries on Yap. These limits define the primary right of a clan to the marine area. However, there is also provision for individual rights to exist in respect of a particular resource, such as a species of fish, or the means of exploiting that resource, such as a fish trap of particular design.

Once upon a time Africa must have been home to many bands of hunters and gatherers. Unfortunately, from the point of view of this study, the course of African history prevents us from knowing details of territorial arrangements for most of these groups. Roman occupation of North Africa that reached its maximum extent by AD 350 obliterated knowledge of aboriginal territorial arrangements there. By AD 400 domestication of the camel had allowed the Sahara Desert to be crossed and trade developed with the subsistence groups in the Sahel south of the desert. Islam reached Timbuktu and the Lake Chad region by AD 1100 and spread into Hausaland, now northern Nigeria, by AD 1250. Penetration along the coast of East Africa reaching Sofala by 1200 and down the Nile Valley into Nubia created contacts and cultural shocks that transformed aboriginal patterns of settlement.

The Moslem empires and kingdoms of the Sahel and the Christian empire in Ethiopia conquered adjacent areas and started ripples of migrations and wars that affected distant areas. Powerful kingdoms developed in areas now occupied by Zaire, Angola, Zambia, Zimbabwe and Uganda, and their conflicts also sent cultural shock waves throughout central Africa and caused the displacement of other groups.

Then the slave trade, the activities of missionaries, the colonisation of southern Africa by the Dutch, the depradations of the Zulus and Amandebeles, and the Great Trek of Boer farmers contributed to the dislocation of populations or their transformation from hunters and gatherers to farmers and pastoralists. The process has been well described (pp. 253-4) by one of the contributors who produced the restricted handbook, *The Belgian Congo*, prepared by the Naval Intelligence Division (1944) for use in World War II under the editorial supervision of Mason, then Professor of Geography at Oxford.

> If the distribution of the population in the Congo is to be appreciated it must be remembered that only within the memory of man have some of the tribes been anchored to their present areas. Before the advent of settled government there were sudden often unexpected migrations of peoples from north, south and east of the Congo basin. These irruptions were caused by distant wars, slave-raiding, famine, pestilence, the search for fresh pastures, or, in some cases, by a mere lust for conquest. They displaced not only those who were directly in the line of advance but also, indirectly, tribes further afield ...
>
> Such movements are impossible today. Tribes have been obliged to settle where the European administration found them. Some of the tribal areas are larger than an English county and some have been split into scattered fragments by the intrusion of alien tribes. The whole pattern of tribal settlement is irregular and is like that of a jig-saw puzzle. Exhaustive information about the tribes, their numbers and the boundaries between them is not available.

In modern times only the Pygmies of modern Zaire and the Bushmen, properly known as San, have retained a hunting and gathering economy. These groups survived into the present in the dense forest of the Congo basin and harsh desert of the Kalahari respectively. No description of the Pygmies' territorial arrangements has been found but Forde (1952) and Post and Taylor (1984) were certain that the San had clearly defined territories and that trespass across the boundaries that fixed them was a very serious affair.

> Each [San] band had its own clearly defined territory which was respected by the neighbouring bands. They understood the ways of nature in the most

complete manner, for they knew themselves to be part of its intricate and divinely-ordered system . . .

Bushmen had little sense of property . . . But they did have a sense of territory—the area within which they hunted game and each group respected the territory of their neighbours. To do otherwise was a clear act of aggression. (Post and Taylor, pp. 11, 15)

Forde (1952, pp. 26–7) notes that the territory of a San band might appear unnecessarily large during the short wet season when there are extensive areas of surface water and teeming herds of game. But during the dry season many of the herds migrate and water becomes scarce. So the extent of territory is set by the carrying capacity of the land in the dry season not in the time of plenty. Post (1988, p. 189) gives an indication of the precise knowledge about the location of boundaries:

Accordingly they divided the desert into two zones, promising never to cross the demarcation line between them. They, and Dabé too, assured me that none of them to this day would go from one zone to the other.

'But how d'you know which zone is which?' I asked, thinking of the thousands of square miles of identical sand, dune and bush.

They laughed at my innocence and with that wonderful Bushman laugh which rises sheer from the stomach, a laugh you never hear among civilised people. Did I not know, they exclaimed when the explosion of merriment died down, that there was not a tree, expanse of sand or bush that were alike? They knew the frontier tree by tree, and grass by grass.

Many of the senior men we have worked with in identifying traditional boundaries of Aborigines in Australia would have joined in the laughter that greeted Post's question.

This review of some of the literature dealing with territorial arrangements of aboriginal hunting and gathering groups in the Americas, the Marquesas and Hawaii and the Kalahari Desert demonstrates that most of those groups had the primary or exclusive use of territories that were clearly defined by boundaries. The inhospitable territory of the Seri was bounded on land by a desert frontier; the Yaghan seemed less concerned with landward limits than those at the coast and this appears to have also been true of the Inuit amongst whom the interface between groups can be found in the dialects in which the names of places are spoken. This means therefore that there is nothing unusual or unique in our claim that Aborigines in Australia defined their clan territories by precise boundaries in many cases and by frontiers in the remaining cases.

The review of the literature also provided information about the restrictions that these hunting and gathering groups imposed on access to their territories, their spiritual association with the land, and the internal sub-divisions of their territories for various purposes. The evidence for these features has not been provided because their existence in traditional Aborigine society is not disputed. Aspects of these features will be provided in the case studies that make up most of this volume.

Cartographic Evidence for the Existence of Aboriginal Boundaries

Since 1788 settlers, administrators, anthropologists and historians coming into contact with Aborigines have been aware of what Peterson referred to as the 'remarkable persistence of association between people and place'. Foolish people like Hamilton, who wrote regarding Aborigines that 'Here was a country without a geography, and a race of men without a history' (Clark 1991, p. 43), were in a minority. The views of Lang and Grey in the 1830s were more typical of the general understanding. Lang wrote to a missionary organisation in the following terms:

> The whole race is divided into tribes, more or less numerous, according to circumstances, and designated from the localities they inhabit; for although universally a wandering race with respect to places of habitation, their wanderings are circumscribed by certain well-defined limits, beyond which they seldom pass, except for purposes of war or festivity. In short, every tribe has its own district, the boundaries of which are well known to the natives generally ... (p. 233)

Grey (1841, vol. 2) was equally emphatic:

> ... and the limits of his property are so accurately defined that every native knows those of his own land and can point out the various objects which mark his boundary. (p. 232)

Since the earliest times attempts have been made to record the location of Aboriginal groups on maps either for local areas or wider regions. If we look first at the Northern Territory as an example, because that is an area where fieldwork on this question is still possible today, one of the first maps was produced by Father Angelo Confalonieri in 1846 (Powell 1988, p. 60). The priest produced vocabularies of seven Aboriginal dialects and a map that showed the names of six groups written on the map to show their approximate location. Thus the Binanolombo were shown as occupying the southwestern shore of the Cobourg Peninsula. The same technique, that does not try to portray any boundaries, was used by Parkhouse (1895) when he produced a map of Aboriginal groups in the area between Pine Creek and Port Darwin. Groups identified as 'Waggait', 'Larrakiha' and 'Wulnar' are shown in the same relative positions as the Wagaitj, Larrakeya and Wulnaminitja on modern maps.

Spencer (1914) continued this technique of showing the approximate location of Aboriginal groups in his map of the Northern Territory. Numbers were placed on the map to indicate the location of groups that could be identified in a table. The distribution of numbers honestly showed a lack of knowledge about northeast Arnhem Land and the central sections of the borders with Western Australia and Queensland. Stanner (1933) used the same cartographic method. He was portraying the distribution of groups in the vicinity of the Daly and Fitzmaurice rivers, outside the area settled by whites. The Warrai (Warray), Kungarakan (Kungarakany) and Madngella (Mgangele) are three groups that appear in the same relative position on Stanner's map that they occupy today. It would not be safe to assume that the numbers were placed at the geographical centre of the groups' territories as they existed in 1933. Certainly today the numbers are located at the centre of the current Kungarakany territory and at the western and eastern margins respectively of the Warray and Mgangele groups.

A possible improvement on these generalised locations is shown on maps by Elkin, Davidson (1938) and Clark (1991). In each case the individual groups are shown by a number or letter but the maps also include the boundaries that surround those groups that share a common language or cultural basis. So Elkin plots the distribution of 45 groups that together are called the Karadjeri tribe. The boundary between the territories of the Karadjeri and the adjoining Yauor, Nygina and Mangala 'tribes' is shown together with the boundary between parts of the territories of the Nygina and Mangala. All these groups were located near the coast of Western Australian and the map was reproduced by Davidson (1938).

Davidson (1938) produced a similar map for the distribution of groups in Gippsland in eastern Victoria. His map is not explicit but he appears to mark groups known as 'hordes' by precise boundaries. These groups include the Brtaua-Lung in the west, including Wilson's Promontory and Kurauatunga-Lung in the extreme east. He also shows letters within these boundaries that probably indicate the general location of family hunting territories. Most of the precise boundaries follow watersheds, a few follow the shores of the Gippsland Lakes.

Gippsland is one of the areas where Davidson shows territorial boundaries on his general map of Australian groups at a scale of 1:8.5 million. The other areas are western Victoria around Portland, northeastern New South Wales, the Victorian bank of the Murray River below Mulwala and northeastern Arnhem Land. Elsewhere on the general map of Australia the distribution of groups is indicated solely by their printed names. This interest by Davidson in the distribution of Aboriginal groups was revealed in a paper published a decade before. In it (1928, p. 619) he expressed confidence that the territories of groups were defined precisely:

> Boundaries of the local group territory are well known ... It is undoubtedly true that, in general, no artificial means are used to indicate the extent of a local group's holding, but on the other hand the natives seem to have carefully described boundaries, based upon such natural features as streams, lakes, clumps of trees, waterholes, ridges of land and the like.

Clark (1991) based his work on fieldwork undertaken by George Robinson, the Chief Protector of Aborigines, in 1839 who instructed his assistants as follows (p. 1):

> ... [discover] the boundaries and Aboriginal names of districts occupied by each tribe, the Aboriginal names of mountains, lakes, rivers and other localities.

Use of the archives left by Robinson enabled Clark to create a map of the Djab wurrung language area in west-central Victoria. The limits of the language area are shown and within them the general location of 39 of the 41 recorded clans are indicated by numbers. More than half of the clans were associated either with specific hills or named rivers and streams.

The really detailed work on the precise location of Aboriginal boundaries began in the 1920s when first Tindale and then Strehlow started fieldwork. Tindale worked on Groote Eylandt in 1921 and submitted his first paper showing exact boundaries in 1925. The editor, believing that Aborigines roamed at will over the whole country, refused to allow the boundaries to be shown as solid lines (Tindale 1974, p. 3). They were shown as dotted lines! Tindale was introduced to the concept of Aboriginal boundaries by an informant who regularly travelled to take stone blades from the mines east of Katherine River to distant groups. The comprehensive survey of Aboriginal boundaries was published in 1974 in the form of a book and a map of Australia in four sheets at a scale of 1:2.5 million. The boundaries are of tribes and they are solid when they have been established with confidence and dashed when their establishment is less certain. For Tindale the tribe is composed of a number of hordes or clans, which are each composed of a number of families. The family is the smallest social unit in Aboriginal society. According to Tindale under normal circumstances Aborigines prefer to live in a unit composed of a number of families. Nevertheless he notes that there is communication with other hordes or clans. This communication creates the tribe that is the limit of political organisation. For Tindale this is the largest group within which a man can take part in community life and share his thoughts while still feeling he is among his own kind (p. 30).

While Tindale travelled widely he had to rely in some areas on the work of others and there are four areas where most of the boundaries are shown as dashed lines because their establishment was not certain. The first of these areas is located in the western part of the Great Victoria Desert centred on Lake Jubilee. The coordinates that bound it are 122 degrees and 130 degrees east and 26 degrees and 31 degrees south. There were 15 separate boundaries shown by dashed lines in this area. The second area occupies parts of the Gibson and Great Sandy Deserts within the graticule 120 degrees and 129 degrees east and 20 degrees and 25 degrees 30 minutes south. This region showed 23 boundaries as uncertain. The third area is mainly in the Northern Territory and extends from just west of Tennant Creek to the southeastern shore of Joseph Bonaparte Gulf. The 29 uncertain boundaries lie in the area bounded by 129 degrees and 134 degrees east and 15 degrees and 19 degrees south. Finally west of the Diamantina River centred in Lake Philippi there is an area with 26 boundaries shown as uncertain. Its limits are 136 degrees and 141 degrees east and 22 degrees and 26 degrees south.

The tribal distributions shown on Tindale's map have many similarities to linguistic maps of Australia (O'Grady et al. 1966; Wurm 1972) and there is disagreement about the level of social organisation or group that he mapped. These are also doubts that the boundaries shown are consistent in concept across the map or in the quality of the fieldwork that fixed them. For example, although Tindale discovered that sometimes Aboriginal groups were separated by strips of territory of various widths he always reduced that zone to a line.

Strehlow (1947) did outstanding work on the Arranda in central Australia. He had the decided advantage of having learned the Arranda language as a child at Hermannsburg Mission. The fieldwork done by Strehlow from the 1930s to the 1960s enabled him to draw maps showing precisely the boundaries separating Arranda groups. He found that the boundaries tended to coincide with water courses and topographic features.

This brief review demonstrates that most of the mapping of Aboriginal boundaries has been done by anthropologists. Further, most of the discussion and comment has also been by anthropologists such as Hiatt, Lee and Pilling (1968), Peterson (1976) and Stanner (1965). Davidson

(1938) and Peterson have drawn attention to the special interests of anthropologists that influence their attitudes to boundary studies:

> Although a political map of [Aboriginal] Australia should portray the distribution of hordes, since they are the political units, it seems obvious that such would be impractical regardless of how desirable it might be ... we have relatively little detailed information of this character, for very few investigators have sought information of a purely political nature. The reasons for this condition are not difficult to ascertain. Most Australianists have found the social structure of the Aborigines so intricate that it has absorbed all their attention or interest. Furthermore the purely political aspects of the Australian cultural pattern are relatively unimpressive and of local character when contrasted with social institutions which constitute the dominant role in Australian life ... (Davidson, pp. 662–3)
>
> Further, until recently, little of the work on territories was done by on-the-ground mapping over a long period by people with a deep concern for spatial organisation, most writers being interested in place only because of its relationship to totemism and mythology. With physical demarcation of boundaries by cultural means or patrolling absent, it is easy to assume that boundaries are insignificant. (Peterson and Long 1986, p. 54)

The approximate definition of boundaries has been sufficient for most anthropologists who are seeking a framework within which they can describe and analyse, for example, genealogies, ceremonies and customs related to birth, marriage and death.

Recently Taylor (1976) and Memmot (1983) have undertaken mapping of political boundaries as part of wider anthropological studies. Taylor produced detailed maps of the Edward River area in Cape York showing Aboriginal place names indicating clan ownership, ritual and mythological associations including dreaming tracks, ceremonial sites, the location of camp and burial sites, water sources, vegetation and topography. Memmott mapped the countries of the Lardil Aboriginal people of the north Wellesley Islands in the Gulf of Carpentaria, as part of his documentation of Lardil social structure. He found there were clear boundaries defining the extent of each patrician country, referred to as cut-off lines by the Lardil in Aboriginal English.

Study of Boundaries in Political Geography

The study of boundaries has been an important part of political geography since Ratzel published his famous *Politische Geographie* (Political Geography) in 1897. It is a matter of lasting regret that the book was never translated into English for it has not been studied as widely as it deserves. Fortunately his analysis of boundaries has received appropriate attention. Ratzel, in the scientific fashion of the day, sought territorial laws related to boundaries. Since he regarded the state as a living organism it followed that its boundaries were the epidemis, providing protection and allowing exchanges to occur. His laws included the following assertions:

> The law of the evolution of boundaries can be defined as a striving towards simplification and in this simplification is contained a shortening of boundaries. (p. 555)
>
> In accordance with the general law of growth of historical spatial phenomena the borders of the larger areas embrace the borders of the smaller one. (p. 557)
>
> Political balance [between countries] is to a large extent dependent on the [characteristics of] borders between them. (p. 584)

These assertions can be shown to have no general validity today but Ratzel was writing at a time when colonial competition was at its height and when boundaries were being negotiated in Asia, Africa, and South Pacific by European empires and in South America by the indigenous successors to the collapsed Spanish and Portuguese empires. Boundaries in various areas were being altered by wars or threats of force.

Ratzel's views found favour with disciples of *Geopolitik* a pseudoscience that emphasised the role of geography in the development of policies to make Germany great again during the 1920s and 1930s. For example, Haushofer (1927), the arch-priest of *Geopolitik*, classified boundaries into categories labelled 'attack', 'defence', 'decay' and 'growth'. Whilst East (1937), Hartshorne (1935) and Gyorgy (1944) were exposing the intellectual aberrations of *Geopolitik* and, in the case of the first two authors, trying to steer political geography back on an objective course, an important book on boundaries was published by Lapradelle (1928). Lapradelle was a French lawyer and his major contribution was to identify the stages through which boundaries tended to evolve. This theme was brilliantly developed in English by Jones (1945) who wrote a handbook for statemen, treaty editors and boundary commissioners that has remained a classic in the field.

All the studies mentioned to this point dealt with international boundaries. That was not surprising since the period from 1890 to 1945 was one of major changes in international boundaries in colonial areas and Europe. The problems associated with boundaries and the decay of empires after World War II ensured that international boundaries remain a major focus of political geographers. Publications by Prescott (1987) dealing systematically and regionally with international boundaries and by Schofield (1991) who produced the definitive study of the Iraq–Kuwait boundary are examples of the continuance of this main theme. Thankfully it is very rare these days that partial or subjective accounts to support a particular national viewpoint are encountered. A most welcome development has been the establishment of the International Boundaries Research Unit at the University of Durham in England which holds annual conferences and publishes their proceedings and a useful newsletter.

Three other themes are important in the study of boundaries by political geographers. The study of internal boundaries of the state, whether they are electoral, planning or administrative limits has burgeoned. There is an awareness that such boundaries often have a greater immediate impact on the lives of citizens of democratic countries than the international boundaries. Since 1945 there has been a scramble for maritime zones by the coastal states of the world. The analysis of maritime limits of territorial seas, fishing zones, exclusive economic zones and continental margins has been the fastest growing point of boundary studies by political geographers (Prescott 1986, 1990). Finally the study of border landscapes has started to receive the level of attention that was overdue. The excellent collection of papers edited by Rumley and Minghi (1991) has placed this theme on a solid foundation.

Two themes consistently underrated by political geographers concern political frontiers and the limits of aboriginal groups. Having noted earlier that a frontier is a zone it is important to distinguish between two kinds of frontiers. Political frontiers are used to separate neighbouring states. Settlement frontiers are located within a single state and separate the settled from the unsettled areas. Of course the distinction between these two kinds of frontiers might depend on which side of the settlement frontier an individual is located. American writers, such as Turner (1953) regarded the American frontier as being of the settlement variety. Chiefs of the Sioux and Cherokee might well have thought of it as a political frontier. The same differences of view might have existed as Australia was dominated and settled by migrants from Europe between the migrants and the Aborigines.

But the chief point of this discussion is that political frontiers in the strict sense have now disappeared. They have been replaced by boundaries, and the analysis of ancient political frontiers in Europe and Asia is mainly undertaken by classical scholars, historians and historical geographers. Political geographers appear to believe that these political frontiers are too remote from present conditions to merit study, even if any individual was equipped with the necessary skills in language, archaeology and the interpretation of very old documents, many of which are incomplete.

Reynolds (1987) has made very important contributions to the study of the settlement–political frontier in Australia as whites took possession of Australia. Perry (1963) produced the classical study of Australia's first settlement frontier in New South Wales. However, our focus is on those occasions where traditional elders have been able to describe what appears to have been a political frontier between the territories of Aborigines in central parts of Australia.

The neglect by political geographers of the boundaries between groups pursuing an existence based on hunting and gathering occurs for similar reasons to the neglect of political frontiers. In most cases these groups ceased to exist as hunters and gatherers before accurate maps and records were available. The information was fragmentary and included statements that could never be verified by explorers who relied on interpreters of unknown ability and honesty. Where the descendants of such groups are still alive the work in the Americas has been mainly pursued by anthropologists such as Cooper, Kelly and Parker. They had the language, conceptual and cartographic skills that such analysis needed. For political geographers there was no evidence that these aboriginal boundaries, if they could be located, had any relevance to the international and internal boundaries that characterise modern states. Nicholson (1954) noted this situation in his study of the boundaries of Canada's Provinces and Territories. He observed (p. 116) that any relationships between aboriginal limits, which he regarded as frontiers, and later boundary evolution were entirely fortuitous.

Of course in many inter-colonial boundaries in Africa and southern Asia the exact extent of indigenous states was often the most important issue in the negotiations. But these indigenous states had passed far beyond the hunting and gathering societies of yore. So the demarcation of the boundary between Portuguese Angola and British Northern Rhodesia turned on the identification of the western boundary of the Barotse Kingdom. The matter was eventually settled by arbitration by the King of Italy in 1905. The foot soldiers in the scramble for Africa were the adventurers and traders who signed treaties with petty and major chiefs and included in those treaties for protection or preferential trade descriptions of the chief's territory.

The study of aboriginal boundaries around the world where that is still possible is not for the purpose of understanding the subsequent development of international limits. It is because there is now a view, in Canada, Hawaii, New Zealand and Australia at least, that aboriginal societies, where they still exist, should be granted land rights in one form or another. We have now passed beyond the situation described by Davidson in 1938 (p. 664):

> In addition it should be pointed out that there has been no necessity to determine the names and boundaries of the [Aboriginal] political units of the continent from the point of view of government authorities.

That situation has changed. In the Northern Territory there is legislation that allows Aborigines to claim seas and unalienated Crown Land and to be granted those areas if it is established that they are the traditional owners of the area within the meaning of the Act. Heritage legislation allows Aborigines to give evidence of affiliation with particular sites and areas where economic development of those areas is proposed. It was such an intervention in 1990 and 1991 that persuaded the federal cabinet to prevent mining at Coronation Hill. There have been calls by a number of Aborigines for the establishment of an increased number of Land Councils in the Northern Territory. Finally the creation of the Aboriginal and Torres Strait Islander Commission (ATSIC) involved the definition of administrative boundaries that were acceptable to the Aborigines and Torres Strait Islanders.

As Australia moves towards the end of the first century of federation the Minister for Aboriginal Affairs has announced a decade of reconciliation between Aborigines and white Australians. Part of that reconciliation will involve the issue of exclusive Aboriginal rights over land and, where appropriate, adjoining seas. It is our view that whatever arrangements are made they should be based on the most precise information available. This means that the best possible information on the extent of clan territories should be collected and verified where that is possible. There is an urgency about this activity because of the rate at which traditional knowledge held by senior elders is being lost by their reluctance in some cases to pass it on before their deaths to successors who do not seem to be interested.

The accumulation of this detailed knowledge will demonstrate that in large parts of Australia outside the tropics precise information about Aboriginal boundaries has been lost forever. This variability in the completeness of historical knowledge about patterns of Aboriginal ownership will be relevant when either state or federal legislation on land rights is composed.

In this book we show how political geographers can contribute to knowledge about Aboriginal political boundaries. This is not a preemptive academic claim to the entire field. There is plenty of work in the time available for geographers, historians and anthropologists. We will show the research methods of political geographers that have evolved over recent decades and describe the outcomes of that research.

Research Methods

The prime research method is fieldwork involving visiting Aboriginal people and often travelling with them. Preparation for these fieldtrips, that were sometimes lengthy, involved reading what others had written about the area and its inhabitants and acquiring the best possible topographic maps and, when necessary, charts.

In visiting and working with Aboriginal groups details of the identity and extent of territories over which they exerted primary political influence were recorded. Arrangements were then made to be introduced to senior custodians of adjacent groups so that the boundary could be checked from both sides. This procedure is essential to establish that the adjacent territories are separated by a boundary and not by a frontier or, in some maritime situations, by a zone of common use.

Attending traditional ceremonies often afforded the opportunity to gather and cross-check data with senior Aboriginal custodians from a wide area and sometimes distant regions who had gathered to play their part in the ceremonies. While Aboriginal people provided information during informal situations such as conversation around the camp or during hunting trips, the formal structure of the ceremony provided an intensity of detail contained in the song cycles and dances performed and in the designs and other symbolism such as ground sculptures and ritual paraphernalia which were constructed for the ceremony. Of course, being present for the preparation and conduct of ceremonies often necessitated prolonged periods of fieldwork.

Only rarely did fieldwork involve senior Aboriginal women in the absence of Aboriginal men. Those rare occasions involved older women with whom Davis's family had lived or when Julie Davis was present. Male–female interaction within Aboriginal society is hedged about with particularly strong prohibitions in terms of name-use, physical proximity and body language. The great majority of fieldtrips were therefore conducted with senior Aboriginal men only or with mixed groups. Coincidentally, most information detailing and confirming the identities and distributions of territories seems to be held by men. This view is held because of field experience and the small amount of archival data that can be attributed to Aboriginal women.

At the conclusion of fieldwork in each area the senior Aboriginal people were provided with a copy of the map of their territory constructed on the basis of their information. This is also an essential part of fieldwork so that there is no misunderstanding between the people and the researcher. We have found that it is a procedure that is welcomed as the following letter from the Muralag Tribal Torres Strait Islander Corporation on Horn Island shows:

> Dear Stephen,   10 May 1991
>
>   Myself, Chief Elders and other Elders of the Kaurareg Tribe appreciate the work you have put into the Kaurareg Territory maps in which you have drawn up. We would like to thank you also for the accuracy in which the maps contain. All the information included on the maps boundaries names etc. are to our satisfactory because this is exactly the information in which we told you.
>
>   Thanking you for your help and I hope to do more work with you in the future.
>
> Yours faithfully,
> Ronsy W. Wasaga President, Adie Paul Chief Elder, Eselina Nawie Chief Elder, Maleta Luta Chief Elder, Billy Niba Wasaga (JP) Elder, Lela Eseli Elder. (original held by Davis)

Plan of the Book

The next four chapters deal with case studies selected from different environments. Chapter 2 details the Yolngu and its constituent clans of northeast Arnhem Land as a case of boundary delineation in marine areas. Reference is also made to the Tiwi, an island-based group north of Darwin on the Northern Territory coast, who also evidence an outstanding precision in marine boundary delineation. The lack of dispute over boundaries among these groups is unexpected given data from other regions of the world. However, disputes which do arise focus on rights to the territory and not the location of the boundary itself. The process of succession to territories of deceased groups is examined and further discussed in later chapters.

    Chapter 3 examines the Jawoyn, an example of a group which has been subject to intense, prolonged contact leading to the loss of traditional knowledge without which claims to territory and succession to other territories cannot be sustained. The Jawoyn have used legislation skilfully to facilitate their claims to territory in a mineral rich area of the Northern Territory with controversial results.

    The Luritja of Central Australia are described in Chapter 4 as a group which has been subject to a violent contact history resulting in a massive, forced dislocation of the Aboriginal population. The Luritja is shown to be an identity which bridges the transition from boundary dominant groups to frontier-dominant groups. Chapter 4 examines the process by which the Luritja identity has been successfully used to reassert traditional frontiers and boundaries in an arid zone.

Maluigal is a Torres Strait identity used to denote four tribes which focus on Mabuiag (Jervis Island) and surrounding territory. In Chapter 5 detailed research spanning more than a century of sustained contact is compared to reveal any changes in territoriality among the Maluigal tribes. As with the Yolngu and Tiwi in Chapter 2 the physical basis of their political boundaries and natural features of the landscape co-incident with Maluigal political boundaries are described, as are the attendant rights of access.

Chapter 6 summarises the generalisations about Aboriginal boundaries that can be derived from the case studies and the dozens of other completed studies not recorded in this book. Those generalisations will deal with the degree of correspondence between Aboriginal boundaries and the landscape, the restrictions and transit rights that apply to them in traditional society, the variation in size of territories in different parts of Australia, the subdivision of territories into sites or localities for particular purposes, and the way in which the limits of any territory might change. This concluding chapter also outlines those aspects of the traditional Aboriginal society and the administration of Aboriginal affairs by state and federal governments to which political geographers can make a contribution as useful as the boundary studies.

2

Tropical Coast

Arnhem Land is located in the northeast region of the Northern Territory of Australia. The northern coast of Arnhem Land lies generally along latitude 12 degrees south facing the Arafura Sea between longitudes 130 degrees east and 137 degrees east. The western section of the Arnhem Land coast is heavily indented around Cobourg Peninsula with several large estuaries flowing into Van Diemen Gulf. The central north coast is incised by only two major estuarine systems which both flow into Boucat Bay. The northeast coast is heavily indented by Castlereagh Bay, Buckingham Bay, Arnhem Bay and Melville Bay with the Crocodile Islands, Wessel Islands and The English Company's Islands providing a mixture of inshore fringing islands and offshore islands.

There are approximately 126 Aboriginal groups whose traditional territories encompass part of the north coast of Arnhem Land. The average size of each territory including both land and marine domains is approximately 235 square kilometres except in the case of Bathurst and Melville islands where territories average 1263 square kilometres.

Two examples of the precise definition of estates will be drawn from this region: the Tiwi of Bathurst and Melville islands and the Yolngu clans around Castlereagh Bay. These communities are treated first because they have preserved their Aboriginal traditions in a more complete fashion than most other groups. This is plainly related to the lower levels of European contact through mining and pastoral activities. It is interesting that these groups survived the earliest external contacts with Macassans in entirely different ways. The Yolngu incorporated many aspects of Macassan life into their traditions in contrast to intense European contact such as occurred in the Katherine area (Chapter 3) which decimated Aboriginal traditions. The Tiwi, on the other hand, rejected the Macassans.

The landward area flanking and generally lying south of Castlereagh Bay may be described as a low coastal plain which is drained by the Glyde River to the south and the Bennett, Darbitja, Djigagila, Djabura and Ngandadauda creeks in the west. The Glyde River, a large meandering river system which drains the 400 square kilometres of the Arafura Swamp has a heavy freshwater flow during the wet season (Messel et al. 1980, p. 6). The Woolen River, immediately east of the Glyde flows generally northwest, draining higher elevated sandstone areas south of the Napier Peninsula. At its mouth lies Banyan Island.

Water flows between the Woolen River and the south entrance to the Hutchison Strait which separates Howard Island from the mainland at higher levels of the tide. The Hutchison Strait is flanked by mangroves for its entire length, whereas both the Glyde and Woolen rivers are characterised by mangrove communities only in their highly saline coastal regions, otherwise being flanked by open woodland or savanna grasslands and floodplains. The creeks on the western side of Castlereagh Bay to Cape Stewart are similarly flanked by mangrove vegetation often giving way to paperbark swamp and savanna grassland in their upper reaches.

Castlereagh Bay possesses a number of fringing islands which effectively screen the mainland from a seaward view. One of these, Howard Island, is the most southwesterly extension of the Wessel Islands. The islands which lie within Castlereagh Bay, with their Aboriginal name in brackets, are as follows: Darbada (Darpada) Island, Crocodile (Nilpaywa) Island, Milingimbi (Yurrwi) Island, Yabooma (Räpuma) Island, Gananggarngur (Ganangkarrngur) Island, Mardanaingura (Mararrtharrayngur) Island and Boojiragi (Buthyiriki) Island. They are all members of the Crocodile Islands group and all have significant expanses of mud flats and mangrove vegetation. Mooroongga (Murrungga) Island, North West Crocodile (Gurriba) Island and North East Crocodile (Burrulpurrulngur) Island all lying north and seaward of Castlereagh Bay are also members of the Crocodile Islands group but are offshore islands surrounded by clear water and sandy beaches. Several other islands are contained within this group but are not named on any maps of the region. The remaining named feature in this area is North Crocodile Reef (Gunumba) lying in the Arafura Sea, approximately 80 kilometres north of the mainland. In all, the Crocodile Islands and Castlereagh Bay area cover approximately 5500 square kilometres of the marine area immediately adjacent to the north coast of Arnhem Land.

In contrast Bathurst and Melville islands, which lie 380 kilometres west of Castlereagh Bay and approximately 80 kilometres north of

Darwin, between longitudes 130 degrees east and 132 degrees east, have a total land mass of 7870 square kilometres. Melville Island is separated from the Australian mainland by the Clarence Strait which at its narrowest point is only 25 kilometres wide. This gap is bridged by the Vernon Islands, the most northerly of which lies only 13 kilometres from Melville Island.

It seems that territoriality among the Tiwi and the Yolngu and their inherent knowledge of frontiers and boundaries have not been seriously eroded by European contact despite the erosion of many aspects of social customs such as polygamy. A curious aspect of Tiwi territoriality, however, is that, unlike the Yolngu, it is not a well-developed case of maritime tenure even though the Tiwi live on islands.

The Tiwi did not travel extensively by canoe and hence did not have a detailed knowledge of maritime navigation as do the Yolngu of northeastern Arnhem Land (Davis 1984, 1989). The Tiwi used canoes primarily to hunt turtle and fish on inshore areas and to cross estuaries. While the Tiwi invariably paddled their canoes, the Yolngu not only used paddles during turtle and dugong hunting but used woven pandanus sails for long voyages. Bathurst and Melville islands have only two small adjacent islands which both lie only a few kilometres offshore. One of these, Seagull Island on the north coast, was visited probably only once a year to collect the eggs of crested terns and turtles. The other, Buchanan Island on the south coast, lies close inshore and was easily accessed across a narrow channel at low tide primarily to collect shellfish. Its seaward side is the confluence of two sacred or imunga sites which would generally be avoided by the Tiwi people. Hence, despite living on islands the Tiwi were a land-based rather than marine-based people. Tiwi territoriality is exercised only within sight of land thereby allowing marine territorial rights to be extrapolated by reference to landmarks. Tiwi do not hunt or fish out of sight of land and do not exercise or claim territorial rights to the open sea:

> That open sea . . .
> That belong to Government.
>   Raphael Apuatimi (Davis 1989)

Environment

Lying 12 degrees south of the equator the north coast of Arnhem Land experiences a tropical climate characterised by typical northwest monsoon rains of the wet season from December to April followed by the southeast trade winds of May to November which are noticeably cooler in the early months of the dry season.

The saline muds under the mangroves extend up to 13 kilometres seaward from the mainland in Castlereagh Bay at 0.1 metre low tide and are also extensive around Buchanan Island at the southern entrance to the Apsley Strait between Bathurst and Melville islands. Sandy beaches are characteristic of those areas where freshwater inflow is initiated in higher elevation areas. Islands close to the mainland, such as Milingimbi (Yurrwi) Island, typically are surrounded by extensions to these saline muds in sheltered areas, with sandy beaches on the more exposed sides. Islands further seaward such as North West Crocodile (Gurriba) Island and the north coast of Bathurst and Melville islands are free of the saline muds with an increasing predominance of sandy beaches stabilised by vegetation, being clear of the influence of estuarine deposition.

Most reefs in the Crocodile Islands appear only as rocky outcrops at mean low tide but are often shown to have extensive associated sand-bars at lower tidal levels. Minimal land vegetation dominated by the mangrove tree *Avicennia marina* exists on only a few reefs, with coral species being extensive around the seaward islands and reefs especially along the south coast of Melville Island.

Reduction in water turbulence, current velocities and the coagulating effect produced by the mixing of river-borne sediments with sea waste at river mouths, result in extensive areas of fine grained, anoxic, saline substrate or muds. This substrate is an extension of the mangrove substrate which is richer in organic materials. North East Crocodile (Burrulpurrulngur) Island, North West Crocodile (Gurriba) Island and Mooroongga (Murrungga) Island are free of the extensive mud flats which surround all other inshore islands of the group apart from the small parts of Yabooma (Räpuma) Island and Crocodile (Nilpaywa) Island which are exposed to the action of the open sea.

The numerous creeks which flow into Castlereagh Bay behind the complex of small islands on its western side combine with the backflow of currents around the islands to maintain the large amounts of sediment which constitute the mud flats. The central area of Castlereagh Bay possesses extensive sand-banks which are traversed from north to south by large channels through which the outflow of the Woolen River, Glyde River and Hutchison Strait flow to the deeper channels of the open sea immediately south of Mooroongga (Murrungga) Island. Channels which carry the bulk of faster flowing water through regular tidal recessions and inundations are well marked, with depths averaging from 2 to 6 metres in those running along rocky shorelines and further out to sea.

Due to the low gradient of the inshore regions and a large tidal amplitude of up to 8 metres in Castlereagh Bay, tidal inundation covers large areas. Likewise the exposed area from mean low water to lowest astronomical tide may be several kilometres in width. Bathurst and Melville islands are subject to much smaller tidal amplitude and thus tidal inundation is not as extensive as in Castlereagh Bay. In the mouth of the Glyde River, Woolen River and Hutchison Strait, the tidal action is particularly strong, the area exhibiting a large tidal amplitude at extreme tides often exaggerated by strong freshwater inflow. Some habitats or sub-systems which occur within estuary systems of particular importance to Aboriginal people include such areas as beds of eel grass (*Zostera sp.*), mud flats, tidal pools and reefs all of which may harbour dense populations of molluscs and other bottom dwellers. Estuaries then are a major source of nutrients to adjacent deeper water along the coastline indicating that the marine areas of the Crocodile Islands and Bathurst and Melville islands as a whole are very rich environments supporting a large population of species.

The tall open forests are generally dominated by *Eucalyptus tetrodonta* and *Eucalyptus miniata*, both about 11 metres high, with mainly annual grasses of variable species and height. Soils are wet, sandy or gravelly laterite. The mixed open forests contain the same eucalypts but not with the same frequency of occurrence. Rather, they are dominated by *Terminalia, Buchanania obovata, Planchonia careya* and *Gardenia megasperma. Ampelocissus cetosa* is a common ground cover, among other prostrate vines which scramble over *Cycas media. Dioscorea nummularia, D. sativa var. elongata, D. transversa* and *Similax australis* are among the vines clinging to tree trunks and generally found among soil types similar to that of the tall open forest. In the semi-deciduous forest, trees vary in height from 1 to 13 metres without the layering characteristics of rain forest. The vegetation is dense, with occasional open and well-lit areas. The litter is deep, especially in the dry season when the forest is particularly open due to the deciduous nature of most trees, resulting in an organic soil usually of a sandy type.

The savanna grasslands comprise a scattering of trees over grasses. *Eucalyptus polycarpa, Grevillea pteridifolia* and *Pandanus spiralis* are the dominant species of trees. *Pandanus* clumps are sparsely scattered throughout the grasses which cover most of the coastal plains and are often dominated by communities of *Hetropogon contortus*.

Melaleuca leucadendron, up to 15 metres, is almost the only tree in the dense paperbark communities edging the landward zone of the coastal plains. A more mixed form of paperbark forest occurs along freshwater streams and billabongs. *Melaleuca* are interspersed with *Acacia auriculiformis, Barringtonia, Eugena, Pandanus, Terminalis* and *Morinda* over organic soils usually on estuarine deposits or freshwater alluvia.

Where mixed scrub occurs it is dominated by low non-eucalypts of dense habit. There is a typical domination of *Grevillea pteridifolia* and *Livistonia humilis*, each within relatively small communities of under 7 metres in sandy residual or skeletal soils.

The mangrove scrub is nearly all in the littoral land system characterised by tidally inundated soils and immature cracking clays from which eleven species are recorded. Typically there is a mangrove succession from the seaward zone dominated by *Aegialitis annulata* and *Avicennia marina*, *Sonneratia alba*, *Rhizophora stylosa*, *Sonneratia alba*, *Ceriops tagal* and *Avicennia marina*. Many saline creeks are, however, almost solely dominated by *Rhyzophora stylosa*.

Seasonal Use of Resources

Within the Crocodile Islands and Castlereagh Bay area, the seasonal movement of Yolngu between the islands is closely tied to the shifting emphasis on different marine resources. The total territory of each clan group may be composed of several discrete tracts of land and sea. This, coupled with access to adjoining territories made possible through kinship relationships, allows for considerable latitude in the movement of any one group seeking seasonal abundance or palatability, as evaluated roughly in terms of perceived fat content, of various marine species. The movement of Tiwi groups is more confined to the land, with foraging and hunting patterns of any one clan much more likely to occur totally within their own territory.

During the northwest monsoons of the wet season, which lasts approximately from December to March (Figure 1), shellfish form a major part of the daily Yolngu diet and, to a lesser degree, that of the Tiwi. The seas may be quite rough, precluding line fishing. The rough seas and heavy discharge of water from large estuarine systems make the spearing of fish and stingrays almost impossible. Yolngu therefore tend to move to sheltered areas adjacent to inshore shellfish beds. At such times these shellfish beds, in association with molluscs from nearby mangrove communities, constitute a high proportion of the food resources taken from the sea. In general the heavy rain of the wet season dictates a sedentary existence. Camp sites are invariably centred around beach areas offering shelter and good drainage under spreading trees, and ready access to shellfish beds and fresh water. As the wet season draws to a close, forest areas yield fruit, fish from habitats further afield become 'fat', and so the mobility of food-seeking groups increases rapidly.

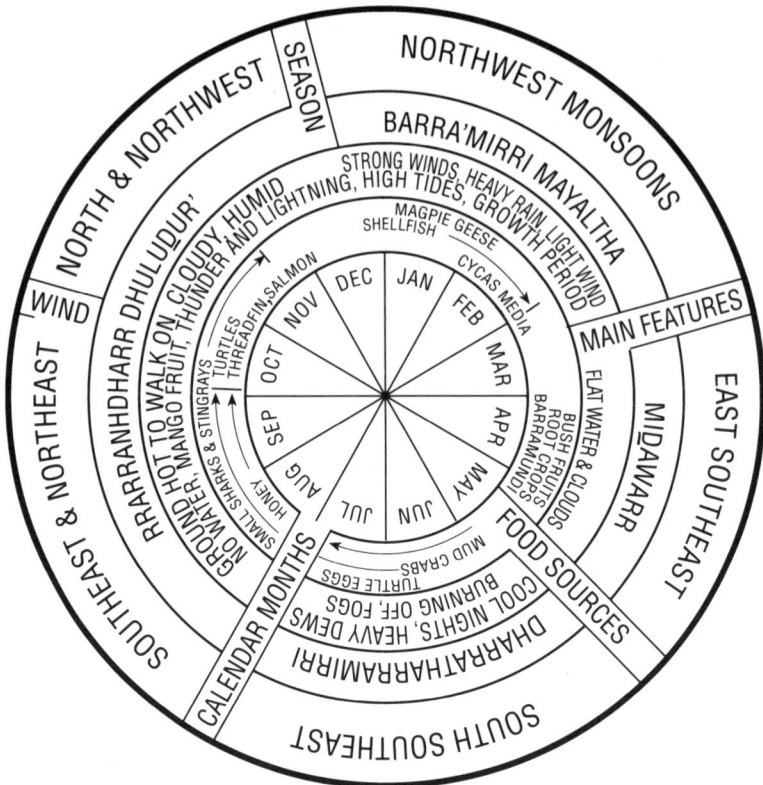

Figure 1 Seasonal Change in the Environment and Resource Availability in Yolngu Territory

The late wet season and early dry season see a revival in fishing, with barramundi (*Lates calcarifer*), specifically, being hunted with spears across the totally inundated floodplains. Mud crabs (*Scylla serrata*) are fat and turtles are also harvested. As the wind settles to the southeast during the dry season, which extends from approximately April to October, fishing with spears and lines, and turtle and dugong hunting become the primary activities of coastal hunting groups. Such activities for Yolngu are now centred on the outer islands of the Crocodile group. During the mid-dry season young sharks and stingrays are hunted with pronged spears. Stingrays, young sharks, fish, turtles and shellfish alike are judged by Yolngu to be significant and desirable food sources when they possess fat (*djukurrmirr*), although no satisfactory commonality has yet been established in the fat-possessing nature of each species. Toward the end of the dry season, the offshore reefs and sand-bars are heavily fished and scoured for particular species of shellfish, such as oysters (*Saccrosta sp.*). The beach areas are significant for spearing fish at this time.

In each of the major seasons, camp sites will be as closely allied to the hunting and foraging grounds as possible. Fresh water is a major inhibiting factor. Many sites may only be established for short durations with small wells or soaks used to sustain the daily hunting party.

The People

In 1931 Arnhem Land was reserved by legislation for the use of Aboriginal people who had traditionally occupied the area. Within this area the coastal Aboriginal people of northeastern Arnhem Land may be considered an homogenous group in terms of their exploitation of marine resources. They refer to themselves as Yolngu, a vernacular term meaning Aboriginal person, and are variously referred to in the literature as 'Murngin' (Warner 1937), 'Wulanba cultural bloc' (Berndt 1951) and currently as the Yolngu bloc.

The Yolngu world is divided into two complimentary halves or moieties called Dhuwa and Yirritja with membership of each based on patrilineal descent. Each person is born into a patrilineal group (hereafter called 'clan') within one of the moieties which afford them, among other things, economic and ritual use of tracts of land and sea (hereafter called 'territory'). They also obtain rights to other tracts through their matrilineal affiliation (Williams 1983) and various other affinal ties.

The language most commonly spoken in the Crocodile Islands and Castlereagh Bay is Gupapuyngu, a dialect of the Yolngu sub-family which has been described by Schebeck (1968), Wood (1978) and Zorc (1979). There are forty Yolngu dialects in northeast Arnhem Land (Ross and Walker 1983). Gupapuyngu is not the first language of any of the land owning clans in the Crocodile Islands and Castlereagh Bay area. However, it is spoken in most northeast Arnhem Land communities such as Galiwin'ku (Elcho Island), Gapuwiyak (Lake Evella, from which the Gupapuyngu clan originates) Ramingining and Yurrwi (Milingimbi). It is closely related to speech varieties such as Liyagawumirr, Djambarrpuyngu, Djapu and Gumatj, spoken in the same area and often in the same communities. Speakers are polylingual, knowing the above dialects and understanding, if not speaking, several more distantly related members of this Yolngu sub-family, such as Gälpu, Ngaymil, Rirratjingu, Wangurri and Warramiri (Zorc 1982; personal communication).

Within the Crocodile Islands and Castlereagh Bay there are seventeen clan territories. There are no living descendants for at least six of these territories. Members of two other territories reside in the area intermittently. Members of the remaining nine territories comprise approximately half of the population of the area. The other half is predominantly members of five major clans, including Gupapuyngu, Birrkili and Wangurri, who settled in the area with the advent of the Methodist Mission in 1922.

Many groups among the Yolngu are now moving back to their own territories, reversing the trend to residence in a central community which accompanied the establishment of missions and government settlements. The Tiwi were similarly attracted to central communities but they were still within Tiwi territory and afforded the thirteen Tiwi clans the opportunity to participate in and maintain their traditions. Tiwi generally identified themselves as one entity to the outside world while retaining their separate identities down to the level of family groups within the infrastructure of Tiwi society. 'When at home on the Islands, a man thinks of himself as Tiklauila or a Manupula, or whatever his horde [clan] may be . . . When in contact with other tribes, however he thinks of himself as Tiwi' (Hart 1930, p. 171).

The Tiwi, like the Yolngu, are no longer geared economically only to the resources of their islands. They participate in the wage and cash economy of wider Australia. Their consequent need for employment and education has resulted in them moving to centres established by the mission and government. Consequently, many people use the natural resources of the islands less frequently than in pre-contact times. Employment and education are not the only reasons why some people do not visit their territories as frequently as they want. Incursions by non-Aborigines, such as by inshore commercial fishing, deter them. However, it must be borne in mind that some family groups have always chosen to live away from the major settlements, and others move away for varying periods in order to take full advantage of the natural resources of their territory.

There is little suggestion of Tiwi ownership-rights over extensive offshore areas although travel does seem to have taken place, with some frequency at various times, between the islands and the mainland. Generally, the foreshore down to the low water level provided the majority of foraging sites to meet the daily needs of Tiwi family groups. That the foreshores were of particular importance is indicated by Mountford's totemic map of Bathurst and Melville islands (Mountford 1958) which indicates 37 of the 51 totemic sites shown as lying either on the coastline or in the seas itself. The remaining 14 sites are located on the headwaters of rivers and creeks or are associated with bodies of water such as springs, billabongs or paperbark swamps.

Non Aboriginal Contact

Prior to European contact with Aboriginal people in Arnhem Land there were at least three sources of non-Aboriginal contact (Berndt and Berndt 1954).

Aboriginal people speak of the Baydjini people who came from the northwest beyond the Arafura and Timor seas, travelling during the monsoons in praus and bringing with them women and cloth. They stayed long enough to cultivate the land and build permanent stone dwellings. Berndt and Berndt (1954) record stories from older people which suggest the Baydjini originated from the East Indies.

Contact with another group known by Aborigines as the Badu is recorded in a cycle of songs which deals with pre-European contact (Berndt and Berndt 1954, p. 65). The Badu people came from the northeast, an area which is mythologically associated with the spirits of dead Aboriginal people.

The third and major group were the Macassans of Celebes. These contacts, which began perhaps as early as the sixteenth century, were much more frequent and continued until as recently as forty years ago (Berndt and Berndt 1977; MacKnight 1969, 1976).

Several sites in Castlereagh Bay were heavily used by Macassan trepangers because of the sheltered anchorages and availability of fresh water. On Banyan Island and Milingimbi (Yurrwi) Islands remnants of Macassan camps are still visible. Here, they smoked their trepang in preparation for sale on the Asian market. On these occasions, Yolngu travelled considerable distances to trade for rice, steel, gin, cloth and other items (MacKnight 1976). Milingimbi was also the focus of Yolngu ritual life (Keen 1978, p. 16). The Wangurri and Birrkili clans, for example, travelled west from Arnhem Bay to the Milingimbi area to participate in the collection of warraga (Cycas media) which is still prepared as a food for use in rituals. Vast amounts of warraga fruit called ngathu are collected by women early in the dry season when there is sufficient fresh water to leech the poison from the nuts rendering them edible. The resultant damper-like cakes may be stored for many weeks until sufficient food is accumulated to maintain the appropriate number of people required in the performance of a specified ritual.

With the establishment of the Methodist Mission on Milingimbi Island some members of clans such as the Wangurri, Birrkili and Daygurrkurr (Gupapuyngu) who had regularly migrated to the Castlereagh Bay area stayed on, encouraged by the availability of food, clothing and trade goods from the mission staff. The majority of the 600 people now living in the Castlereagh Bay and Howard Island area are not owners of that country. Rather, it belongs to the clan of their mother, mother's mother (MM) or mother's mother's mother (MMM) (Keen 1978, p. 17) and therefore they may reside in the area and exercise rights in the economic exploitation of the territories and participate in ceremonial life through close affinal ties with the local clans.

Unlike the Yolngu contact experience, the Tiwi vigorously defended Bathurst and Melville islands against any Macassan landings. The hostility shown by Tiwi to those unfortunate trepangers who happened to be shipwrecked was a constant warning to all others to stay clear. After intermittent contact with various navigators the Tiwi felt the first sustained European contact with the establishment of British settlement at Fort Dundas on Melville Island in 1824. An aggressive relationship ended in the British abandonment of the settlement for a more favourable situation on the mainland at Cobourg Peninsula in 1829. Hostile Tiwi encounters with government parties continued sporadically. Meanwhile the Tiwi also resisted the constant advances of the Iwadja tribe who travelled from Cobourg Peninsula by canoe to capture Tiwi women to become their wives.

Discoveries of commercial quantities of pearl shell on the south coast of Melville Island brought cautious contact with Malay and Japanese pearlers. Buffalo shooters were attracted to Melville Island in 1894 to secure hides from water buffaloes abandoned during the British withdrawal from Fort Dundas. Rifles, horses and a contingent of Iwadja tribesmen helped them overcome Tiwi resistance.

European contact was expanded in 1911 by the establishment of a Catholic Mission on Bathurst Island which has continued to operate and become integrated with the community.

Clan Territories

It has been a perplexing task to find a label for that level of Aboriginal organisation which exercises primary political responsibility for a territory. The most common are 'clan' and 'tribe' but the use of these terms like most others has been the subject of considerable and continuing anthropological debate. We are concerned with a sociopolitical group being one embedded in social relationships which exercises political responsibility over a defined territory.

We note that at times in the anthropological debate the definition of the clan has come exceedingly close to our adaptation of the term. The most prominently named social group among the Yolngu is referred to as the clan. Warner (1958, pp. 16–19, 338–92) denotes clan as the land owning group throughout the area. Clans are composed, Warner (1958, p. 16) states, of those 'individuals who possess a common territory'. Peterson (1972, p. 30) defines the clan as the smallest of land owning groups. He similarly notes corporateness of rights in land when he states that 'the only corporate property of the clan is the territory and the sacred songs, rites and paraphernalia that constituted the title deeds to it' (p. 15).

With the foregoing in mind we refer to the sociopolitical group so identified as the clan and use the term without any of its diverse anthropological implications. Each clan is identifiable with a discrete territory for which the boundaries can be defined.

As with territory among other Aboriginal groups the Yolngu and Tiwi territories are composed of a number of regions which are themselves a composite of sites. Among the Yolngu the territory of any one clan may be composed of several distinct regions separated by one or more intervening territories belonging to other clans. Most often, adjoining territories belong to clans of the opposite moiety producing a checkerboard effect of moiety ownership along the coastal region of Castlereagh Bay. In many cases the disparate regions belonging to one clan may be separated by distances in the order of fifty to sixty kilometres. Each separate region belonging to one clan may be denoted as being owned by a sub-group or lineage of the clan and termed a sub-territory. Warner (1937, p. 18), on the basis of his fieldwork among the Yolngu from 1926–1929, made similar estimates: 'A clan's countries are usually separated by up to sixty kilometres'.

Any member of the sub-group may claim identity not only with his sub-territory but also with the total territory of his clan. However, within the clan structure particular ritual emblems, for instance, may identify individual responsibilities for particular sub-territories. Ritual designs and the performance of dances and particular songs may be considered to be the exclusive property of particular persons related to separate sub-territories. However, where the sub-territories are not exclusively identified with any one lineage, ritual paraphernalia, songs and dances may be accessible to all senior custodians of the clan.

Beyond their identity with their own territory, clans may claim membership of a wider grouping of clans through common ritual affiliation. In line with the primary function of the wider membership of clans being common spiritual affiliation, we have chosen to label such groups as 'ritual groups'. Any one clan has rights in more than one ritual. Affiliations in such rituals will 'form many cross-cutting sets' (Keen 1978, p. 29) linking clans of different ritual groups on various occasions. The clan's territory, however, is not subject to the common rights of the ritual group.

The overall ritual cycle is held in common and so member clans come together to contribute to the performance of the ritual while holding separate rights in ritual paraphernalia. Among the Yolngu the Mandjikay ritual group, for example, shares the mangrove wood (*Rhyzophora stylosa*), rock and barramundi (*Lates calcarifer*) *wangarr* (ancestral beings). The connection between the Wubulkarra, Wangurri, Walamangu and Batjimurrungu clans of the Mandjikay ritual group through the *wangarr* (ancestral being) is described by Buwa'nandhu (Liyagawumirr clan, senior custodian for deceased Batjimurrungu clan) as follows:

> This wangarr name ... yindi wangarr [most important ancestral beings] like madayinmirri wangarr [the most sacred being]. That Meliway [Hutchison Strait] like the biggest, most important wangarr. That's like England or Jerusalem. Like that ... sacred. Jesus' big place ... Jerusalem ... that's like Meliway for us. That's a big place from outside the mouth of the Strait to right up the river ... big place. That's the place for [name of ancestral being deleted]. It belongs to Wubulkarra [clan].
>
> That [name of ancestral being deleted], he came from Meliway, to here [Milingimbi] and he changed bäparru [clan group]. From where he started from he was Wangurri [clan] ... right. When he got to Howard Island he changed bäparru ... to Wubulkarra [clan] ... and [changed] language. Right. Then he started from Meliway coming this way and when he got here he changed bäparru and matha [clan group and language] and became Walamangu [clan] and Batjimurrungu [clan]. Right, they came as one madayin but change, change at each ... different place. He went further, got to another place and he changed bäparru and matha ... But all one song and one madayin.
>
> Recorded at Milingimbi, 4 September 1981

Buwa'nandhu describes a most important feature of the interconnecting travels of the ancestral being wherein he changes his clan identity and his language as he passes from one territory to another. The locality at which this change occurs marks the boundary of the clan's territory. Hence the identity of each group at the clan level remains, as well as their rights in the focal sites of the ancestral being on their territory. The common ritual affiliation of the Wubulkarra, Walamangu, Wangurri and Batjimurrungu clans as members of the Mandjikay ritual group is clearly acknowledged by Buwa'nandhu in the concluding phrase, 'one song and one madayin'.

The path which an ancestral being travelled relates to individual clans who have territories encompassing sites at which he performed significant events. As each clan has an affiliation with more than one ancestral being, so they are related through more than one ritual cycle. Thus ritual cycles intersect in each clan territory.

Warrawarra clan, for example, is a member of the Maḏarrpa ritual group of the Yirritja moiety. They share the crocodile (Baruma, Baru) and fire (Gurtha) ancestral being with Gumatj and other clans of the Maḏarrpa ritual group as related below:

> This crocodile man and Lapakarra [spotted tree goanna: *Varanus timorensis*] were going along. She [Lapakarra] is that Djapu [clan] women. He [crocodile man] was Gumatj [clan] but he changed to Warrawarra [clan]. After the ceremony where he was burnt he came here [Crocodile Islands area] but this crocodile man is the ancestral being of Maḏarrpa bäparru [ritual group]. He is really Gumatj [clan] but after some trouble where he got burnt he came along here [Cape Stewart]. When he got burnt he turned himself into a crocodile and then came along here. He was the Gumatj crocodile man but he said 'I am not Gumatj now. I am Warrawarra here and my language is Burarra'.
>
> Mätjirr, Warrawarra Clan: recorded at Ngamuyani, 14 July 1981

Warrawarra clan (Yirritja moiety) thus has a close affiliation with other clans of the Maḏarrpa (Yirritja moiety) ritual group as connected along the mythical track.

Similarly Gamalangga clan (Dhuwa moiety) is related to a number of other clans of the Dhuwa moiety by right of sharing the same wangarr which usually encompasses sharing the same maḏayin and songs. In each case of a ritual affiliation the ancestral being travels from territory to territory but also voluntarily terminates his travels on each territory, there to metamorphose himself into some feature of the landscape thus giving the most restricted significance to the focal site of the territory. The ancestral being is not diminished by this act and the next clan of the ritual group takes up the story, acknowledging his acts on the previous territory but insisting that he continue his travels and deeds to their territory where he terminates his travels by again voluntarily metamorphosing himself into a feature of the landscape. For Yolngu there is no conflict in the ancestral being repeatedly metamorphosing himself and terminating his travels on each territory.

As noted in Chapter 1 the land was given form by ancestral beings who traversed the landscape, conferring territories and naming each locality. Each named locality within the total territory can be identified by senior custodians of the territory. Names are recited in a particular order. When asking a senior custodian the extent of his territory he will, most often, name all localities on the territory to which the ancestral being travelled and performed all the daily activities of life in the creative epoch. The names are recited in the order in which they were visited. This naming of localities matches the order in which names appear in the song cycle during the performance of rituals involving clans from the wider ritual group with which the clan identifies. 'Names . . . constitute a full description of the group's land' (Williams 1983, p. 99).

Among the Yolngu, two senior men, D̲akawarr (Gupapuyngu clan) and Bininyuwuy (Djambarrpuyngu clan), gave the following account of the extent of the marine region of the deceased Balmawuy territory (as shown in Map 2) in their capacities as senior custodians for that territory:

> D̲akawarr: Balmawuy . . . there at Worralngur. Worralngur, big name. Gapu Gora, that's Balmawuy. Barrapangura, Dhulinhagudirringura, Butjulugalarrbilik. Butjulunalarrbilik . . . they are the same two sisters . . . one, two but one language. They are two different places. One is a little sandy beach near Barrpangura. Both are called Nalarrbilik. Then Gurungura, that's a small name place. Going the other way (up the Woolen River) next there's Barrpangura . . . Dhulkingura, that's its other name. Wait. Dhin'kala . . . more different. Bunhayathanhaminy. Then Worralngur.
>
> Starting from here at Dhipirringur and going that way [towards the Woolen River] there's Gamanngur, Wapudharra, Buthiguli. You've got, Dhulinhamirringu. You've got, Nalarrpilik, Barrpangura. Barrpangura then that small place . . . Min'gala and Bunhayathanhaminy. Min'gala and Barrpangur are the same small peninsulas [*ngurru*]. Then Worralngur.
>
> Bininyuwuy: When you go around the corner near the rocks and the billabong there's Rarrapagarra. Rarrapagarra, there . . . that little creek in the mangroves.
>
> D̲akawarr: Then Gapu Gora.
>
> Bininyuwuy: Winwiniya . . . there in the sea.
>
> D̲akawarr: Dhunthala . . . all that place . . . the sea, mangroves, everything.
>
> Bininyuwuy: Yula, that creek, right through to the bush where the stringybarks are. That creek near the mangroves.
>
> Where that path runs from the landing . . . what's its name?
>
> D̲akawarr: That's a place without a name.
>
> Bininyuwuy: Barrama, that's in the sea. That's the place.
>
> D̲akawarr: It's not in the creek, it's a low tide place [*bandanyngur*]. In the mangroves. I go there and get lots of Ragudha [*Geloina coaxans*], shellfish.
>
> Bininyuwuy: Gurrumattjidhaḻ'yurru.
>
> D̲akawarr: Gurrumattjidhaḻ'yurru, that's the next place.
>
> Bininuwuy: Wait, first there's Buthumirringu then Gurrumattjidhaḻ'yurrunha. At the mouth of Yula is D̲ikarrangura. Then the shore where the mangroves are called Wad̲awad̲amirr . . . that's the spear. Then Ragalmirriway, the creek, lots of snakes there.
>
> Ngalngura, a long way, that's Gamalangga [clan]. They own it. Its Dhuwa. Ngalngur and Walindjuna and Gamalangga . . . and Djiwiwingur . . . that little bit of sand.

Gapuguwalbumara, just past Ragalmirriway. Two young boys died there
... that's where they were swallowed when they went to spear that stingray
but it was the snake.

Gundalgurruma is the creek opposite Gapuguwalbumara. It's not really
Gadayka creek. It's Gundalgurruma.

<u>D</u>akawarr: Djarringura ... that's the next place. All these places follow the
river. These names are for the bush and the river. They are not just in the
river, they are both. Djarringura is this side of the river. Buliyumirri.

Bininyuwuy: Wangurrngura, that's Balmawuy. All these places are Balmawuy.
Wangurrngura ... you got that? O.K. Djin'puwa. Djin'puwa ... you got
that? Right. Gora. Gora is near the mangroves, near the creek. Malarinydju
... bad place, angry ... and Dokngura. Garirri. Guninyimirram there,
where there's lots of stringybark trees at that point. That's Gamalangga
[clan] from there on.

<u>D</u>akawarr: All those places are Balmawuy [clan].

Recorded at Dhipirringur, 17 July 1981

Evolution of Boundaries

There is very little historical data to assist us in establishing the continuity of boundaries. The earliest reliable ethnographic data available for northeast Arnhem Land was that of Warner, 1926–1929. Warner's mapping of the area shows several clan groups and a number of language groups. However the work he conducted was not detailed in respect of boundaries and the only conclusions we can draw is that there appears to have been reasonable continuity since the time of his fieldwork.

Available knowledge of the African and European regions shows that boundaries may be subject to dispute with subsequent dispute resolution resulting in agreed boundaries or agreed boundary changes. It has proved possible in some such cases to show how peoples have expanded their territorial holdings and eventually met with other groups expanding in the opposite direction. There is no evidence of similar situations among the Yolngu. However, reference to other Aboriginal groups such as the Tiwi of Bathurst and Melville islands shows signs of such situations developing. Following marine survey work around Bathurst and Melville islands and the delineation of clan boundaries, the Tiwi Land Council has agreed to fix and maintain those boundaries which are presently recognised among Tiwi. This is the first instance along the north coast of Australia of the agreement and adoption of clan boundaries, freezing them in time, for purposes other than those traditionally recognised among the indigenous group.

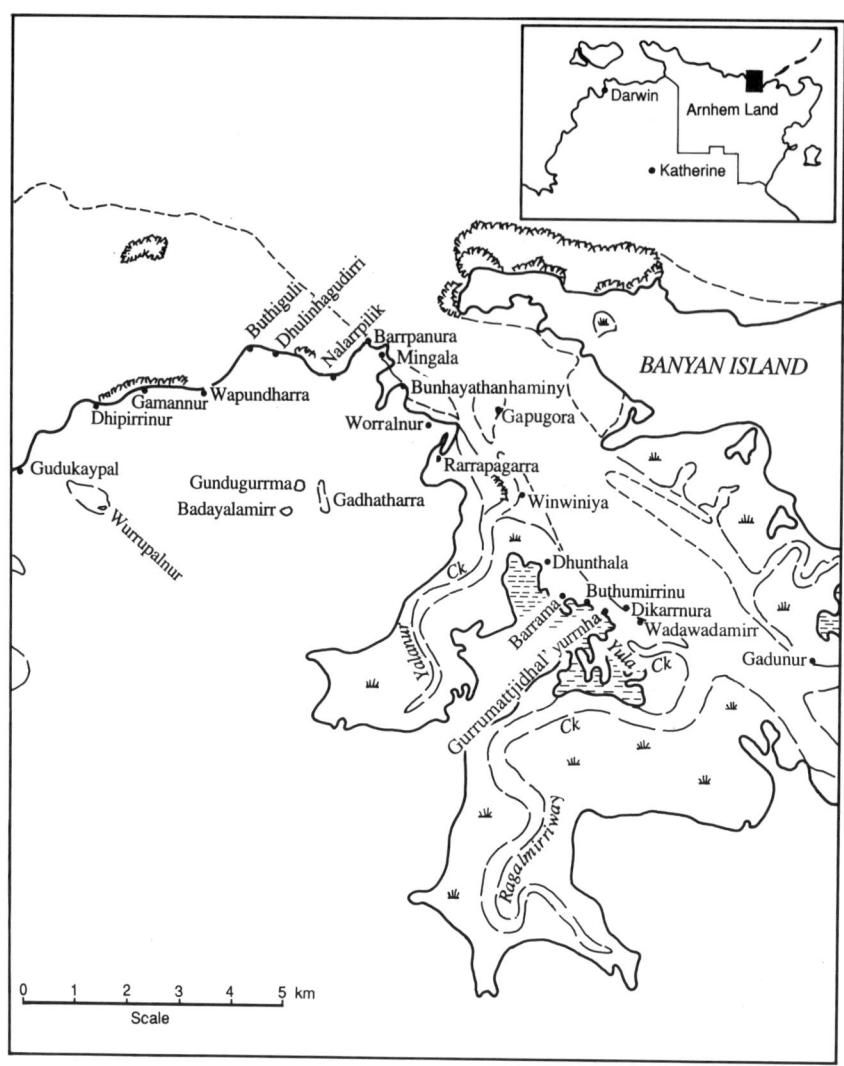

Map 2   Named Localities on Balmawuy Sub-Territory

We cannot come to any conclusions as to the evolution of boundaries as delineated among Aboriginal groups and so must take them as ready-made at the period which can be reached by historical analysis. The Bathurst Island case does, however, afford us some information as to the permanence of boundaries. On the south coast of Bathurst Island the boundary between the Tikalaru and Mantiyupwi clans at the site known as Pipiyanyuwumili extends from the sea directly north through a small creek fringed by mangrove vegetation and tidally inundated floodplains. The boundary follows the creek through the low tide elevation areas, winding its way upstream into the higher elevation regions of the island. Evidence from coastal geomorphologists (Bird 1983; Rosengren 1984) shows that the tidally inundated area was formerly a bay which has silted up and vegetated within the last 300 to 400 years. Assuming the coast was occupied 300 to 400 years ago, the creek presumably always represented the continuation of the deepest channel in the bay. The boundary prior to siltation would have followed the marine channel from the open sea and through the bay to the upper reaches of the creek. Thus the present boundary accords with the criteria of boundary delineation used by the other thirteen Tiwi clans. We can assume then that the boundary between the Tikalaru and Mantiyupwi territories has been maintained for at least 300 to 400 years. However, evidence of such boundary maintenance in the Crocodile Islands and Castlereagh Bay area is not available.

Among the Yolngu there is at least one available indicator that succession may have taken place. The distribution of Yolngu clan territories along the coastal fringe evidences an alternating pattern between the Dhuwa and Yirritja moieties. This is to be expected because women from the adjacent clan group are of the opposite moiety and therefore available as marriage partners. However, where the territories of two clans of the same moiety abut, we may speculate that territories have changed hands and there has been either some change in ownership or some reordering of territories in the intervening areas. We may further speculate that there was, between these two groups, another parcel of land which has been subsumed into one of the territories, containing a focal site of a previously known clan group. However, this does cause some anthropological problems, as territories of either clan are subsumed generally within the territories of clans of the same moiety.

Boundary Definition of Territories

Watersheds more often form part of a territorial boundary between adjacent clans than a specific site boundary. Although the boundary between the two adjoining territories accords with the watershed and limits of a catchment area, it inherently accords with higher elevation areas and physical barriers such as mountain ranges. In terms of human ecology, one would not expect such barriers to be traversed in the course of daily food gathering. However, in ritual and spiritual terms the morphology of freshwater flow often delineates the extent of the activities of ancestral beings associated with the area, and thus during the wet season the watershed itself denotes daily the extent of those activities.

In the case of the Tiwi people of Bathurst and Melville islands the majority of landward boundaries between adjoining territories denote catchment areas formed by surrounding higher elevation areas. Along the north coast of Arnhem Land where major river systems enter the seas the situation is similar, i.e. the extent of catchment areas either side of the river generally accords with the extent of the territory.

In several notable cases along the coast of north Australia, major water courses denote the boundary of adjoining territories. Where a major water course is wholly contained within one territory, the boundaries of the territory are often delineated in accordance with catchment or vegetation criteria. However, where rights in the water course are shared between adjoining territories adjacent to the sea coast, the main channel of the river most often forms the boundary (Map 3). Further upstream at the intersection of other territories, the water course will most often be encompassed within one of the territories with the boundary being the vegetation line adjoining the bank or the major change in gradient delineating the bank. Straits, rivers, estuaries and bays are treated separately.

Boundary delineation in reference to vegetation takes two major forms. The first is species specific in that a particular species of plant is associated with a boundary. The second focuses on vegetation types such as monsoon forests and mangroves. Vegetation as a criterion of boundary delineation is used extensively in the case of sites. In the case of the species specific boundary delineation, the boundary is aligned with that point or line marking the interface between the focal species and abutting vegetation. It not only demonstrates the existence of a particular species but highlights the change from one species to another. Where clan boundaries are concerned, the change of species often occurs at a prominent position from which a straight line is projected to another prominent position or in a seaward direction to denote the differing territories.

When viewed from the sea the common boundary between Manharrngu and Mildjingi clan territories in Castlereagh Bay, for example, is marked by the interface between the mangrove species *Avicennia marina* and *Rhyzophora stylosa*. The prominent distinction between

2 Tropical Coast

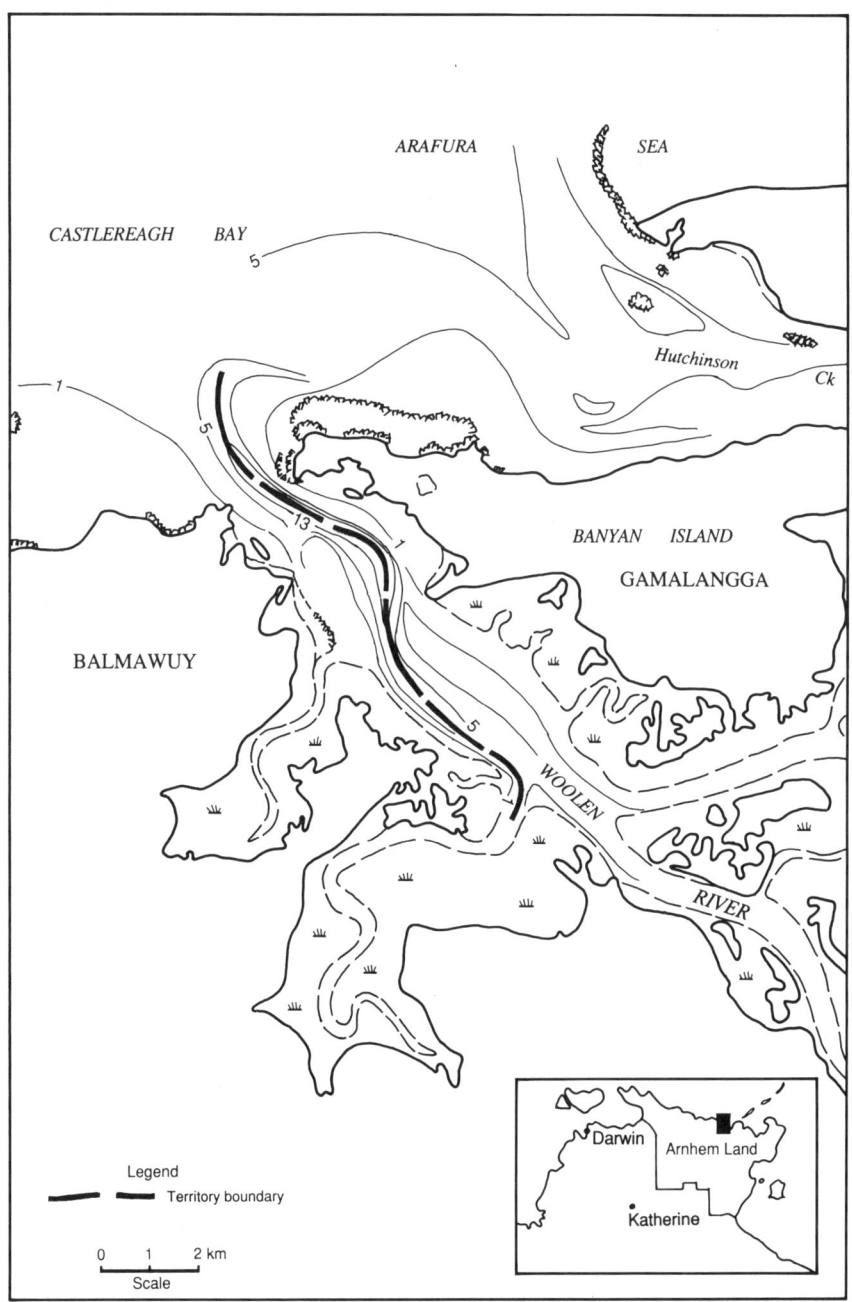

Map 3   Boundary between Gamalangga and Balmawuy Territories

species lies in leaf colouration. While *Avicennia marina* displays a grey/white trunk and a light grey underside to the leaf, *Rhyzophora stylosa* is characterised not only by the aerial root system, but by dark green foliage. It is the colour distinction which is prominent from a considerable distance and not the general habit of each species.

Boundaries between Tiwi territories or countries are, in all cases, defined with reference to water courses. Territory boundaries are not projected from the land into the sea. Such a notion extends from our predisposition with land. However, the predisposition of Tiwi people is with the sea, as it is with most Aboriginal groups along the north coast of Australia. This is reflected strongly in Tiwi mythology (Mountford 1958).

Tiwi ancestral beings, as with those of most other Aboriginal groups along the Northern Territory coast, entered the land through water courses. Europeans conceptualise such water courses as being the natural outflow of water resulting from landward catchment. Tiwi are not ignorant of this, but perceive the further significance of the land in terms of those acts performed by ancestral beings entering through the water courses. In this way Bathurst and Melville islands are indented with bays, rivers and creeks, all carrying life-sustaining significance to Tiwi land as arteries and blood vessels sustain the body and reach into every part of it.

Delineation of territory boundaries in water courses seems almost arbitrary. However, mapping the features on the sea bed reveals a consistently high correlation between the territory boundary, as delineated on the surface, and some natural features on the sea bed. Sometimes the boundary is indicated on the surface by a line of white foam. At other times there seems to be no surface indicator. About delineation of territory boundaries in the littoral zone a senior Tiwi man territory said:

> Pipiyanyuwumili ... creek ... boundary between Mantiyupwi and Tikalaru [clans].
> Pirrawakirri ... boundary of Tikalaru and Tikalawila country.
> They gotta split him in half, make him two pieces.
>
> Raphael Apuatimi: recorded at Melville Island, May 1982

The Snake Bay depth sounding profiles have named localities at both ends of the intersections and, as may be expected, the territory boundary also delineated the boundary between the named localities. What then is the response of the Tiwi to the delineation of a boundary in the midst of a water course which has only one name applying across its entire width? Such a case exists in the lower Apsley Strait at Morru point. In this area Munupi and Mantiyupwi territories abut in the Apsley Strait. The boundary then turns north to follow the course of Mirrapoka Creek. A Tiwi custodian of the Munupi country said of this area:

> Half of the sea belongs to him [John Baptist, a patrilineal custodian of Mantiyupwi clan] and half to Munupula [clan].
>
> They [Mantiyupula people] own sea [Apsley Strait] from Yuwurawu [Euro Creek] through to here . . . Muwaryi [Morru Point].

Depth sounding profiles reveal the correlation between territory boundaries as delineated by Tiwi custodians and features of the marine bed.

Of the delineation of a territory boundary, Tiwi custodians of the abutting Munupi and Mantiyupwi clans observed:

> This it here . . . finished [midstream due west of Muwaryi–Morru Point]. This Mantiyupula country goes straight across here [indicating due east across Apsley Strait with sweeping motion to south over the land both sides of the Apsley Strait].

Of the northwesterly continuation of the boundary through the Apsley Strait the custodians said:

> This [northeastern] side of the sea [Apsley Strait] is . . . Munupula [clan territories]. From that side there [southwestern side of Apsley Strait], that's all Mantiyupula [clan territory].

Here specific reference is made to the sea: the boundary between the clan areas is not itself the Apsley Strait, i.e. the Apsley Strait does not constitute the boundary between two land masses. The boundary itself has no definable width and thus the Apsley Strait itself is divided between and included in each of the two abutting territories. Inherent in the definition of Tiwi territories are both the land and the sea.

The extent of territories is to a large degree tied to the pursuit of economic resources. Tiwi custodians refer to the seaward zones of their territory thus:

> Mantiyupwi sea . . . long way [seaward].
> All out where we get turtles . . . still Mantiyupwi.

Tiwi consider that the width of their territorial seas extends from the land, across the littoral zone to the horizon, with that area beyond the horizon being 'for government'. This was a principle adopted occasionally in Europe in making maritime claims.

Prescott noted that 'the horizon seen from the shore . . . was obviously a distance which would vary according to the height of the shore, the prevailing visibility and the keenness of the observer's vision' (1975, p. 36). However, this practice remained in use for a considerable time as a basis for making maritime claims as Prescott further notes (p. 37): 'as late as 1740 Naples and the Ottoman Empire signed an agreement that ships would be protected within sight of their shores'.

Hunting for dugong and turtle generally takes place in shallow water where the victim cannot dive to any great depth to dislodge the harpoon and elude the hunters. It is to be expected then that low tide elevations of large area will be the focus of such hunting activities at the appropriate time of year. Wide flat sand-banks which are exposed at mean water often fringe a relatively narrow channel. Turtles are hunted as they move from the channel across the shallow water covering the sand-banks. Hence, such low tide elevations are usually included within territory boundaries rather than dissected by them.

Among those Yolngu whose territories encompass marine areas, the economic zones for shellfish collection extend down to Lowest Astronomical Tide (LAT). This is true also of the Tiwi. When LAT occurs, false trumpet shells (Syrinx arnanus) are particularly sought, for they are exposed on the outermost reaches of the sand-bars. The foraging methods employed are the same as for other shellfish in beds adjacent to land, reinforcing the classification of LAT as being the seaward extremity of 'land'. Above LAT the concept of 'sea' is restricted to the sea water itself which inundates the land as spring tides inundate salt flats. Hence all low tide elevations above LAT are considered to be land in the sense of 'earth' rather than 'sand'.

Changes in Boundary Location

It has been exceedingly hard to assess whether boundaries change as the landscape changes. The Admiralty chart (AUS16) constructed in 1943, which shows low tide elevations in the southern regions of Castlereagh Bay, evidences a continuity in the physical landscape of the marine areas when compared with mapping constructed in the course of this research. Although it is generally speculated that this is an area of rapid marine geographical change, little change is revealed by these maps over the intervening forty years, and hence no conclusions may be drawn as to the change of boundaries through physical changes. However, the instance on the southeast coast of Bathurst Island of a river mouth which is about to breach the foreshore some 400 metres west of its present mouth will prove instructive. Similarly Andiraningoo Creek on the north coast of Melville Island is about to breach the foreshore 1 kilometre east of its present mouth. Although neither situation involves clan boundaries, they do constitute changes in a physical landscape which may possibly affect the constitution of the area to which named localities apply. The problem is that the Tiwi Land Council has adopted particular named localities which are unlikely to change. This is a problem not to be ignored in mapping any clan of an Aboriginal group. Where rapid change in the course of a river is possible, it should be identified and rechecked at later dates.

When succession occurs and the territory of a deceased clan is incorporated into that of an existing clan, the boundaries of the resulting territory is a composite of the boundaries of both original territories.

Succession to Territory

Among the Yolngu the patrilineal descendants of a territory are considered to hold primary rights in the territory. They acquire these rights patrilineally from their forebears, by virtue of membership of that patrilineally defined land owning group (Williams 1983, p. 103). Primary rights are complemented by other rights held by members outside the patrilineal group–most often termed secondary or subsidiary rights.

Where the patrilineage exists, the clan's territory remains vested in that group. Williams (p. 106) states that 'a patrilineage must be seen as viable' with viability being 'determined by a number of factors, principally demographic and political'. It has been pointed out on a number of occasions by senior Yolngu custodians that wherever the names of senior patrilineal custodians of a clan territory can be remembered, and although the clan patrilineage may be deceased, the territory is recognised as still belonging to the deceased patrilineage. It retains its identity, with custodial responsibilities being conducted on behalf of the deceased by uterine kin or other persons with subsidiary claims.

Where a patrilineage ceases to be viable, because the remaining custodians are reaching the end of their lives, steps are initiated for fusion with other groups. Such groups are generally linked through common myths and are part of one ritual group and may share common rights and affiliations to the major sites of the myth cycle. This is presently the case among the Gorryindi clan of the Yanhangu language group (Dhuwa moiety) in the Crocodile Islands. That patrilineage is no longer seen as viable, as the remaining senior patrilineal descendant has no children and is at such an age that there is little likelihood of any children being born to him. Therefore, the Mälarra and Gamalangga clans have begun a process whereby Gorryindi territory will be fused into the remaining clans of the Yanhangu language group and responsibilities for their territory will be apportioned between the surviving groups. To this end, several of the sub-territories are now no longer identified as Gorryindi but as Yanhangu, thus making them available for re-identification at a later stage as either Gamalangga or Mälarra. As with the now deceased Dhäbitjin, the major sites of the Gorryindi will still be identified by their Gorryindi names as these are parts of the wider Yanhangu language group. There is constant friction between the Mälarra and Gamalangga groups over succession to the Gorryindi territory. Gamalangga men set up a permanent camp site on the north side of Murrungga Island which was part of the Gorryindi territory, thus advancing their claim to that territory. Few of the Mälarra patrilineal custodians are resident in the Crocodile Islands area and thus Gamalangga advances on claims to Gorryindi territory continue unchecked until the Mälarra custodians visit the area for ritual purposes or otherwise. Then friction flares over claims of succession to the territory. However, it would seem that Gamalangga clan has proceeded much further in affirming its claim by re-emphasising the relative importance of the major sites in the Yanhangu ritual cycle.

Within the Gamalangga territory, which includes Banyan Island, lies a major site at which an ancestral being of primary importance to the Yanhangu group performed specific acts which gave that area significance. He then travelled north-northwest to an offshore reef northwest of Murrungga Island. The site of this reef was, according to senior Gamalangga men, of subsidiary significance to the site on Banyan Island. However, as the offshore reef lay within Gorryindi clan territory the Gamalangga claim was strengthened when it became known that the ancestral being who was resident of Banyan Island and visited the offshore reef site daily had now taken up residence at the offshore reef, and only visited Banyan Island. With this shifting in the emphasis of the relative importance of the sites from Banyan Island to the offshore reef, the ancestral being, which had been primarily identified with the Gamalangga and continued to be so, gave more significance to the Gamalangga claim over the offshore reef through his continued presence there.

The daily action of the tide flowing across the reef and through several holes in it evidences the daily activity of the ancestral being on that area. The reef in question is now the focal site of all Yanhangu myth cycles and therefore is elevating Gamalangga clan to a level whereby, at the passing of the senior remaining Gorryindi patrilineal custodian, Gamalangga clan will assume custodial role for the Gorryindi territory. The Gorryindi territory may then reasonably be expected to become a sub-territory of the Gamalangga group, retaining the same language and moiety affiliation. There is no doubt that Mälarra clan members will continue a counter claim over the Gorryindi territory, however it may be that some agreement is reached between Mälarra and Gamalangga clans whereby Gamalangga for instance may cede to Mälarra a sub-territory which previously may have been identified with the deceased Dhabitjin clan, which was also of Yanhangu language affiliation.

Rights of Access and Permission

Rights in territories accorded to Aborigines by ancestral beings were dependent upon the Aboriginal owners continuing to perform ceremonies and care for the sacred objects and places. People who are generally seen to be using an area for economic purposes may have what could be termed a 'standing invitation' to enter and use the resources of that clan's territory. A standing invitation most often exists where people claim affiliation to that territory through uterine relatives of the patrilineal descent group.

In the Yirrkala land case, *Milirrpum v. Nabalco Pty Ltd and the Commonwealth of Australia* (Gove 1971) the solicitor for the defendants wished to establish the right of access between moieties for the purpose of hunting. Milirrpum Marika, Rirratjingu clan, Dhuwa moiety replied to the solicitor's questions as follows:

> Milirrpum: If I go hunting by myself on yirritja [moiety] land I ask first, except when I'm hunting with a yirritja man, then it's all right.
> Solicitor: Well, when you go to Port Bradshaw to hunt, do you ask anybody?
> Milirrpum: We Rirratjingu people talk together and then we go.
> Solicitor: Yes, but you don't ask any yirritja people?
> Milirrpum: The yirritja people hear us.
> Solicitor: Yes, but you don't ask them if you can go there.
> Milirrpum: No.
> Solicitor: ... if Munggurruwuy [a yirritja man] goes to Dundas Point, to his house ... does he ask your permission?'
> Milirrpum: He tells me, not asks, at the mission for the people; then he'll go because that's his country, Gumatj [clan] country.
> Solicitor: Does he ask for permission?
> Milirrpum: He lets me know but he doesn't ask.
> Solicitor (later): You would never say 'No', to Munggurruwy, that right?
> Milirrpum: If there's no trouble, we would say 'Yes'.
>
> Milirrpum 1971

As Peterson (1975, p. 74) points out:

> Only the solicitor's wilfulness prevented him from accepting this as a clear indication of the direct exercise of ownership rights.
>
> It is important then that the style in which rights are exercised is not allowed to obscure the existence of such rights.

However, even where such a standing invitation exists, a prospective user of the territory will most often inform the principal custodians, generally being the patrilineal descent group, upon his return from their territory and subsequently share with them the foods he has collected there.

It is common practice at Milingimbi for a turtle hunting party to include at least one member of the patrilineal descent group of the territory to which the party is bound, ensuring rights of access and subsequently avoiding any possible dispute over entry into the area. Members of the Liyagawumirr clan, whose territory lies at Garriyakngur on the northeast end of Howard Island, were resident in Milingimbi as custodians of the deceased Batjimurrungu territory comprising the southern portion of Milingimbi Island. Therefore, members of the Liyagawumirr clan exercised relationships through uterine kin to claim access to the economic resources of the Yanhangu language group to which Batjimurrungu clan belonged. As at least one other of the clans of the Yanhangu language group, the Dhabitjin clan, was already deceased and another, the Gorryindi, had only one male remaining alive, the Gamalangga clan assumed primary responsibility for the Yanhangu language group as a whole; the remaining clan, the Mälarra, were resident to the west of Cape Stewart in the Blythe River area. To ensure avoidance of dispute over access to economic resources the men of the Liyagawumirr clan most often included some men from the Gamalangga clan in their hunting party. Upon the return of the successful hunters the product was distributed through both clans and subsequently through further extended kin relationships.

During the period 1979–1984 there was no case of violation of a clan's territorial boundaries by any other clan for economic purposes or otherwise, nor are such violations evidenced in any literature (Davis 1984). However, violations of clan boundaries by non-Aborigines are many, particularly in relation to commercial fishing vessels. Such incursions have been variously met by displays of force from the Aboriginal custodians of such estates. In some instances firearms have been discharged, but more often displays of force with spears are directed at fishermen, who subsequently return the threats.

The violation of a clan boundary by Yolngu is virtually unheard of among the Yolngu. Such a violation would be tantamount to depriving the patrilineal custodians of the violated territory of their identity, for a person's being and therefore identity is their patrilineal territory from whence their spirit was conceived and shall return upon death. To violate the boundaries of that territory amounts to claiming primary affiliation and responsibilities for it, therefore depriving the patrilineal custodians of their relationship with the territory and making them a non-entity. No case of such an act has been recounted to us by any member of the clans in the Castlereagh Bay and Crocodile Islands area.

Some marine areas in the sea are held in common by adjacent groups. Such areas are not seen as belonging to Group A and Group B but as being available for use by all Aboriginal people of the area. They are usually access routes and no really viable alternative access is generally available in such cases. They provide access through channels sheltered from open and particularly unpredictable areas of ocean or merely through the only navigable channel. Such access routes may lead to a cluster of bounded areas owned by various groups, a ceremonial site or settlement. The main approach to Shark Bay on the north coast of Melville Island is an area held in common, as the channel is the only means of access for both the Munupula and the Wilirangkuwila groups whose common boundary dissects the bay itself. In this case the area held in common also serves as a hunting area of shared rights. Of this area, shown in Map 4, a Tiwi custodian of the Munupula group said:

> All this just hunting ground [north and northeast of Cook Reef]. They [Munupula people] own rock, land and beach . . . This [central section of Shark Bay] hunting place.

The economic importance of the area to adjacent groups is such that both groups publicly acknowledge common rights in access and forego exclusive claims. Custodians made the following statements in reference to this area while on site:

> We are in the middle . . . nobody owns this [Point H on Map 4].
> I'll tell you when we are in Wilrangku . . . when we are level with that island [Karslake Island].
> This is it [Point I]. We are in Wilrangku now.
> All that Wilrangku. See all that break there [referring to water awash on the reef] . . . all down to that mud low [low tide which exposes all the mud– indicating the adjoining bay].

The joint responsibilities in the area in which rights are held in common are confirmed in social alliances through marriage. In this case the clan groups on adjacent sides of the shared area exchange women in marriage:

> Man from there [Cook Reef] . . .
> women from here [Cape Lavery].
> They get that woman.
> Man from here get woman from there.
> They change women . . . swap.
> Man live here [Cape Lavery]
> and man live there [Cook Reef] . . .
> they relation.

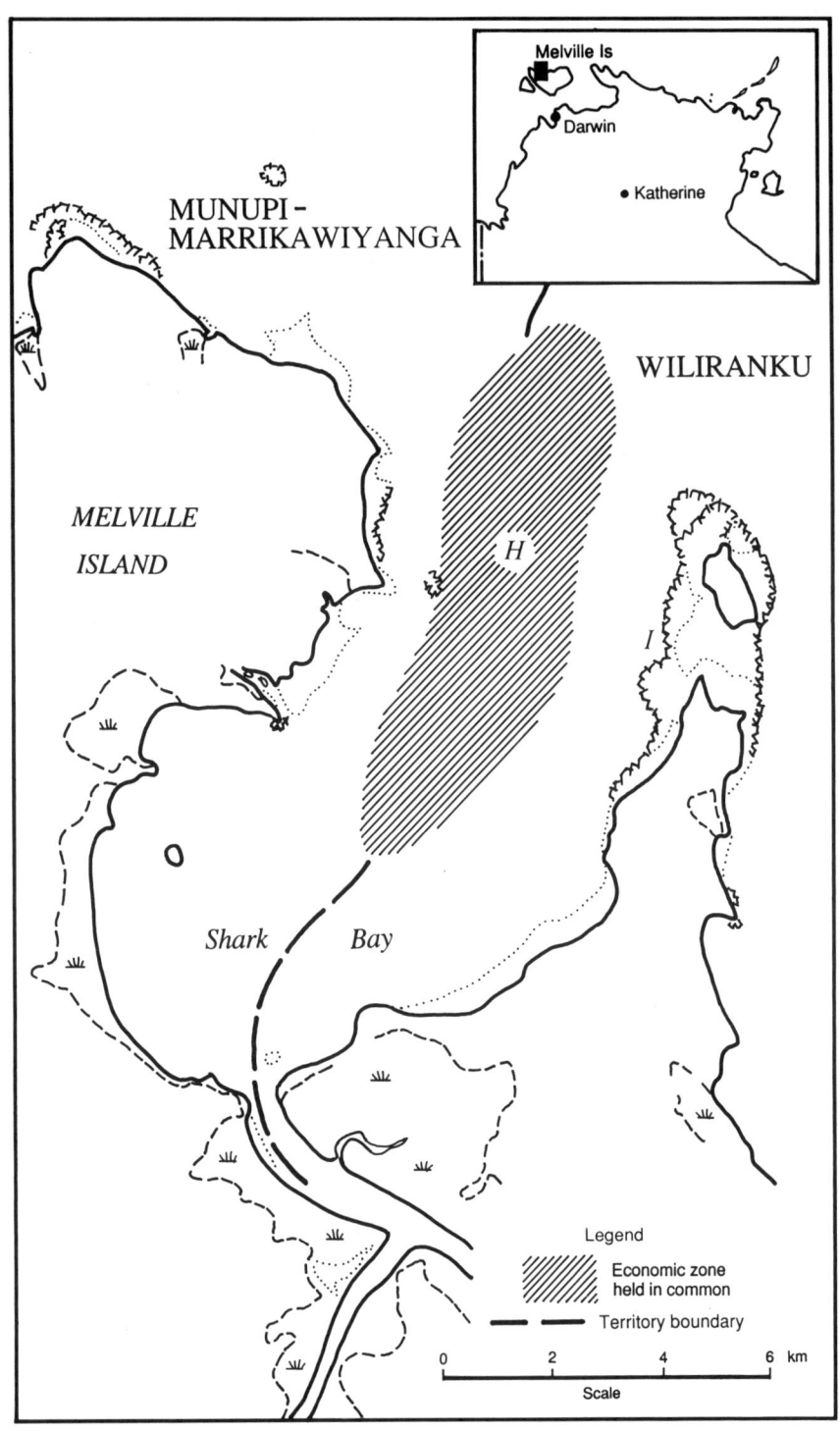

Map 4 Area Held in Common by Munupula and Wilrangkuwila Clans

The social alliances then form the basis for the joint exploitation of economic resources. The following quotation by a senior Tiwi man specifies the common membership of adjacent clans through kinship in one group hunting over the shared area:

> One creek
> one straight [main channel in Shark Bay].
> They hunt turtle . . .
> one hunting group.
> They know each other . . .
> relation.
> This part of everyone' [Central area of Shark Bay–see Map 4].

Thus rights in an area held in common by adjacent groups may be reflected in the social, economic and political structure of those groups.

Often where the access route leads to a cluster of areas owned by clan groups of both moieties, that route is common to all and owned by none, but access is nevertheless denied to strangers. Where the route leads to areas owned by two or more clan groups of the one moiety, the access route belongs to that moiety. For example, in the Crocodile Islands area a deepwater channel south of Murrungga Island is a Yirritja moiety channel which gives deep sea access to Walamangu and Ngurruwulu clan territories (both clan groups being of the Yirritja moiety). The main seaward access channel to Milingimbi Island similarly is a shared access route for clans of both moieties.

Thus the permeable nature of boundaries means that disputes which were common in the case of settled states of Europe centuries ago, and of pastoral and military empires of North America, North and West Africa and central Asia were largely avoided among the Aboriginal groups in Australia.

It is not so much a case of disputes over where boundaries lie as over who has priority of rights to the territories contained within the boundary. As mentioned earlier, there is no record of disputes over boundaries among the Yolngu either in the literature or orally from any living members of Yolngu clans. Again it less often a matter of disputing Yolngu's claims to territory than of avoiding disputes over various areas. In the case of the Yanhangu, the Gamalangga clan generally accede to the Malärra clan of their own language group affiliation and withdraw from the dispute. This is a common practice in that Yolngu generally avoid confrontation and dispute.

In the resolution of a dispute within a clan group the name of the sub-territory, as identified with the focal site of that territory, may be used by members of the disputing group to mark their sub-territory as distinct from other sub-territories of the same clan. In this way they are defining their boundaries or marking them as being distinctly different to those of the total clan and therefore maintaining their identity as a separate entity. Conversely, in the resolution of disputes it may be propitious for a Yolngu to identify himself with the more generic grouping of the total clan, thereby identifying the total boundary of the group and thus solidifying himself as a member of the total group's unity:

> As long as focusing on a unity is the intention, he will use names that indicate that common boundary of the grouping rather than what might set its components apart. (Williams 1983, p. 100)

Members of the Birrkili clan which have five separate sub-territories may variously identify themselves with those regions. For instance Djikula, a patrilineal custodian of the Birrkili clan group, identifies himself as Burrumngur Yolngu, signifying that his identity is of the Birrkili territory focusing on the site of Burrum on the southern shore of Buckingham Bay. Others such as Mamakun consider themselves to be Lunggutja, being Hardy Island in Buckingham Bay. Together with the people of other regions they may consider themselves to be Birrkili Yolngu as a clan group containing all Birrkili sub-territories, or more inclusively still consider themselves to be Gupapuyngu, along with Daygurrkurr clan. It is clear that Yolngu will use names at more generic or more specific levels to suit their purposes of affiliations in the course of dispute avoidance or resolution. In all these cases it is not a matter of disputing the boundary, but disputing or confirming the affiliation to areas contained within the boundary.

It is not unusual to witness at Milingimbi a dispute over claims to rights in a deceased territory which may have flared intermittently over several generations. In such circumstances the person making the claim may be very emotionally charged and will posture back and forth in the main camp area calling out the names of his forebears and his genealogy, and tracing his claims to forebears whose claims were stronger than his are now and hopefully indisputable, thereby affirming his present claims to the territory. There will be no denial of such claims directly to the person making the claims. However, there may be a similar demonstration at a later time in the same locality by a person who makes a counterclaim to that area. Direct confrontation will be avoided wherever possible.

Conclusion

Territorial knowledge among the Yolngu and the Tiwi has, to a large degree, been maintained throughout the pe riod of contact with

Europeans and operates equally well on land and sea. Although often obscured and submerged by European dominance, Yolngu and Tiwi territoriality have maintained the boundaries and frontiers of the pre-contact period. The boundaries between territories are defined in a variety of ways and their location is well known to owners of the territory, adjacent clans and other clans who may possess rights of access. The associated rules of access across boundaries and frontiers are strictly controlled and are firmly entrenched in the social, economic, political and spiritual life of the people. There are no disputes about the location of boundaries between territories although occasionally disputes may arise concerning access across boundaries primarily to pursue subsistence activities.

3

Southwest Arnhem Land

This area has been selected for two reasons. First, it experienced a century of sustained and intense contact by pastoralists and miners which caused major dislocation of Aboriginal groups and extremely high death rates—creating deceased estates in the area between Pine Creek, Katherine and the Upper South Alligator River Valley. Second, the Jawoyn, who occupy parts of this area, have made repeated and determined efforts through land claims and proceedings of the Resource Assessment Commission's heritage hearings to establish influence over and title to areas in the headwaters of the South Alligator River, for which they do not appear to have the normal proofs within Aboriginal tradition including ceremonies, ritual paraphernalia, songs and body paintings. These attempts might provide precedents for other groups in areas where deceased estates exist or boundaries have been lost.

The early pastoral interest was precipitated mainly by the construction of the Overland Telegraph Line and the discovery of gold during the course of its construction. While pastoral interests around Katherine flourished from the outset and have been continuously sustained, the more rugged country northeast of Katherine around the headwaters of the South Alligator and Katherine Rivers (Map 5), has not proven conducive to profitable pastoral operations.

The mining industry was, in contrast, no more intense anywhere in the Northern Territory than in the Pine Creek–Katherine area (Map 6). The effect on Aboriginal society of the violence and disease which accompanied the contact situation became obvious. Violent contact in Arnhem Land became increasingly common, resulting in some cases in punitive police expeditions being sent north from Roper Bar. Leprosy and opium brought to the goldfields by the Chinese was prevalent late in the 19th century. The dislocation of groups of Jawoyn people from the north of the Jawoyn territory, and the disappearance and dislocation of adjacent Aboriginal groups, has left large areas vacant for several generations. The introduction of the *Aboriginal Land Rights (Northern Territory) Act 1976*, coupled with recent discoveries of highly prospective mineral deposits in the South Alligator Valley, have heightened Aboriginal interest in the area.

The substantial competing interests in the Upper Alligator Rivers area have considerably escalated the case for establishing the integrity of current Aboriginal claims to the area and thereby considerably accelerated the process of succession and expansion as it would naturally occur within Aboriginal tradition.

Environment

The Jawoyn territory lies within the humid zone of north Australia where open eucalypt forest or savanna dominates with a ground cover of coarse, tall, annual grasses, collectively referred to as tropical tall-grass woodland. The grasses of the the region are mainly *Sorghum* spp. which occur on the stony, sand or lateritic soils, and perennial grasses, including Kangaroo grass (*Themeda australis*), golden beard grass (*Chrysopopogon fallax*), white grass (*Sehima nervosum*) and bunch spear grass (*Heteropogon contortus*) on loam soils (Mollah 1986). The humid zone provides a rich environment for fauna and flora, sustaining a much higher carrying capacity of the land for the needs of Aboriginal people and pastoralist alike.

In southwest Arnhem Land riverine-based food sources including fish, turtles and fresh water mussels are more consistently available than larger animals such as kangaroos. The valleys flanking the river systems provide an abundance of fruit and vegetable foods in comparison to other areas of savanna and open eucalypt forest, which are usually burnt off early in the dry season. Aboriginal territories in the humid zone are thus generally smaller than those Aboriginal territories in the arid zone.

Within the humid zone the coastal Aboriginal territories, which average approximately 235 square kilometres, are much smaller than those in southwest Arnhem Land, which vary from 15 319 square kilometres for the Jawoyn to 8258 square kilometres for the Yangman, 11 281 square kilometres for the Mangarray and 10 306 square kilometres for the Wagaman. Despite this range in size, they are generally smaller than territories in the arid zone, which may range up to 116 000 square kilometres as in the case of the Walpiri.

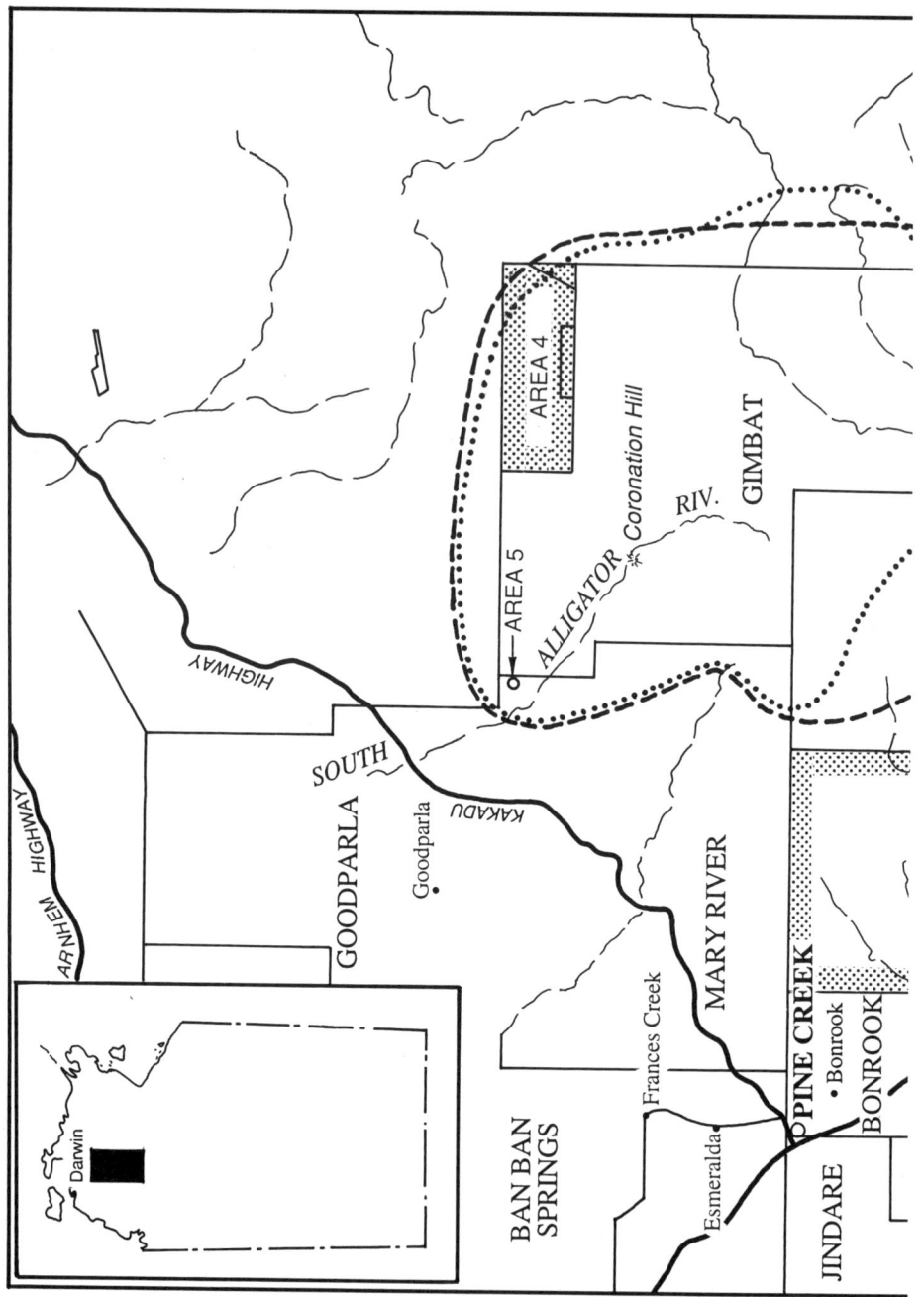

3 Southwest Arnhem Land

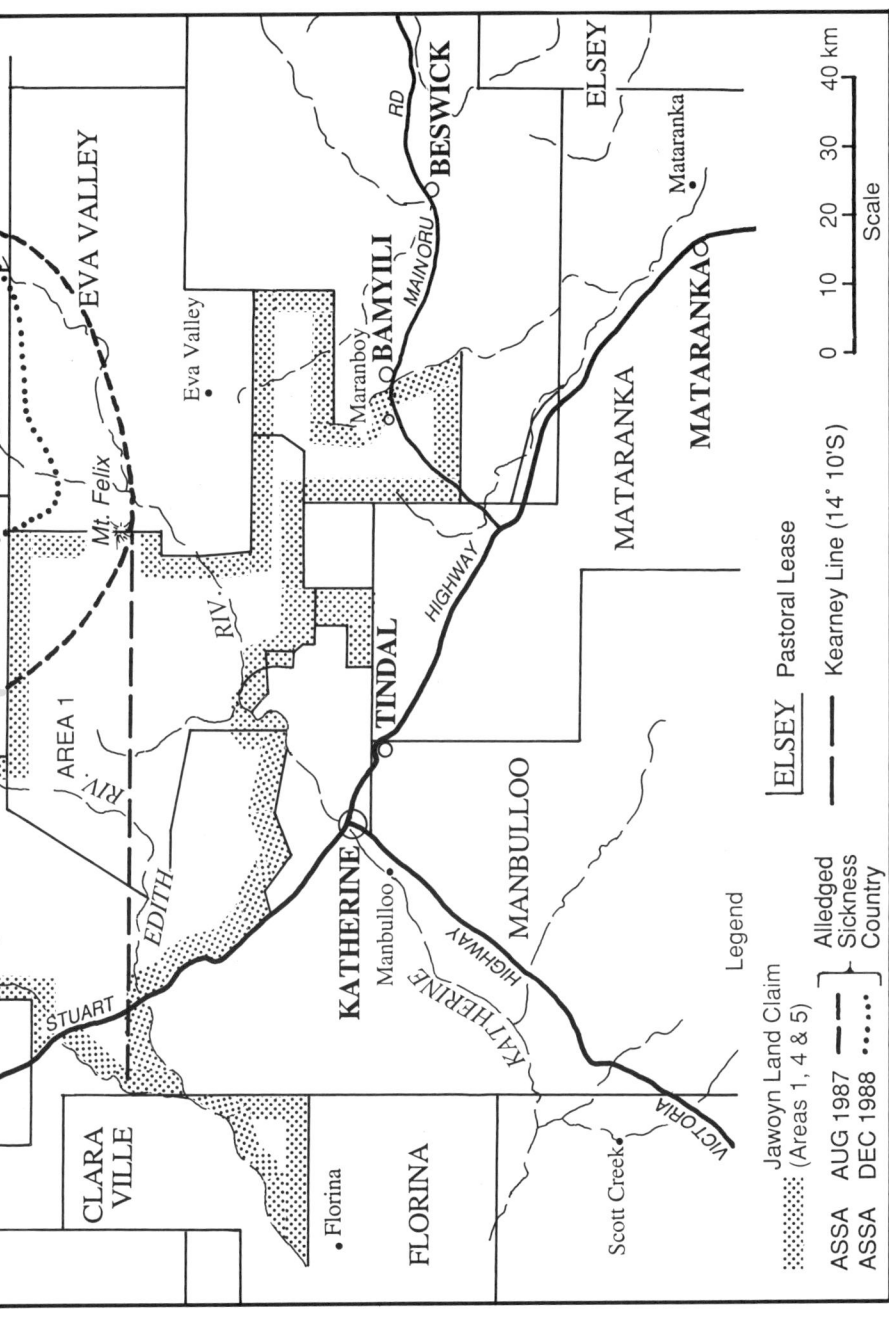

Map 5 Aboriginal and Pastoral Interest in the Katherine and South Alligator River Area

There are few perennial streams as may be expected with strong seasonality of rainfall. The Katherine River which is the major river system in Jawoyn territory maintains water throughout the year. Adjoining the Jawoyn to the southeast are the Mangarray and Yangman territories through which flows the Roper River which is fed by ground water and maintains its flow for an average of 350 days per year (Northern Territory Department of Mines and Energy 1984). The close association between the Jawoyn and the adjacent groups has afforded access to good water for the Jawoyn throughout the annual seasonal cycle, particularly when stream flow is at a minimum in the dry season between May and November. Ground water resources vary markedly through the humid zone, but recharge to ground water reserves generally by direct, local percolation provides reliability each year (Mollah 1986).

Exploration and Non-Aboriginal Settlement

Between 1845 and 1870 Leichhardt, Gregory and Stuart travelled through the region. After reaching the headwaters of the Katherine River in November 1845 Leichhardt took a more northerly course towards his destination of Port Essington on Coburg Peninsular. He saw a valley extending far ahead flanking a large river which was joined by many tributary creeks coming from the east, southeast, southwest and west. The river was the South Alligator, named by the maritime explorer King in 1818 (Feeken *et al.* 1970, p. 143). Leichhardt followed it to its floodplains and crossed the East Alligator before turning northwest up Coburg Peninsular to reach the military outpost, Victoria, on 17 December 1845.

In July 1862 Stuart, while attempting to find an overland passage across Australia, crossed and named the Katherine River at a point about 80 kilometres northeast of the present Katherine town site. That day he wrote, 'The country gone over today . . . is good for pasturage purposes; in the valley it is of the finest description' (Stuart 1865, p. 386). His positive reports on the pastoral potential of some of the areas he crossed weighed heavily in South Australia's ultimately successful pursuit of the annexation of the present Northern Territory in 1863. Stuart travelled parallel to Leichhardt's earlier track, and about 60 kilometres west of it, as he crossed the headwaters of the Mary River. Two years later the site of Palmerston had been established at Escape Cliffs, and in 1864 McKinlay explored the country between the Adelaide River and the East Alligator River.

Large scale land speculation of the mid 1870s to 1890s period, which was fired by Stuart's glowing reports, saw a vast area claimed by the Travers and Sergison syndicate. By 1878 this venture had not crystallised and the area was subsequently held by W. J. Browne, a wealthy South

Australian pastoralist. In 1879 Browne stocked Springvale Station near Katherine, but had over-reached himself. Further pastoral ventures were left to smaller scale pastoralists.

It was Nat Buchanan with 1200 head of cattle to stock the Top End's first station, Glencoe, north of Pine Creek, who showed that the Gulf Track was open to overland large mobs of stock. A pastoral rush followed, with the era of the overlander financed by the optimism of the gold rushes and encouraging reports of pastoral potential. In 1881 Buchanan overlanded another 20 000 head for Glencoe. Woods and Giles brought 3000 cattle and 12 000 sheep north along the Overland Telegraph Line to Springvale, near Katherine, arriving in June 1879 to establish the Top End's second station. The third was Elsey Station near Mataranka where Abraham Wallace had taken up country along Elsey Creek 'off the map', in 1877 and stocked it in 1881.

Duncan Campbell, the head stockman on Elsey Station, was fatally speared in 1882, and reprisals by Europeans quickly followed. Following a number of transfers of ownership of the station between 1886 and 1902, Elsey was sold to the Eastern and African Cold Storage Company (the 'Arafura' company) which was initiated by Joseph Bradshaw and backed by a number of London investors. As stations were established, the Aboriginal people were displaced by cattle. In common with other parts of the Territory, it soon became apparent to the Aborigines that their choice was either to 'come in' to the homestead and work for Europeans in return for basic rations, or to retreat into distant unsettled country. The company proceeded with what has been asserted to be the most systematic extermination of Aboriginal people in Northern Territory history. It has been claimed that the company employed two gangs of ten to fourteen Aborigines under the direction of a European or part-Aborigine to hunt and shoot wild blacks on sight (Bauer 1964). While written evidence of the activities of such gangs may be sparse, Aboriginal oral history in northeast Arnhem Land gives clear and vivid accounts of massacres by pastoralists.

The construction of the Overland Telegraph Line led to the discovery of gold near Pine Creek late in 1871 by men digging post holes. The presence of Europeans and mining activity has continued ever since in the area (Map 6). The mining boom saw a dramatic increase in the non-Aboriginal population which was sustained at a substantial level until the First World War. Labour intensive operations were widespread throughout the region. Intermittent declines in mining activity saw corresponding increases in demand for non-Aboriginal labour such as occurred in the late 1880s with construction of the Palmerston to Pine Creek railway and again in the mid 1910s with the extension of the railway from Pine Creek to Emungalan near Katherine. Among the effects of this early contact

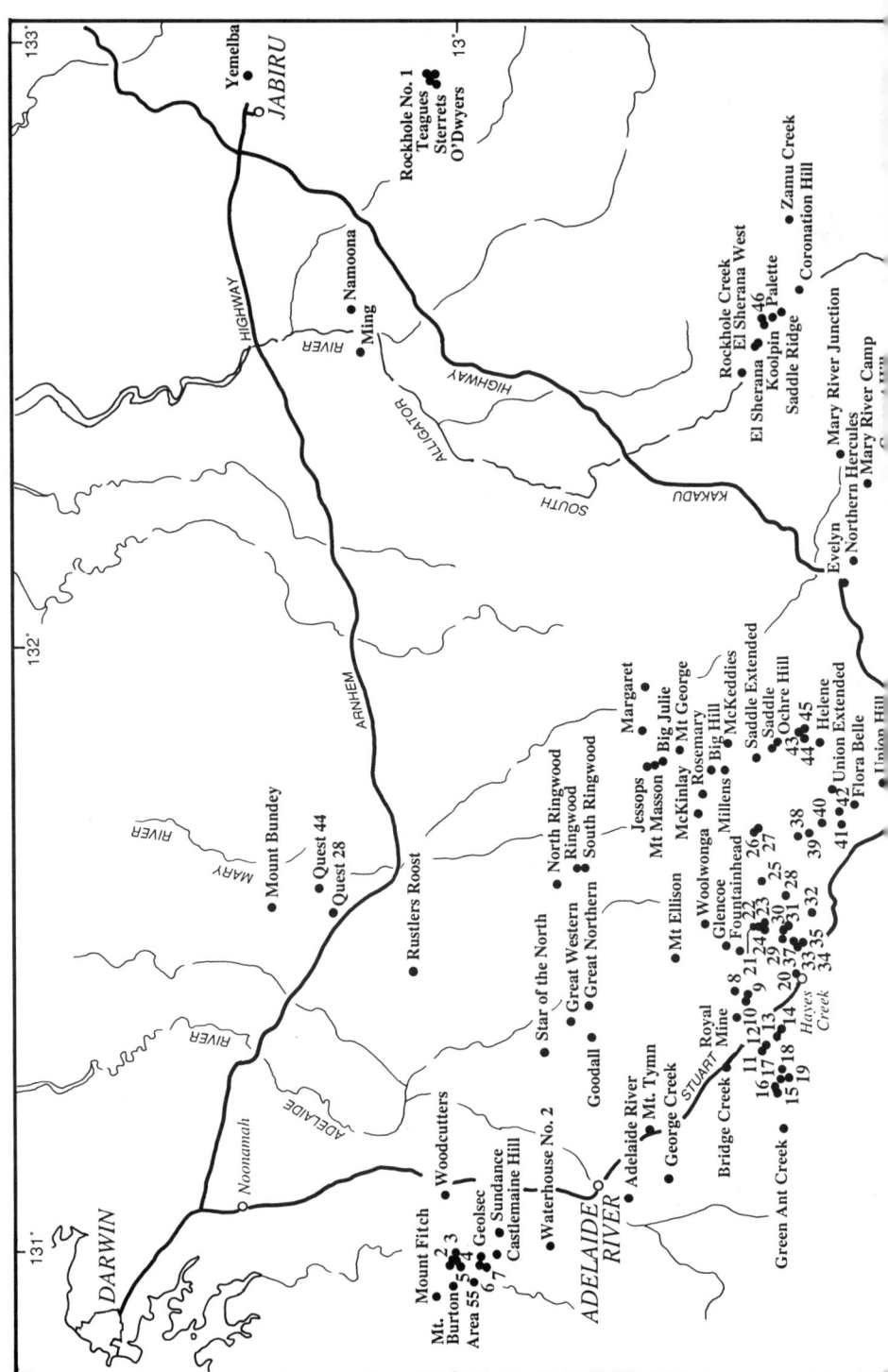

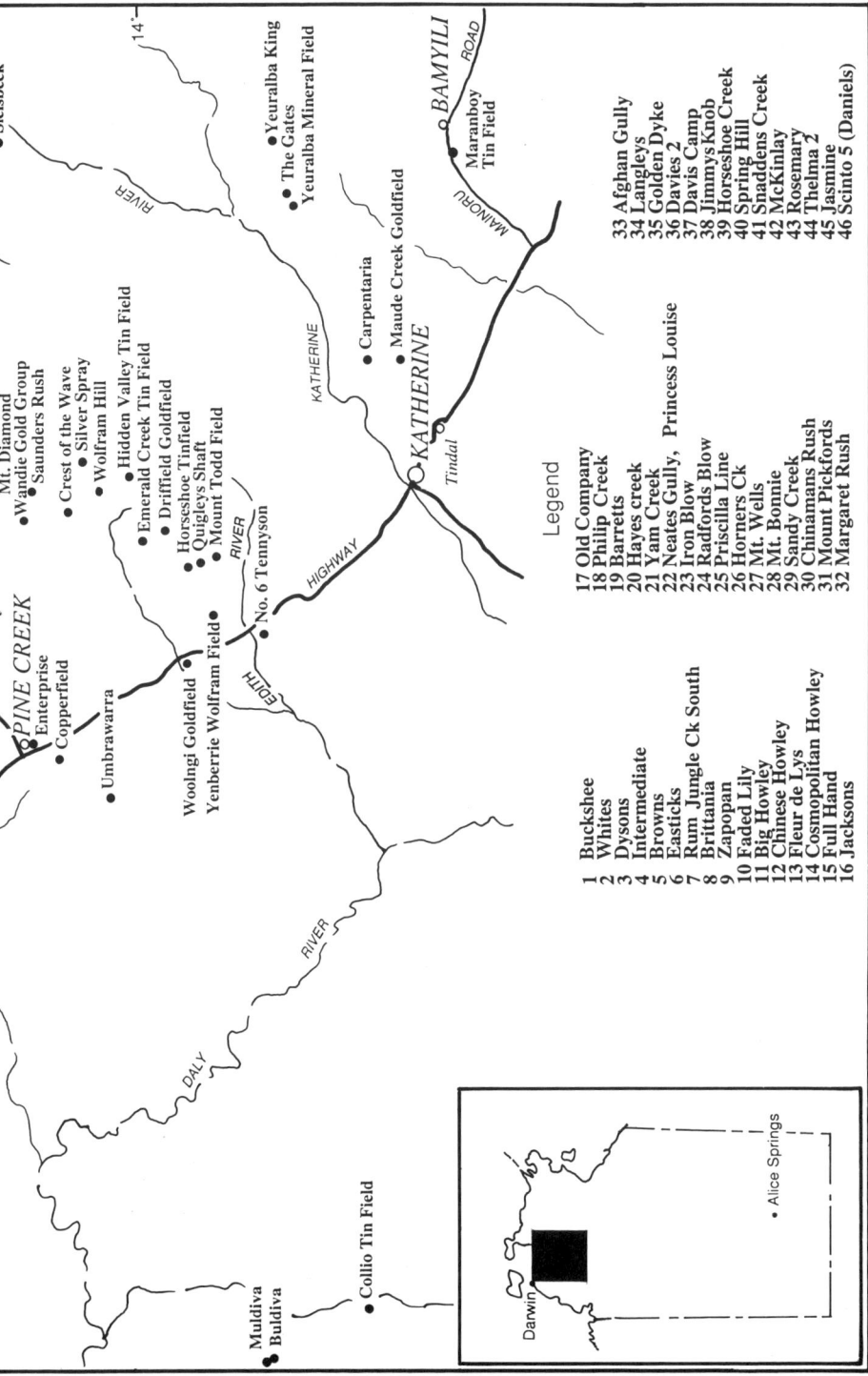

Map 6 Mineral Activity in the Alligator Rivers–Pine Creek Area

were the sexual exploitation of Aboriginal women, the supply of opium and alcohol to Aborigines, and their dislocation from the areas with which they had close association (Toohey 1981, p. 10).

The initial gold discoveries focused on Yam Creek northwest of Pine Creek and were quickly subject to a high level of speculation. During this early period, mining operations were predominantly alluvial and labour intensive as was characteristic of most Australian goldfields in their early stages. There was no machinery on any claims until 1874. With a severe labour shortage the Government acceded to pressure to import Chinese labourers; the first group of 196 arrived in late 1874, although not all found their way into mining. Discoveries soon spread southeast to the Fergusson River, although Yam Creek remained central to the main rushes. The Mining Warden estimated the population on the mining field in 1876 as 259 Europeans and 97 Chinese with working mines being 200 and 84 respectively (South Australian Parliamentary Papers 106/1876 cited in Bauer 1964, p.86).

Despite intermittent declines, mining continued as the most important industry in the north. Operations were returned to the hands of Chinese tributors soon after the turn of the century, and the depletion of the mining population was temporarily arrested. Tin and wolfram discoveries saw a concentration of activity at the headwaters of the Fergusson River and Wandie Creek. The liquidation of the major English companies in 1906 precipitated further decline of the mining population, and the mining industry was further degraded by the fall in tin and copper prices in 1907 and 1908 respectively.

The First World War promoted a major interest in metals other than gold, and copper, tin and wolfram prospects attracted a significant concentration of Chinese workers. The discovery of the Maranboy tin field initiated a sustained European presence which attracted Aboriginal people to the southern boundary of the Jawoyn territory. After the war Chinese workers began disappearing from the mining industry until only 18 remained at Maranboy in 1929 out of a total presence of 78 in the mineral fields. The extension of the railway line from Pine Creek commenced in 1914 but progressed slowly until its completion in 1917 at Emungalan, a site a few kilometres north of Katherine. Many of the Chinese formerly employed in mining were engaged in its construction. The production of gold slumped from 7277 ounces in 1911 to only 13 ounces in 1930 (Bauer 1964, p. 237). Most other metals showed substantial increases in production during the war years but collapsed disastrously thereafter with only a partial recovery in the mid 1920s.

The development of Maranboy, which began in 1914, was a significant factor in the drift of Aboriginal people away from the headwaters of the Alligator Rivers. As Merlan (1986, p. 1), states, 'It attracted a considerable Aboriginal population, mainly from Southern Arnhem Land and from the immediate area'. The operation of the tin field over an extended period to at least 1946 served to ensure a continued Jawoyn presence in the area. Jawoyn people became associated with the area and particularly with Elsey Station while Giles was the manager from 1928 to 1946 (Merlan 1986, p. 7; Thonemann 1949, p. 118).

Maranboy remained the pre-eminent mineral producer with a brief revival in 1925. At that time Aboriginal people had a constant presence in the area and became keen tin chasers, selling it to Europeans (Jones 1987, p. 181). A mining engineer, C. F. Francis, noted that in 1931 it was common to see Aboriginal people in the Pine Creek–Grove Hill–Brock's Creek area. Francis states that Aboriginal people bought much adultered opium from the Chinese (Jones 1987, p. 186).

Interest in gold mining in the Pine Creek area was revived in the early 1930s with capital investment on some old mines and options for purchase being given on other leases. However, despite the considerable paper speculation, actual work conducted was not substantial. Work continued in the established prospects east and southeast of Pine Creek with significant new activity in the South Alligator Valley.

The rapidly expanding population which attended the establishment of each new mining field was a major encouragement to the first attempts at permanent pastoral settlement. Glencoe near Hayes Creek, and Springvale near Katherine were stocked in 1879 in an effort to capitalise on the local demand for beef. The gold discoveries in the Pine Creek area also encouraged the South Australian Government to build a railway line south from Darwin to reach Pine Creek by 1889.

The sudden presence of a large non-Aboriginal population in the area quickly brought Aboriginal people into the contact situation. Such contacts often had disastrous results such as the killing of European miners at the Daly River coppermine and subsequent reprisals against Aborigines in 1884. The movement of Aborigines, temporarily or permanently, toward the settled areas which straddled the Overland Telegraph Line, coupled with the impact of diseases, violent contact, punitive expeditions and the social pressures which followed the disturbance of traditional occupation patterns, resulted in a serious depopulation of the traditional country and displacement of many groups. This is currently reflected in a general lack of knowledge of boundaries of traditional territories among Aboriginal people who claim affiliation with the area.

Stanner noted that there was also a voluntary movement of Aboriginal people away from traditional country to centres of European occupation and activity. For every Aborigine who had Europeans thrust upon him, so to speak, at least one other had sought them out (Stanner 1958, cited in Toohey 1981, p. 12). In the Finniss River Land Claim, Justice Toohey agreed with the submission supporting an eastward movement of the Kungarakany group towards the Overland Telegraph Line, the railway, the mines and the dubious benefits of flour, sugar, tea, alcohol and opium. The focus for the Kungarakany became the Adelaide River township (Toohey 1981, p. 14).

In the Oenpelli area the Aboriginal people are today generally known as the Gunwinggu. However, as Cole (1975, p. 6) notes:

> They appear to have arrived in the 1920s, as they, with other major tribes of Western Arnhem Land, slowly made their way westwards towards the buffalo camps, the mining settlements and Darwin, drawn by curiosity and the availability of western goods including tobacco and alcohol.

Cole's view of the Gunwinggu influx is supported by the Berndts who record the first movement of Gunwinggu people into the Oenpelli area as taking place prior to the establishment of the Church Missionary Society at Oenpelli in 1925 (Berndt 1970). Elkin (1938) documented the Mangari at Oenpelli as almost dying out and being replaced by the Kakadu (Gagadju) who subsequently suffered the same fate and were replaced by the Gunwinggu, who originally came from the hill country south of Goulburn Island.

The contact period in this region, then, is typified by incursion of non-Aborigines and dispersal of many Aboriginal groups, the extinction or removal of some Aboriginal groups, and displacement of still others. The effect on traditional boundaries has been such that the groups who originally straddled the Overland Telegraph Line and railway have generally remained and thus maintained their knowledge of the extent of their estates and boundaries. The attraction of groups from both the east and the west to the telegraph line and railway has resulted in a blurring of boundaries that should not be mistaken for frontiers. A large area of western Arnhem Land is now only vaguely identified with specific groups. The rough and generally inaccessible nature of the country has not been conducive to its re-occupation by other groups, who themselves have been drawn from Central Arnhem Land to coastal missions stations, small pastoral holdings and ration depots in the Roper River and Elsey areas to the south.

Claims and Elaboration

The first wave of Jawoyn expansion came with the Jawoyn (Katherine Area) Land Claim (Maps 5 and 7). The preparation in 1982 of a book, *The Jawoyn (Katherine Area) Land Claim*, by the Northern Land Council was a catalyst for pursuing a Jawoyn identity. The Wagaman, Wadaman and Yangman abutting the Jawoyn territory to the west, southwest and southeast respectively did not present any opportunity for Jawoyn expansion. It should not be surprising then that the land claim book contended that Jawoyn identity extended north, well into the former 'Wulwulam country and through the Upper South Alligator Valley. In the absence of any other Aboriginal group living in the area or having asserted any form of primary affiliation with the area, the Jawoyn expansion to the north remained unopposed by Aboriginal people. However, the evidence as presented in the claim did not convince Mr Justice Kearney, the Aboriginal Land Commissioner, that Jawoyn claims to the area in the Upper South Alligator Valley could be substantiated by Jawoyn within Aboriginal tradition. The Kearney Line (Map 5) delimited the land to which the Jawoyn currently have spiritual affiliation (Kearney 1987, p. 96).

In the Jawoyn land claim book, Merlan and Rumsey (1982, p. 37) contend that the term 'Jawoyn' is synonymous with a people, a language and a territory. The term denotes a social group and a language. While language proficiency as such is not a defining characteristic of group membership, it often coincides with it. Jawoyn, like their near neighbours including the Ngalkbon, Ngalakan, Rembarrnga and Mangarray, is a language-owning group rather than a language-using group. Sutton and Palmer (1981, p. 30) make the distinction that groups referred to by language labels are language-owning rather than language-using groups. The social group is affiliated with a particular language because the language is identified with a defined tract of country to which the group is also affiliated. Thus, the land claim book states, the essential factor in group definition is territoriality (Merlan and Rumsey 1982, p. 37). Mr Justice Kearney similarly stated that territoriality is said to be the essence of Jawoyn identity (Kearney 1987, p. 20).

Although much of the South Alligator Valley was not subject to claim, evidence of common spiritual affiliation to sites in the valley which lie outside the claim areas was called upon by the Jawoyn to support their claim to the northern areas of the claim in the vicinity of the South Alligator Valley. However, as the Judge points out (para. 149):

> Where those sites are outside the claim area, they must be sufficiently linked by cogent evidence to the claim area, when affiliations to those sites are relied on to support the claim.

Further, in an attempt to establish 'common spiritual affiliation' (para. 150):

> ... members of the claimant local descent group must show that they possess associations of a spiritual nature with sites on their traditional country, and

demonstrate that they hold those associations more or less equally, that is, that the associations are not just the association of a few knowledgeable individuals. The claimants should show that they possess a spiritual knowledge of their country independently of what they may have learned in connection with the enquiry into the claim; and they should demonstrate some continuing relationship with their traditional country—for example, by visiting it from time to time for spiritual purposes.

In the light of evidence relevant to an assessment of the commonality of spiritual affiliations to sites, the Judge states (para 16):

I consider it is clear that the spiritual affiliation which the members of the Jawoyn group now have in common to sites, is to sites in the southern part of their traditional country.

Such was the gravity of the court's rejection of claims of spiritual affiliations in the northern section of the claim area, both to the south and the north of the South Alligator Valley, that the Judge gave special consideration to the implications of that conclusion (paras 162, 163):

While several sites in the vicinity of Areas 4 and 5 were named and their associated Dreamings identified, no evidence to establish common spiritual affiliations by the claimants to these sites or the performance of spiritual responsibilities for those sites was given either in open or closed session of the enquiry.

The traditional evidence put forward in relation to Areas 4 and 5 is insufficient to enable any finding to be made that the members of that group (or any group, for that matter) are the traditional Aboriginal owners of those areas, within the meaning of the Act. While there are sites on both areas and Dreamings to which the Jawoyn have links, for example, through the travelling Dreamings Gupu [Kangaroo] and Na-gorrko at Gunlom . . . the existence of common spiritual affiliations to sites on Areas 4 and 5, or to sites which can be linked with those areas, is not established, nor is there evidence of a strong traditional attachment to Areas 4 and 5 . . . Accordingly, the claim to Area 4 and 5 fails.

Mr Justice Kearney commented that generally the spiritual affiliation of the Jawoyn diminishes the further north one moves. In an attempt to delimit the area over which the Jawoyn currently have spiritual affiliations, he produced a description (para. 165) which delimits the 'country within the sphere of influence of the sites to which the Jawoyn have etablished common spiritual affiliations'. The northern extremity of the area so described is found to lie approximately along a line of latitude 14 degrees 10 minutes south (the Kearney Line) which generally connects Edith Falls in the west to Mount Felix in the east, and clearly does not include the South Alligator Valley or Coronation Hill which lies a further 65 kilometres north. The western extension of this line through the Edith River is consistent with the boundary which Tindale (1974) asserted for the Jawoyn at the time of contact and excludes the Jawoyn from the entire South Alligator Valley and headwaters of the Katherine River (Map 7).

The land claim was only partially successful. It did not secure title to Areas 4 and 5 for the Jawoyn people and thus they were unable to exercise territoriality based on title to the land gained through the *Aboriginal Land Rights (Northern Territory) Act* 1976. However, the registration of a vast tract of the South Alligator Valley by the Aboriginal Sacred Sites Authority effectively enabled territoriality still to be exercised in favour of the Jawoyn people (apart from the decision to grant a work permit in July 1986).

In support of their claim to traditional ownership of land in the South Alligator Valley the Jawoyn described events which took place in the creative epoch whereby ancestral beings identified with the Jawoyn travelled across the landscape and performed activities which have become synonymous with particular localities. The special properties of these activities or events define the limits of Jawoyn territoriality. During the land claim process the onus rested on the Jawoyn to establish the integrity of such events, that these events are synonymous with the Jawoyn people and that such events feature significantly and are actively maintained within Jawoyn tradition.

It is common within Aboriginal tradition to define the limits of territory through the spatial properties of events which are described by reference to location names in song cycles. These song cycles are often sung in the course of ceremonies to accompany dances which re-enact the events performed by the ancestral beings in the creative epoch. The archaic nature of the Bula ritual synonymous with the Upper South Alligator Valley largely negated the ability of the Jawoyn to push the limits of their territoriality far enough north to encompass the South Alligator Valley. The Jawoyn were not able to establish current spiritual affiliation in terms of the *Aboriginal Land Rights (Northern Territory) Act* 1976 to land north of this line to Mr Justice Kearney's satisfaction.

The extinction of the 'Wulwulam and their northeastern neighbours the Wat:a left a considerable area vacant and subject to the process of succession. However, the adjacent groups had themselves withdrawn from the contiguous areas and the process of succession was forestalled for many generations.

The failure of the Jawoyn to establish their spiritual affiliation north of the Kearney Line did not effectively rebutt Jawoyn attempts to establish their territoriality over the South Alligator Valley. It became obvious that

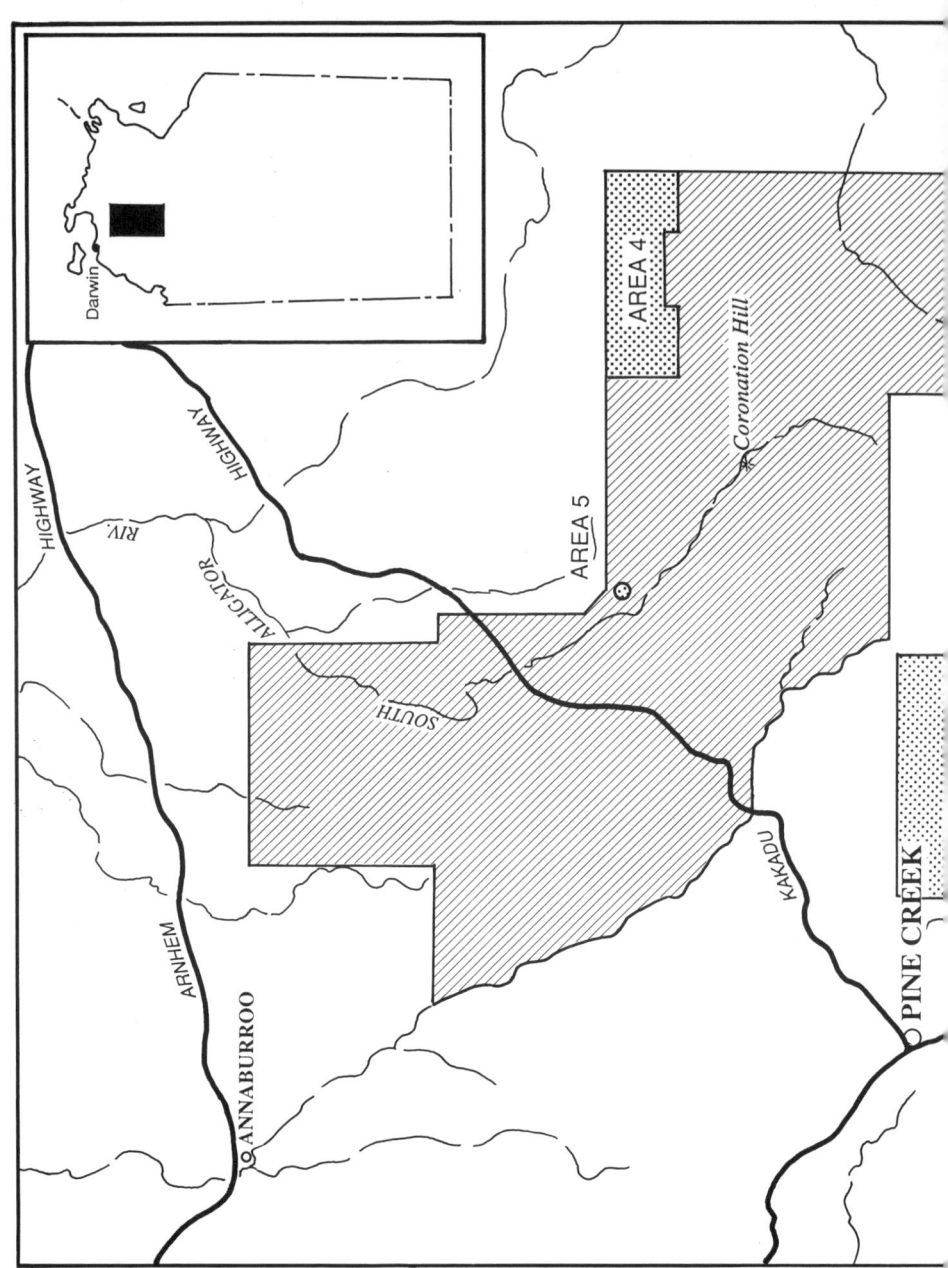

3 Southwest Arnhem Land

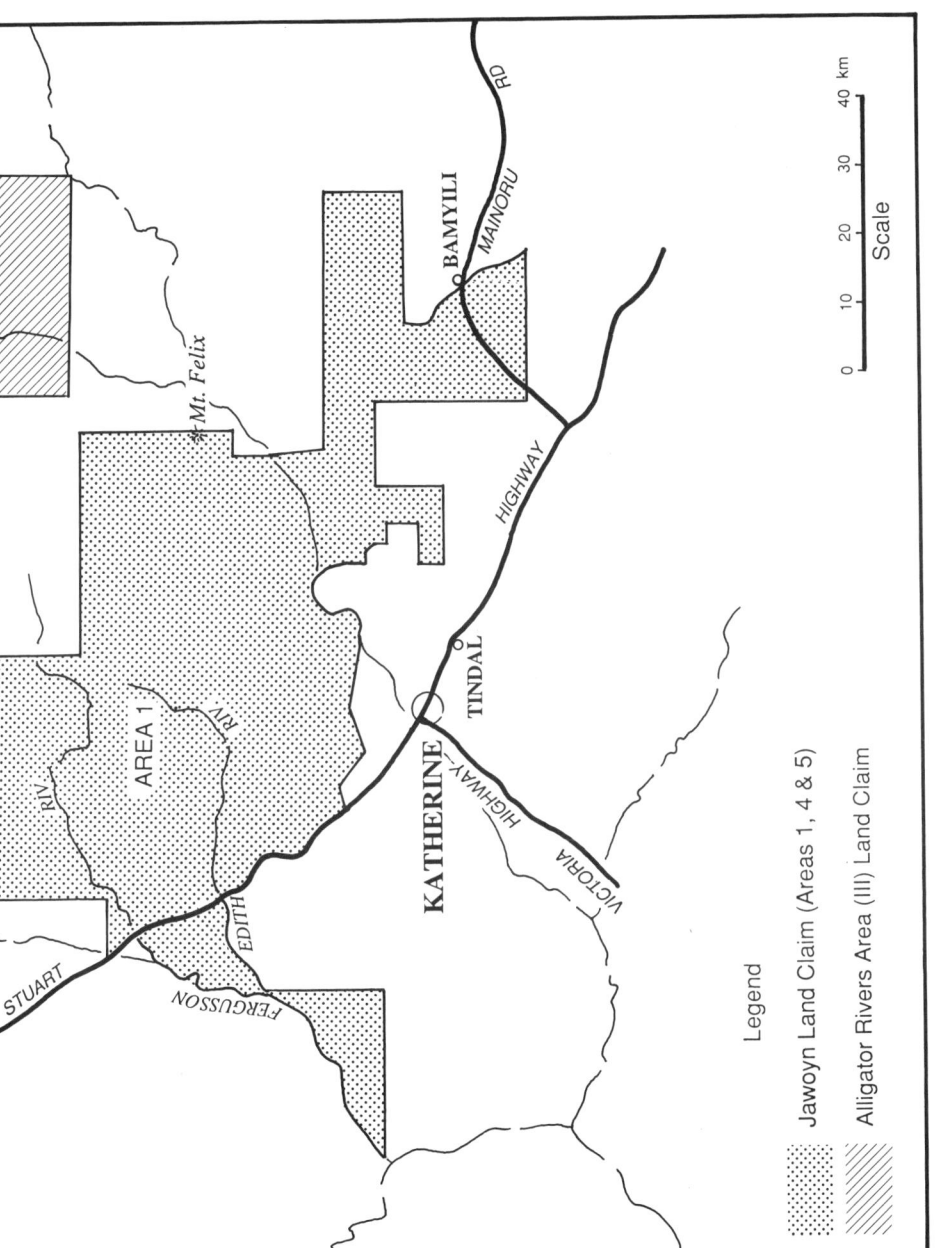

Map 7 Land Claims in the Katherine and South Alligator River Area

the Jawoyn may have proceeded in the reverse order to that of a pre-European contact situation or a situation not influenced by the surrounding events, including the extension of a national park and applications for mineral exploration.

The Jawoyn proceeded to embrace the deceased 'Wulwulam estate as Jawoyn country in the course of the construction of their claim in 1982. However, by 1984 senior Jawoyn custodians still could not exhibit any specific knowledge of sites north of the Edith River when they were employed on survey work designed to avoid Aboriginal sites during the construction of the Amadeus Basin to Darwin gas pipeline. The same senior Jawoyn custodians who were at the forefront of the claim, and have since often been held to be the traditional owners of the Upper South Alligator Valley with all the attendant detailed knowledge of sacred sites and Aboriginal tradition in the area, were engaged in detailed survey work by foot, vehicle and helicopter in the Katherine to Pine Creek area specifically in relation to Aboriginal sites. At that time they were clear that their knowledge of sites did not extend north of the Edith River.

In October 1985 the Aboriginal Sacred Sites Authority registered an area of approximately 260 square kilometres known as the Upper South Alligator Valley Bula Complex. The registered area falls substantially within the boundaries of the 'Wulwulam territory as previously mapped by Tindale (1974). The Authority attributes custodianship of the site to the same Jawoyn custodians that were employed on the gas pipeline survey work in 1984. By early 1988 the Authority had entered on their register more than 40 additional sites in the South Alligator Valley, attributing custodianship in each case to Jawoyn people, and in particular to the same Jawoyn custodians employed on the survey for the Amadeus Basin to Darwin gas pipeline.

It would seem that in using an incremental approach through the registration and recording of sites to achieve Jawoyn rights over the South Alligator Valley, new events are being produced and expanded on behalf of and in conjunction with the Jawoyn to extend Jawoyn territoriality over vacant territory. This is a clear example of the elaboration of traditions. While it is true that setting particular places apart, hedging them about with ritual prohibitions and imbuing them with a metaphysical significance is a displacement effect of territoriality, this is not in itself sufficient to establish territoriality.

The continued process of registering and recording sites by the Aboriginal Sacred Sites Authority is acting as a tool for defining the knowledge and responsiblities of the Jawoyn. The Authority's actions in publishing documents containing maps which circumscribe an area of almost 7000 square kilometres and denoting it as the 'Bula Sickness

Country' (Map 5), a tradition uniquely associated with the Jawoyn, is promoting a union between people and place; between the Jawoyn people and the South Alligator Valley. In doing so, the Authority is assigning an identity which is corporate in the territory, for the very corporateness of the Aboriginal group itself lies in its identification with a territory.

In 1989 the Federal Government was confronted with the prospect of making a decision as to whether to allow mining at Coronation Hill in the Upper South Alligator Valley. With the prospect of an election looming in which the Green conservation vote was to prove critical, it temporarily side-stepped the Coronation Hill issue and referred the matter to a commission of inquiry, the Resource Assessment Commission. The Commission specifically addressed the issue of the elaboration of traditions to serve land ownership ambitions (Resource Assessment Commission, vol. 1, pp. 171–5) and reported that elaboration of Jawoyn traditions had indeed occurred. A specific example cited the identification of reef gold as the blood of the ancestral being Bula. The gold was only found comparatively recently. The Government subsequently banned mining at Coronation Hill. The Commission conceded that the issue of mining at Coronation Hill was not just a matter of traditional religion but a more clearly political and public matter of resistance to encroachment (vol. 1, p. 155).

The territory of a deceased group cannot be conceptually filled in the short term by the use of a piece of legislation to aid, accelerate and validate the process of succession that might otherwise occur within Aboriginal tradition. However, the process of succession continues as new areas become available for claim under the *Aboriginal Land Rights (Northern Territory) Act* 1976. The acquisition of Gimbat and Goodparla pastoral leases by the Federal Government enabled Stage 3 of Kakadu National Park to be proclaimed in 1987. The area was thus available for claim. Despite the findings of Mr Justice Kearney in the Jawoyn (Katherine Area) Land Claim, the Northern Land Council lodged a claim to Stage 3 of Kakadu National Park on behalf of the Jawoyn people (Map 7). The entire claim area lies well to the north of the Kearney Line. The southern boundary of the Kakadu (Alligator Rivers) Stage 3 Land Claim is latitude 14 degrees South, 17 kilometres north of the Kearney Line, and encompasses both Gimbat and Goodparla pastoral leases. The report of the Resource Assessment Commission will prove to be a considerable encouragement for the Jawoyn in their attempts to extend Jawoyn territoriality north and northwest across the deceased 'Wulwulam estate.

It would seem that the Northern Land Council hopes that the registration of sites in the Upper South Alligator Valley on behalf of the Jawoyn, coupled with the report of the Resource Assessment Commission, would sufficiently shorten the traditional process of succession that the Jawoyn case in the Kakadu (Alligator Rivers) Stage 3 Land Claim will succeed—despite the northern limitation to Jawoyn spiritual affiliation described by the Kearney Line.

Boundaries in the Modern Period

Tindale's 1974 publication of *The Aboriginal Tribes of Australia* shows the Jawoyn (Djauan) as extending from Katherine to the Edith River in the northwest, Mt Evelyn in the north and encompassing the headwaters of the Katherine River, Birdie Creek and Fanny Creek in the northeast. To the northwest of the Jawoyn, Tindale placed the 'Wulwulam, who extended from Edith River north to Pine Creek and northeast to Mt Callanan. To the north of the Jawoyn, Tindale placed the Wat:a. To the west of the Jawoyn lies the Wagaman. Tindale asserts the boundaries shown on his 1974 maps to represent the position and extent of each Aboriginal group at the time of European contact.

The impact of contact has been such that the 'Wulwulam have totally disappeared, hence leaving their deceased estate subject to succession by adjacent groups. The intense population collapse, relocation and dislocation of Aboriginal groups in the area has resulted in a considerable flux in the identity and distribution of Aboriginal territories throughout the region. There is little remaining knowledge of the 'Wulwulam and Wat:a people who formerly inhabited the area immediately to the north of the Jawoyn.

The demise of the 'Wulwulam was brought about primarily by intense mining activity in the area, accompanied by a considerable immigration of Chinese and European miners, almost completely displacing the 'Wulwulam people in the first instance and then attracting considerable numbers of other Aboriginal people from adjacent groups to work the mines and later to work on the extension of the railway south from Pine Creek to Katherine. The railway extension resulted in a number of Jawoyn people remaining resident in Pine Creek.

The boundaries shown (Map 8) incorporate the residual knowledge of the deceased group's boundaries as known by the remaining senior custodians in the area. Cowboy Alec, a senior Wagaman man who has lived in the region all his life, recounted the extent of 'Wulwulam country consistent with Tindale's 1974 map as being from 'Edith River to Pine Creek ... That 'Wulwulam, but they finished. They all finished up [all deceased]. They only dust now.' This is consistent with the observations recorded by Francis (Jones 1987) and Norman Ross Mandjal-walkwalk, a senior Wadjak Aboriginal man who was raised in the South Alligator

Valley. Senior custodians also recall the existence of a group to the west of the Garnditbal. Although the identity of that group was no longer known within oral tradition, the boundaries of the deceased territory were still clearly known to the senior Aboriginal men.

The location of boundaries with senior non-Jawoyn custodians, based on their residence in the area from as early as the 1920s and 1930s, confirms firstly the identity of the area formerly as 'Wulwulam and secondly the absence of Jawoyn from the area. The absence of Jawoyn people from the South Alligator Valley and the headwaters of the South Alligator River was formalised during the Second World War when the Army withdrew all Aboriginal people in the region to compounds in the Katherine and Mataranka area. For a number of years, this firmly prevented Aboriginal people from continuing physical contact with the area and conveying traditional information about sites and the country in situ, and focused the Jawoyn identity on the Katherine–Beswick area.

The Wagaman to the west of the Jawoyn, the Wadaman to the southwest and the Yangman to the southeast are firm in the tenure of their territories and do not evidence any pressure from the recent Jawoyn expansion at their boundaries. However, in the north the deceased 'Wulwulam and Wat:a territories have proven to be subject to an accelerated process of succession by the Jawoyn.

Conclusion

The *Aboriginal Land Rights (Northern Territory) Act* 1976 combined with the availability of unalienated land made available through the declaration of Stage 3 of Kakadu National Park has acted as a catalyst to activate succession by the Jawoyn. The succession has been pursued primarily in areas where claims can be foreseen in terms of the Act. The potential gains to Aboriginal people who can prove traditional ownership (in terms of the Act) to Coronation Hill and adjacent highly prospective areas has accelerated and entrenched the succession process to such a degree that it is in danger of being overweighted in favour of the Jawoyn. It may also have prematurely brought it to a stage whereby the attendant details of sites, songs and ceremonies have not been sufficiently developed or restructured as to adequately support the Jawoyn claims to possessing active traditions for the area or to sustain their efforts to exercise territoriality in respect of the area.

The Resource Assessment Commission has apparently simplified and probably shortened the processes of succession to deceased estates. It has also identified and endorsed the elaboration of Aboriginal traditional

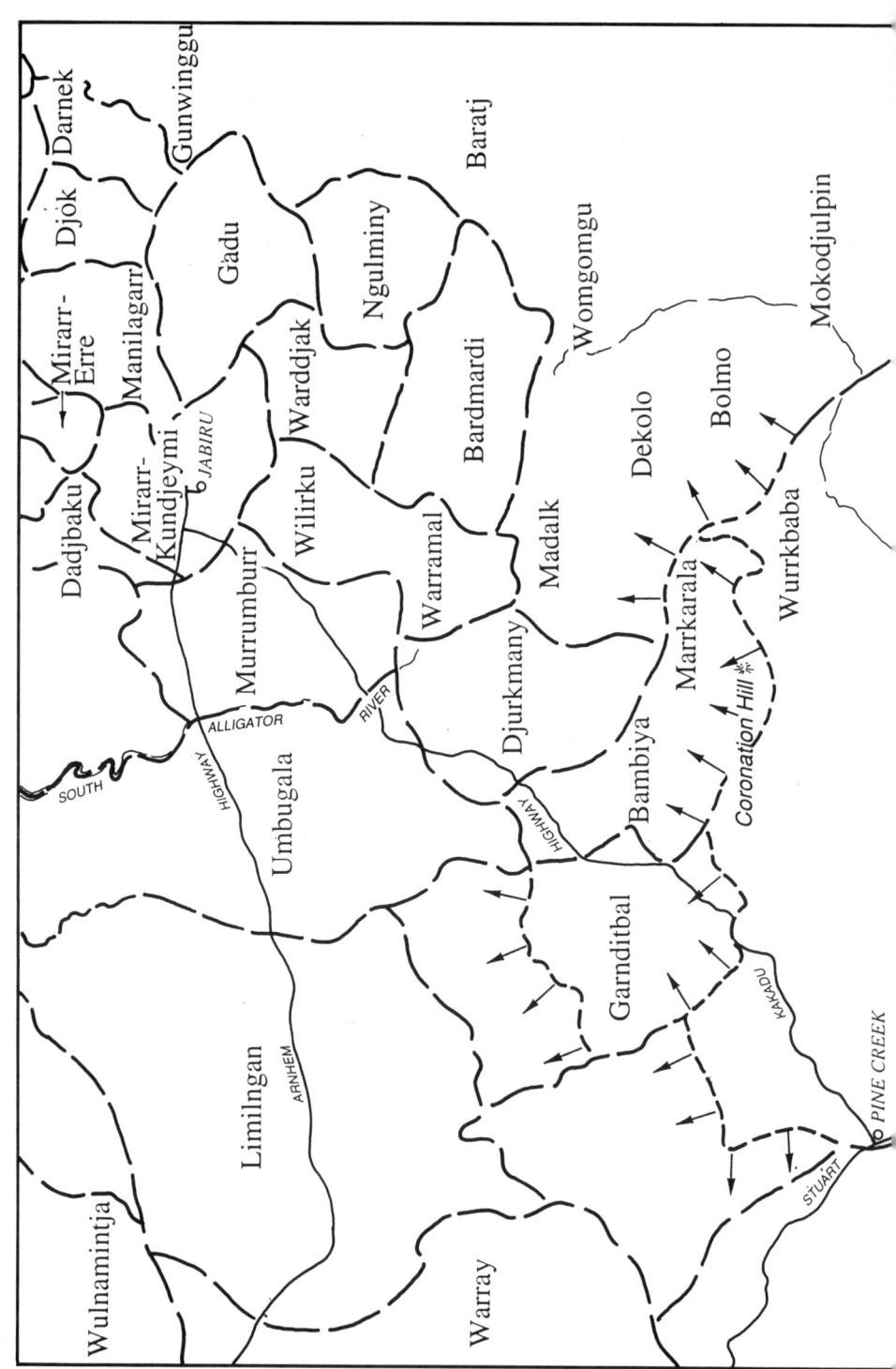

3 Southwest Arnhem Land

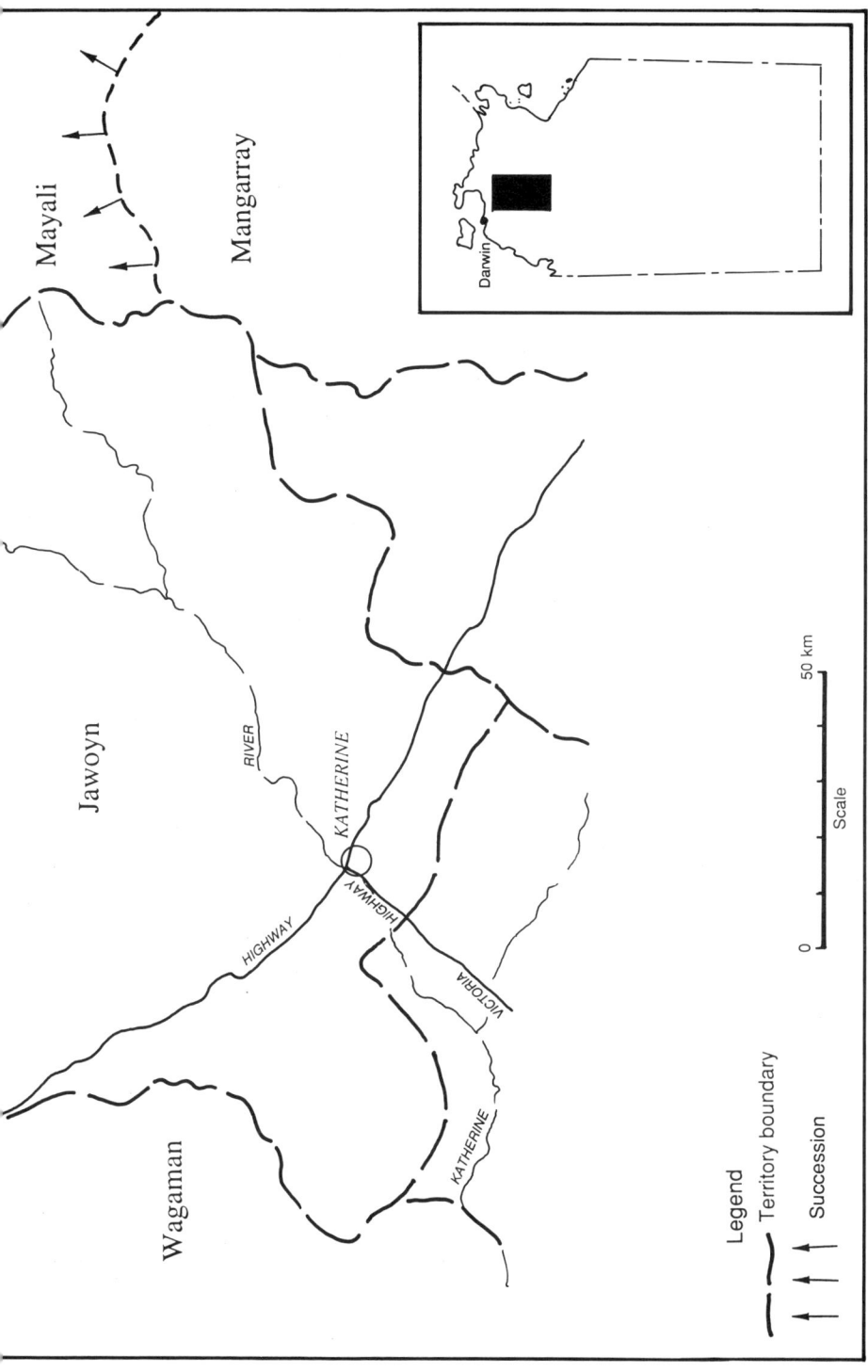

Map 8 Aboriginal Groups in the South Alligator River Area

thought and concepts as new information becomes available. Traditions are being manufactured quite quickly. The techniques used in this case, if widely accepted, will afford better opportunities for other groups to make claims to deceased estates without having the proofs required within Aboriginal tradition. The Resource Assessment Commission reported that the ceremonies related to the area are no longer performed (Resource Assessment Commission, vol. 1, p. 175).

4

Central Australia

This chapter briefly examines territoriality among those often described as the Luritja. It is questionable whether the Luritja is an identifiably separate Aboriginal group. Rather it has a secondary identity, which is a label used to describe the interface of adjacent groups. These adjacent groups typify Western Desert territoriality in the southwest and Arranda territoriality in the northeast of the Luritja area. The Western Desert territoriality is characterised by frontiers whereas the Arranda territoriality is characterised by boundaries. Furthermore, the interface between these two systems is a frontier of contact over which adjacent groups exercise economic rights and within which a transition in the social system is evident.

The most detailed written information about the Luritja is contained in the submissions and transcript of the Lake Amadeus, Luritja Land Claim, a case heard under the *Aboriginal Land Rights (Northern Territory) Act* 1976. The Act provides an opportunity for Aboriginal people to claim unalienated Crown Land. Such a claim necessitates a hearing before a judge of the Supreme Court known as the Aboriginal Land Commissioner. The Commissioner takes oral and written submissions from claimants and objectors both in court and in the field. The case for the claimants is put on their behalf by one of the Aboriginal Land Councils.

The Lake Amadeus, Luritja Land Claim provides an opportunity to examine the transition between Western Desert and Arranda territoriality. The Central Land Council, acting for the Aboriginal claimants to the area, put forward a group of Western Desert people composed primarily of members of the Pitjantjatjara and Yangkunkatjarra tribes. Opposition to this claim was mounted predominantly by members of the Western Arranda and Matutjarra tribes with support from the Walpiri, Kukatjarra and Pintubi tribes who held strong ceremonial responsibilities for the area in conjunction with the Western Arranda. The claim on behalf of the Western Desert people was defeated in favour of the Western Arranda and Matutjarra people whom Mr Justice Maurice, the Aboriginal Land Commissioner, found to be the traditional owners of the area.

Environment

A brief description of the area surrounding the claim area will give context to the specific case. The land systems to a large extent circumscribe the possible degree of usage by Aboriginal people within the traditional systems of tenure. This information was a significant omission from the case presented by the Central Land Council.

The Lake Amadeus, Luritja Land Claim area lies approximately 275 kilometres west-southwest of Alice Springs between Lake Amadeus to the south and the George Gill Range to the north (Map 9). It is dominated by sand plain and dune field with an average elevation of 520 to 550 metres above sea level. The ridgelines trend northwest to southeast, rising up to 60 metres above the level of the plain with some minor occurrences of low sandstone ridges. Rainfall reliability is low, with very high to excessive evaporation rates. Temperature regimes reflect the low minimums and high maximums typical of the arid zone climate. The area south of Lake Amadeus is characterised by stable parallel and irregular sand dunes with minor areas of mobile sands vegetated by spinifex.

Within Lake Amadeus, salt pans with waterlogged clays are common. The lake itself is largely unvegetated or fringed with samphire. The fringing dunes of red sand are vegetated predominantly by spinifex with minor occurrences of tea tree and desert oak. North of Lake Amadeus the stable parallel and irregular sand dunes recur, with minor areas of mobile sands. Sparse shrubs and low trees with occasional desert oak or mulga over spinifex are a feature of the landscape as it encroaches on Kings Canyon at the foot of the George Gill Range to the north. The floor of the canyon is composed of an alluvial fan of clayey sands vegetated mainly with spinifex and some sparse low trees over short grass.

The bold plateau of the range, with rocky summits up to 150 metres high and steep, dissected margins, is vegetated by sparse shrubs and low trees above spinifex or sparse grass, overlying soils which are generally very stoney or sandy. Within the range, sandy plains occur around some creeks with vegetation of sparse shrubs, low trees, mulga, or witchetty

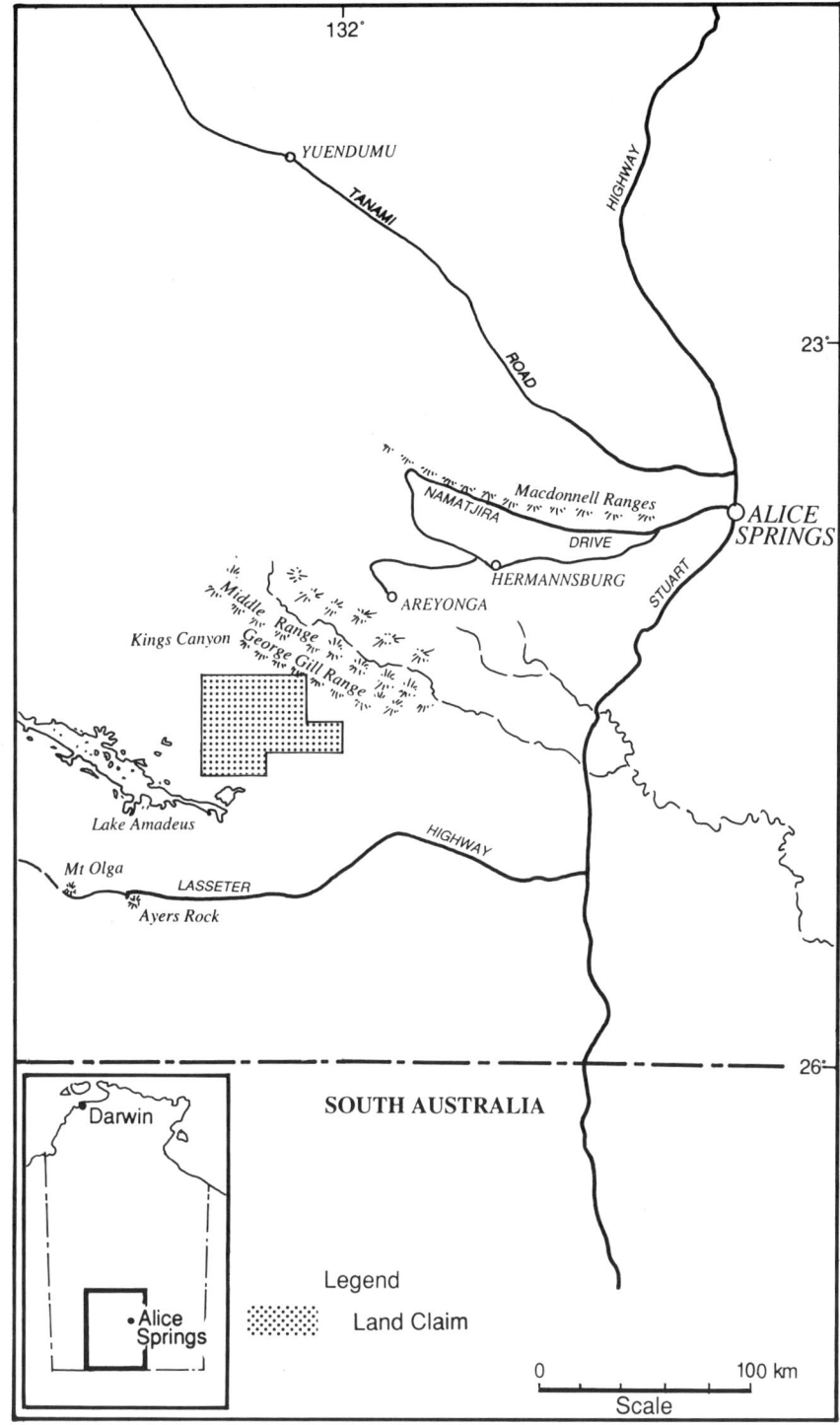

Map 9   The Lake Amadeus, Luritja Land Claim Area

bush over short grass. Further north the ridges and plateaux of Middle Range have bevelled weathered summits with occurrences of ironwood and red gum over grasses.

The water prospects decrease markedly from the large supply and excellent prospects of the Middle Range and George Gill Range in the north to the poor prospects of Lake Amadeus itself in the south. Sources of ephemeral water are many and widespread in the ranges but decrease rapidly as one moves into the sand plains and dunes to the south where small isolated rockholes and soaks present the only surface water available. The decreasing depth of the water-table appears generally to be accompanied by an increase in water salinity from the George Gill Range to Lake Amadeus. Thus the water-table in East Mereenie lies at 125 metres with a salinity of 500 parts per million whereas at Inindia Bore on the north edge of Lake Amadeus it lies at 55 metres with a salinity of 7500 parts per million. Hence even after water boring techniques were developed early this century, they did not significantly enhance the pastoral prospects of the Lake Amadeus area.

The trend to inferior water resources in the Lake Amadeus area is matched by more open vegetation cover and decreasing faunal and floral food sources from the comparatively rich areas of the George Gill Range in the north to the poor areas of Lake Amadeus sand plains further south.

Exploration and Pastoral Settlement

Contact with Europeans began in 1860 when John McDouall Stuart and his small party travelled north through Arranda territory. Stuart returned in 1861 and 1862. As with most of the later explorers, his contact with the peoples of the land he crossed was fleeting and relatively, but not entirely, peaceful.

Stuart's work led directly to the transfer of control of the Northern Territory from New South Wales to the South Australian Government in 1863 and to the construction of the Overland Telegraph Line from 1871. This in turn brought permanent European settlement at the Telegraph Stations in Central Australia at Charlotte Waters, Alice Springs and Barrow Creek from 1872. Although the telegraph line occupied a narrow space and merely connected the stations which were isolated islands in what was otherwise a wilderness to Europeans, it had a significant and wide-ranging impact upon Aboriginals. The European interest in the line had to be protected, and ferocious reprisals followed any actual or presumed Aboriginal hostility toward it. The punitive expeditions which followed the spearings at Barrow Creek Telegraph Station in 1874 almost certainly displaced the Aboriginal population in that region simply because most Aborigines in a wide area were killed. Later, familiarity with the European settlers overcame fear and avoidance, and Aborigines began to be attracted to the telegraph stations by the benefits of Europeans' material culture (Hartwig 1965).

The establishment of the Overland Telegraph Line accelerated and facilitated exploration by parties using the telegraph stations as bases. Ernest Giles, W. C. Gosse, P. E. Warburton and John Forrest all explored the region west of the telegraph line from 1872, and by the time of the Horn scientific expedition in 1894 the Central region had been completely traversed. The passage of these explorers over Aboriginal land was not always peaceful, but it was transient and had little or no impact on traditional settlement patterns (Hartwig 1965; Feeken and Spate 1970).

This was not the case with pastoral settlement, which had begun in Central Australia at Undoolya and Owen Springs in March 1873 and then continued at Idracowra, Henbury, Mount Burrell (Maryvale area), Erldunda and Tempe Downs by 1885 (Map 10). The thrust for new settlement came from South Australia. Ralph Milner and Alfred Giles had shown, during the construction of the Overland Telegraph Line, that Central Australia could be reached by travelling stock, and that the same route along the line could be used to return stock to the home colony. The momentum of expanding settlement in South Australia was maintained by wealthy investors who poured capital into land, and worked the country by using labour-intensive methods. The strategy worked well on stations established on good safe country which repaid investment. The assumption that this method was applicable to the pastoral lands of Central Australia proved disastrously wrong.

This settlement process was undoubtedly detrimental to Aborigines, who were seen as a threat to the security of European lives, cattle and fixed improvements. At first, there was no opinion that the Aborigines might be useful to the station management. Aborigines resisted pastoral settlement by spearing and otherwise harassing the cattle with which they were competing for available natural water. In the ensuing and inevitable conflict, Europeans took the law into their own hands, and then urged and supported vigorous action by the Mounted Police who were stationed at Charlotte Waters and Barrow Creek in 1873, Alice Springs in 1879, Boggy Hole in 1889, and Illamurta Springs in 1891 (Hartwig 1965). At least until 1891 the police and settlers were encouraged to follow a policy which would result in safety for white settlement, rather than to pursue the letter of the law which required apprehension and trial of suspected

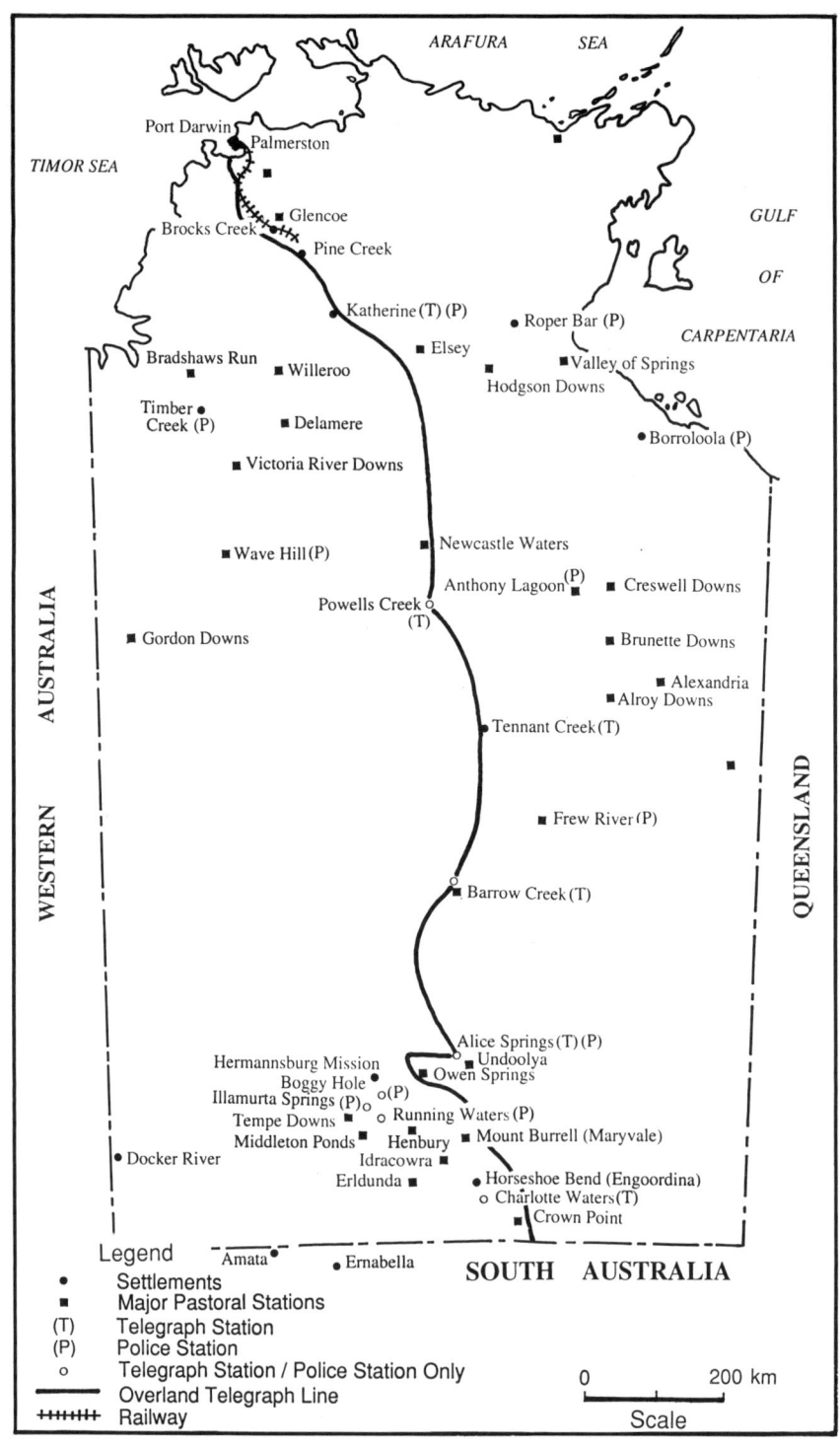

Map 10 Major Pastoral Stations and Settlements, Northern Territory, 1870–1896

Aboriginal offenders. The resultant widespread killing of Aborigines was condoned by the responsible authorities in South Australia. Obviously, this phase was profoundly disturbing to those Aborigines who survived and, by renewing the 'fear and avoidance' reaction, it caused movement away from the main areas of pastoral settlement.

The history of Tempe Downs station exemplifies the issues and events which are central to the changes in the demography of the Aboriginal people in Central Australia. The explorer and geologist Dr Charles Chewings had taken up over 6400 square kilometres of the Western MacDonnell, Krichauff and George Gill ranges from 1881. He formed a syndicate with wealthy partners and began to stock his country from 1885. In that year he also conducted a detailed exploration through the range country to the north and west. A homestead was established on Walker Plain, to the northwest of the present homestead and closer to what was then the centre of operations of the station. By 1889 the syndicate had almost 11 000 square kilometres of country and 6000 cattle in the area (Hartwig 1965). However, the syndicate sold out in 1893, for a mere 2500 pounds, to its manager, Thornton (Hartwig 1965; Duncan 1967). The venture had cost the syndicate 27 000 pounds. Aboriginal harassment of cattle, disrupting breeding and fattening, was considered the sole cause (Duncan 1967).

Clearly, the Aborigines of the Tempe Downs area had progressed from the 'fear and avoidance' noted by Chewings during his early expeditions (Hartwig) to outright resistance. But as early as 1882 the Matutjarra people had obviously heard of firearms and their efficiency as evidenced when about a dozen of them confronted Chewings one day. They 'dropped their spears and vanished as mysteriously as they appeared' once a rifle and revolver were raised by the whites.

Many Aborigines had been shot along the Finke in the early days of the establishment of Henbury Station. This no doubt upset traditional occupation patterns, but so did inter-tribal warfare which may itself have been triggered or aggravated by the tensions created by white settlement. Strehlow (1969) recounts the warfare which raged between the Arranda and the Matutjarra between 1875 and 1891. Although its initial cause is not known, it was certainly perpetuated by reprisals for earlier killings and raids to steal women. When, in the 1880s, the focus of pastoral settlement moved west from Henbury to Tempe Downs, the Matutjarra and Kukatjarra people bore the brunt of the efforts by European authorities to make the region safe for cattle and settlers.

The establishment of Tempe Downs, and the subsequent movement of pastoral interests into an area considered one of the most outstanding for water and wildlife in Central Australia, brought pressure upon its natural resources. There was widespread concern among pastoralists about Aboriginal conflict, primarily over the spearing of cattle.

The European response was to establish police camps at Boggy Hole and at Running Waters. Mounted Constable W. H. Willshire, already notorious for his callous treatment of Aborigines throughout the Territory, applied to be posted to the new police camp which was to be established in the vicinity of Tempe Downs. Willshire wrote that he had noticed that it was the intention of the government to open a temporary police station 'to check the natives in their wanton mischief to the property of the pioneer settlers. I respectfully make this application for the position, as the ways and customs of the wild natives are well known to me, and stopping their depradations is my special forte' (Willshire 1896). Willshire was told to put an end to the cattle spearing. On his own admission, Willshire over the next two years was responsible for the killing of many Aboriginal people in the Tempe Downs locality (Hartwig 1965).

The killings were moderated after 1891 when Frank Gillen of Alice Springs caused Willshire to be tried for murder after killings at Tempe Downs. He was acquitted, but the fact that he had been brought to trial was salutary (Hartwig 1965). In 1891 the Boggy Hole police camp was closed down. However, 600 cattle were allegedly speared on Tempe Downs in 1892, and another police station, this time with two constables and six trackers, was opened at Illamurta Springs. The violent phase probably ended only after Thornton took over Tempe Downs and adopted the policy of using rather than exterminating Aborigines. Thornton was less ambitious than had been the founding syndicate, and he contracted the operations of the station to a more manageable area by surrendering land on the southern and western edges of the station. Thornton sold to Bob and Bill Coulthard in about 1906, and the Coulthards in turn sold to George Bennett in 1918.

While the violence of early pastoral settlement lasted, the only refuges for the Aborigines were the remote hills—which were not completely safe from Willshire and his colleagues—and Hermannsburg Mission which had been established in 1877 by a small party of Lutherans. The mission was in Arranda country, but Strehlow (1969) and others record that in the early years it was not unusual for Kukatjarra people from the southwest and Matutjarra people from the south to seek sanctuary there. Its mere presence was probably a moderating influence on the conduct of pastoralists and police. However, the police outpost at Illamurta was manned until 1912 and this indicates that the pastoral frontier around Tempe Downs was not regarded as being quiet until then.

While Hermannsburg Mission undoubtedly, directly and indirectly, saved many Aboriginal lives by providing a place of sanctuary, it was in its way yet another factor leading to disturbance of Aboriginal occupation patterns in the region. Especially in time of drought, it attracted people from very distant places. These people sought the food and other material benefits of the white man, and some were prepared to embrace Christianity to get those commodities. The Lutherans sent itinerant converts out into the areas to the west to evangelise Aborigines who had not yet had sustained contact.

By the mid 1890s most if not all of the wealthy and optimistic men who had underwritten the first phase of pastoral settlement had lost fortunes. The first stations had usually changed hands several times, at a fraction of the sums invested in them. The big investors had realised that money alone would not buy success in the Centre's pastoral industries. They voluntarily or involuntarily retreated to more favourable and familiar areas.

As they left, smaller resident owners took over the stations. These new pastoralists realised that they needed Aboriginal labour in the stock camps and that Aboriginal women were useful at the homesteads. The Aborigines for their part found that it was safer to 'come in' to the homesteads than to roam in remoter areas where they might be regarded as cattle killers. Aborigines were for the first time seen as a resource, and the pastoralists began to entice them into the homesteads where both men and women could attach themselves in a relationship of mutual dependency with the pastoralist. Physical conflict did not end, because pastoralists would not tolerate 'bush' Aborigines remaining away from the homestead where they could not be watched and where they could continue to spear cattle. However, there was henceforth a choice for the Aborigine—'go bush', far away from cattle, or come in to the homestead. Those who did not elect one of these options risked being shot on sight as a suspected cattle spearer.

This change was yet another powerful factor causing dislocation and severance of Aborigines from their traditional country. Associated with it was a profound change in the way the pastoralists regarded the lands of the Centre. Previously plains had been the most favoured pastoral lands because they most closely approximated the productive grasslands of the settled south. However, the plains lacked natural water and the new cattlemen, with skill and daring rather than money, turned their eyes to the naturally watered mountain ranges. The ranges had been shunned by the first pastoralists who knew that they were Aboriginal retreats and strongholds, and that cattle would be difficult to manage there. The plains were seen as being safer and easier, even though provision of water was costly. The second generation of cattlemen could not contemplate putting artificial water on the plains country so they turned to the ranges where rockholes and waterholes were comparatively abundant. Certainly there were wild Aborigines in the ranges, but they could be cleared out or made to come in to the homesteads. Thus there was change in preference by the cattlemen toward the country which also happened to be favoured by Aborigines—particularly in the area of the George Gill and the Krichauff ranges.

During the Lake Amadeus Land Claim (1987), Arranda people gave evidence of a general movement north due to pressure from the pastoral industry and associated mounted police activity. This is plausible and explains why many groups have remained in the Hermannsburg area despite encouragement by the government of the day to return to their traditional lands.

At the time of the First World War another phase of pastoral settlement began. This was stimulated by improvements in transport technology which reduced the Centre's isolation, and by official efforts to encourage the settlement of smaller scale pastoralists. Typical representatives of this phase were William Liddle and William McNamara. In about 1917 Liddle brought a mob of cattle to King's Creek from Hamilton Downs, and until 1922 he ran a small station in the vicinity of what is today called King's Canyon. Liddle relied on the permanent water in the foothills of the George Gill Range. In 1922 Liddle settled at Angas Downs and that station is held by the Liddle family today. The significance of Angas Downs for our present purpose is that large numbers (at times up to 200) of Luritja people attached themselves to the homestead. It seems that while these people certainly did not abandon their attachment to their country, their regular and traditional association with it was weakened (Rose 1965).

McNamara established his station (variously called Munjara, Munyeroo, Gosse's Range Station, or Bowson's Hole) on country near the future Areyonga settlement. This country had been abandoned by the Coulthards of Tempe Downs in about 1908, and it was taken up by McNamara in partnership with Archie Giles in about 1913 (Pearce 1987). McNamara acquired Giles's interest in about 1921, and at about the same time engaged William Liddle to build a homestead on Areyonga Creek, about 15 kilometres south of the present Areyonga settlement. It was also in about 1921 that McNamara shot a number of Aborigines (between six and twenty-five according to varying accounts) who had speared one of his milking cows (Pearce 1987). The incident had a profound effect on the people of the region and it is still spoken of with awe. There can be little doubt that its disturbing effect was profound at the time.

McNamara's killings near Bowson's Hole were probably among the last 'massacres' conducted on behalf of pastoralists in the region. However, European diseases continued to impact upon a people without immunity to them. Between 1932 and 1940 the Jumu, who had inhabited the country to the northwest of Areyonga, died out as a result of an epidemic. Their country was usurped by the Kukatjarra from the south, and other people from the north and west (Tindale 1974).

The change in pastoral settlement emphasis was not reversed until the 1930s, when better water drilling and earthmoving technology tilted the balance back to the plains country. In the meantime, from about 1890 to about 1930, the George Gill Range, James Range and Krichauff Range area was the venue for further profound disturbance of Aboriginal occupation patterns (Duncan 1967; Hartwig 1965) due primarily to competition between the pastoralists and the Aborigines over rights to use the land and its resources.

By this time other stations had been established in the area, largely due to the advent of the railway line which made turn-off of stock much safer and cheaper. As well as Angas Downs, other stations including Mt Quinn, Middleton Ponds, Curtin Springs, Mount Connor, Lyndavale and Mount Cavenagh were all established between 1922 and the late 1930s. While the first of these stations had enjoyed bountiful seasons in the 1920s, severe droughts followed. The cattle quickly depleted water resources. Aborigines who might normally have avoided the new stations were forced eastward toward them as seasonal conditions deteriorated in the Western Desert. Dependent attachments to the stations and the new railway sidings were formed.

To the south of the George Gill Range and Lake Amadeus region Ernabella Mission was set up in 1937. This was motivated in part by the desire to curb what were seen as undesirable aspects of contact between doggers seeking dingo scalps and Aboriginal people from the Central Reserve. The reserve had been set up in 1920 and the doggers and prospectors who had habitually entered this area were nominally prevented from doing so. The doggers adopted a simple expedient to ensure a steady supply of dingo scalps from within the reserve. They enticed Pitjantjatjara people to collect scalps in the reserve and then bring them to the eastern boundary for trade with the doggers. Thus the social and economic changes caused by contact with the white doggers continued, and yet another factor drawing the Pitjantjatjara to the east and north began to operate.

Ted Strehlow, then a patrol officer with the Northern Territory administration, travelled through the Central Reserve in 1936 and reported that about 700 Aborigines were living there. This number appears to have declined as continuing pressures, notably drought, forced or enticed the Pitjantjatjara eastward.

During the Second World War ration depots were established at Haast's Bluff and Areyonga; later, permanent welfare settlements were set up at those places. A measure of the eastward and northward drift of the Pitjantjatjara is the fact that they now comprise a significant element of the population at Areyonga. After the war new factors reinforced what was by now a well established pattern of human movement from the southwest into country which was less vigorously held by its traditional owners because of numerical decline or population drift.

The Welfare Branch initiated a programme designed to encourage people to come to the various new settlements. Any Aboriginal inclination to do so was strengthened by the drift away from the stations as pastoralists reduced their dependence on Aboriginal labour from the 1950s; by severe drought from 1955; by clearance from the Woomera Rocket Range area; and by Welfare Branch discouragement of continued Aboriginal presence in areas visited by tourists. The eastward movement was so pronounced that alarmed authorities set up new settlements at Amata (1961) and Docker River (1967). These halted the eastward drift, and people returned to the Docker River area from Areyonga and Angas Downs. However, the position did not stabilise for many years and may not have done so yet.

Effects Upon Territoriality

The George Gill Range area has been the venue for significant pressures since the advent of white settlement. These pressures have resulted in movement from the west and south to the north and east, bringing the Matutjarra and Kukatjarra people into a closer and more sustained contact with the Arranda groups than they may previously have experienced. Movement of Aboriginal people in the Lake Amadeus and Western MacDonnell Ranges area clearly affected traditional patterns of tenure of territories, resulting in part in the building of the corporate Luritja identity. The absence of Aboriginal people from the Lake Amadeus area for a prolonged period has had serious consequences for the maintenance of accurate knowledge of boundaries and frontiers.

The site known as Watarrka adjacent to King's Canyon on the southern slopes of the George Gill Range lies on the northern side of the frontier between two systems—the Western Desert social system characterised by frontiers and the Arranda social system characterised by boundaries. In the Lake Amadeus, Luritja Land Claim the Western-Desert group claimed primary rights over the Kuningga native cat dreaming track (Map 11) which was subject to similar claims by the Arranda group. The latter was subsequently able to prove its claim over the entire track from

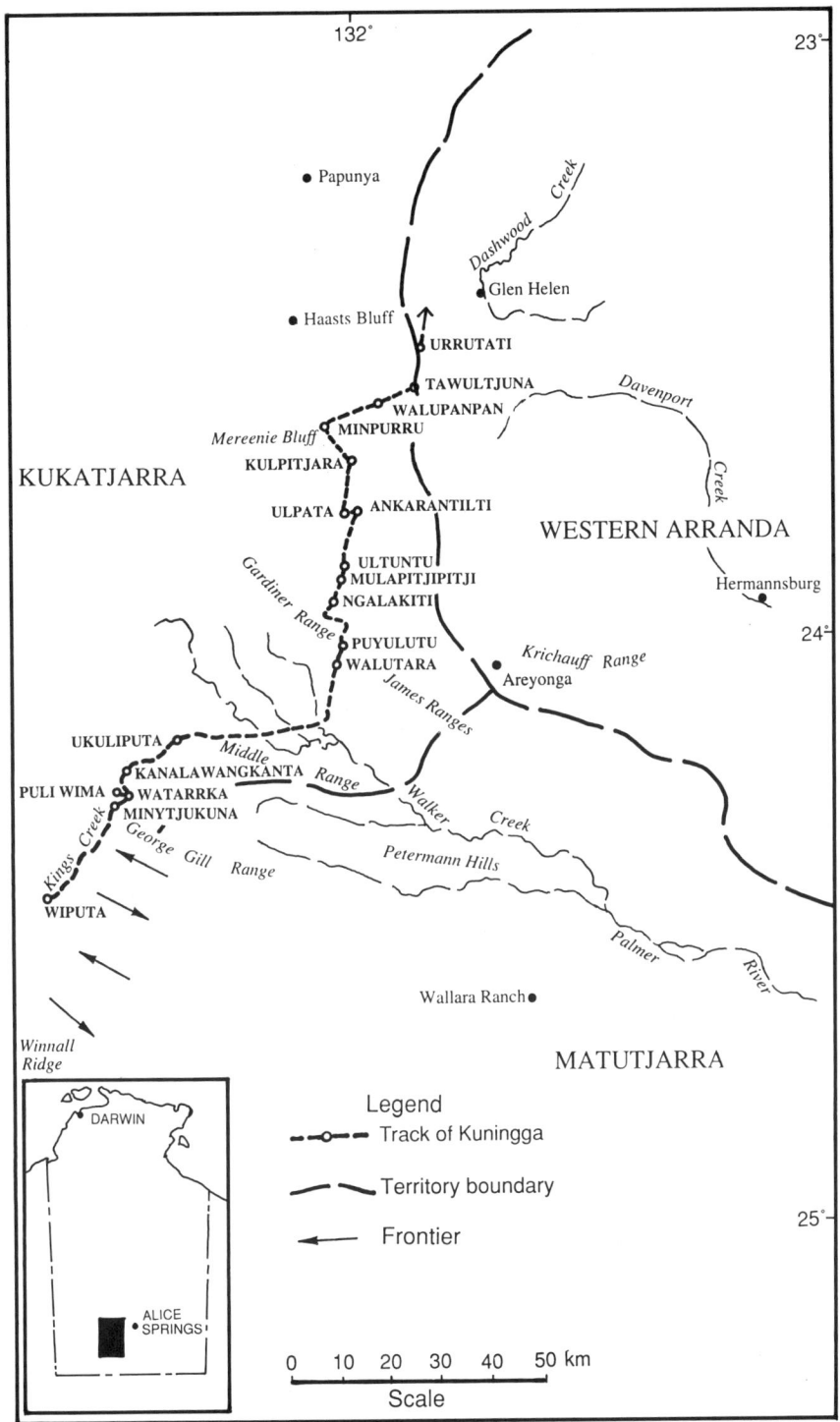

Map 11 Kuningga Native Cat Track

the sand plains between Lake Amadeus and the George Gill Range, north through the territory of the Kukatjarra group before turning northeast into Western Arranda territory. The Western Arranda group indentified itself as the Watarrka family and was able to offer detailed traditional evidence to substantiate their claims to the territory.

The Kuningga native cat track extends from Port Augusta on the coast of South Australia to appear intermittently in the ceremonies of groups along its 3000 kilometre journey to Arnhem Land on the coast of the Northern Territory. Each section of the track is the responsibility of the particular group through whose territory it passes on that segment of its journey. The segment in question in the Lake Amadeus, Luritja Land Claim has its genesis at a site known as Wiputa which also lies within the claim area. The successful claim by the Watarrka group has reaffirmed the Arranda boundaries in an area which had become synonymous with the encroaching frontiers of the Western Desert groups whose extension was made possible by the forced depopulation of the area.

Movement North of the Amadeus Frontier

The Watarrka family lived and foraged around the northern reaches of the Amadeus frontier in the general course of their seasonal movements through the region earlier this century. Many presently live north of the frontier in a number of outstations and at central communities such as Hermannsburg. They did not move from the Watarrka sub-territory voluntarily. There were excellent natural sources of water throughout the ranges which made the region one of the most outstanding areas for water and game in Central Australia.

There was a concerted effort by pastoralists to make it clear to the Aboriginal people that if they stayed in the bush they would be hunted down and shot. They were given the option of going to Hermannsburg, which was established in 1877, or other settlements but were to leave the bush and the immediate vicinity of the Watarrka area (King's Canyon) and Dare's Plain between the James Range and the George Gill Range. The most logical place to move was north where there were good water sources.

The situation worsened in the mid 1890s with the onset of a drought that lasted several years. Cattle spearing by Aboriginal people in the Tempe and George Gill Range area escalated. In June 1898 Constable Cowle noted that 'many of the Gill [George Gill Range] blacks have ... gone over to Mareena [Mereenie]'. In the following year the police apprehended at least sixteen Aboriginal people in the area. This combined with the attraction of the settlements and rations available made the prospect of moving north far more attractive than moving south into the arid frontier area around Lake Amadeus. Thus the continual growth of the pastoral industry between the George Gill Range and the James Range area meant that people were reluctant to move back and became established in the area around Hermannsburg and to its west. The traditionally strong ties between the Western Arranda and the Matutjarra people facilitated this shift in population.

A number of incidents are recorded in the oral history of the Watarrka group including shootings of Watarrka people in the region. Jack Coulthard, a senior Matutjarra man, remembers occasions when Aboriginal people were shot in reprisal for the spearing of cattle. Tralgett Malbangka, a senior Arranda man, remembers for example that he never saw his uncles because they were all shot at Walki, a spring on the northern slopes of the George Gill Range. He remembers Constable Cowle's name being mentioned by his family in relation to the killing, thus dating the incident to around 1900. There are various oral accounts of shootings by others which, although difficult to substantiate, do indicate the fear held by the Aboriginal people over police and pastoral contact. Tralgett states (Davis 1989) that:

> ... all my family got shot at Walki. My mother born there. That's why my family moved back north. They all leave Watarrka. Get frightened. Policeman ... frightened them. They maybe do wrong thing. 'Your grandmother and young uncle finish up there'. That's what my father say.

The Watarrka family evidence their current attachment to the area through the performance of the Kuningga native cat ceremony; the singing of the song cycle which contains at least 52 verses; the possession and maintenance of the *tjurrungga* for the Watarrka area; the ability to name the localities along the dreaming track (Kuningga native cat track); and the knowledge of symbolism associated with the area and ceremonies.

Their knowledge of the ceremonies and song cycles for the area is confirmed by Strehlow (1971), wherein he cites ten verses of the Kuningga song cycle which were not substantially different to that witnessed by Mr Justice Maurice during the hearings of the Lake Amadeus, Luritja Land Claim. It must be remembered that while there are at least four variants of the Kuningga track and cycle (Spencer and Gillen 1899), which splits near the South Australian/Northern Territory border and simultaneously travels along four parallel tracks before rejoining north of the Anmatjerre territory, they remain substantially the same. Slight variations between the ceremony witnessed by the Judge and earlier or other contemporary versions are to be expected and do not form a sufficient basis for rejecting the claims of the Watarrka group to Watarrka sub-territory, contrary to the Central Land Council's contention.

It would also seem likely that the Kukatjarra group moved further north on their traditional territory due to the pressure of the Matutjarra group which had been displaced from the George Gill Range and James Range area due to pastoral pressure. This overall movement north may have pushed the Kukatjarra into the recently vacated area of the Jumu people whose territory was documented by Tindale during his fieldwork of the early 1930s (Tindale 1974). Some living Aborigines still have a vague memory of the Jumu people but their memories are of those people living to the north of the Kukatjarra, close to the Ngalia (Walpiri) territory.

The northern and northeastern affiliations of the Luritja might be best summarised by Strehlow (1947, pp. 154–5) in the context of ownership of *tjurrungga* (boards and stones incised with sacred designs) which are the source of social, ritual and political power:

> The Western Aranda tjilpa [native cat] group, led by the great chief Malbangka, came into Western Aranda territory at Ltalaltuma, after crossing the Krichauff Ranges. Ltalaltuma was a notable ceremonial centre peopled by local tjilpa men before the advent of this horde. The Ltalaltuma clan shoulders the responsibility of preserving the traditions proper to the invading host north of the border. South of Ltalaltuma various Loritja groups took care of the tjilpa tjurunga [native cat sacred objects], and all chant-verses were composed in the Loritja language. The Ltalaltuma traditions are accordingly shared by Loritja and Western Aranda men: the sacred objects, i.e. the tjurunga representing the changed bodies of the visitors, in the Aranda cave are regarded as common property, and many of the chant-verses sung on the inkura ground of Ltalaltuma are still composed in the Loritja language. The njinanga section of Ltalaltuma undertakes to preserve the tjilpa legend and chant as far north as Ilbakarataka, a small place in the southern ridges of the Western MacDonnell system. The account of Malbangka's further journey, and the tjurunga which he left behind, now become the property of the Western Parr' Erultja clan, whose pmara kutata is situated in the MacDonnell Ranges north-east of Mt Sonder. Malbangka stole the tnatantja of the Parr' Erultja ancestors and then continued his march to the north. The Parr' Erultja clan pursues the story as far as the northern foothills of the MacDonnell ridges, whence the account is taken up by the group inhabiting Ulamba and Eritjakwata. Malbangka and his host next plunged into the sandy waste north of Eritjakwata and entered into the territory of the Unmatjera group.

Strehlow's account of the ancestral beings associated with the native cat, and the attendant traditional responsibilities for ritual objects (*tjurrungga*) attests to the native cat connection between the Lake Amadeus, Luritja Land Claim area, and the Loritja (Kukatjarra), Western Arranda and Anmatjarra (Unmatjera) territories to the north.

Boundaries of the Watarrka Sub-Territory

The specific evidence introduced in the land claim proceedings conducted from 1986 to 1988 to support the territorial claims of the Watarrka family are examined in the following sections of this chapter, as this is the only case in which such evidence has been adduced and offers a rare opportunity to reveal and test Aboriginal concepts of territoriality.

The Watarrka family are identified primarily with the Kuningga *tjukurrpa* (native cat dreaming). They emphasised consistently that their responsibilities for the Kuningga track are limited to that part within their own territory. They delineate their area of responsibilities as commencing in the area known as Wiputa at the southern extremity of the Kings Creek floodout, and extending north over the George Gill and James ranges and through to the northern side of the Mereenie Range—encompassing at least seventeen specific sites (see Map 11). The most southerly of these sites are stated by Watarrka men and confirmed in the Kuningga song cycle to lie within the Kukatjarra territory south of Puyulutu or Tent Hill, which was formerly controlled by senior men primarily identified as Luritja. With the passing of these people and the dislocation of their descendants, day-to-day responsibility for these sites would have passed to the Matutjarra, who emphasise their connection with the area through common Luritja ancestors. However, Arranda, who form the core of the Watarrka family, have prevailed in enlisting Matutjarra support to their claim to the area. The remaining thirteen sites lie in the Kukatjarra territory north from the Middle and James ranges to the Mereenie and Idirriki ranges. The dreaming track continues north to Anmatjerre territory after crossing the western boundary of the Western Arranda group.

Helmut Parerultja, who was the senior Arranda man representing the traditional interests of the Watarrka group, described the Watarrka sub-territory as encompassing the localities of Tjungkuba, Ulpinyali, Yarringku, Kutjinti, Palpirrwarra, Wanmarra and Tatunma. Malunga and Nanga were said to form the 'boundary' in the north while in the south Piki was the 'borderline' as was Pantu (Lake Amadeus) (Map 12). Parerultja further stated (Davis 1989) the identity of the claim area to be affiliated with the Matutjarra group:

Matutjarra south to Pantu [Lake Amadeus].
Pantu south to Ayers Rock and Kata Tjuta is Yangkunkatjarra [territory], [and] Luritja [territory].
Kukutja [Kukatjarra] country is north from Tjukalta.

Parerultja again affirmed the sub-territory as being Matutjarra and having Lake Amadeus as its southern boundary (transcript, pp. 514–16). The consistency of this concept of the Watarrka sub-territory is shown in the statement made two weeks earlier at Watarrka Waterhole when Parerultja defined its extent as follows (Davis 1989):

Here [Watarrka Waterhole] to Wanmarra, south to Lake Amadeus, Watarrka, north to Nangga, Malunga, this the Watarrka. East to Palpirrwarra, this way back through Watarrka. West to Ulpinyali . . . Watarrka is this really big place.
Speaking area for Matutjarra.

Senior custodians of the Watarrka group consistently described the sub-territory by reference to localities. This concept of a territory being a constellation or cluster of sites is referred to by Mr Justice Toohey in his report on the Uluru Land Claim (1980). He did not see territories as being enclosed, bounded spaces and in this respect we find Myers (1986) in support of Toohey, based on his work among the Pintupi people of the Western Desert where he found that 'territorial boundaries are highly flexible if not insignificant' (p. 93).

Certainly this would appear to be the case for the Western Desert groups to the west and southwest of Lake Amadeus. However, among the Arranda to the northeast of the George Gill Range, territories may be far more precisely delineated. The main criteria used among the Arranda to define the extent of various tracts of country is hydrology. In formulating the boundary for the Hermannsburg Land Trust each group within the Trust area defined their area in reference to a boundary which accorded with a watershed. Further, each area was identified by using, in a more generic sense, the name of a key site within it.

Northeast of the claim area the Western Arranda strictly define their boundary with Kukatjarra/Luritja and Matutjarra/Luritja. Individual sub-territories are exclusive and do not overlap, unlike those referred to by Mr Justice Toohey in the Uluru Report.

In the southern region of the Lake Amadeus frontier area, Helmut Parerultja ascribed a boundary at Pantu (Lake Amadeus), running from WNW to ESE through Lake Amadeus itself. From his description, the area north of Lake Amadeus falls into Matutjarra country and the area south of it into the Yangkunkatjarra country. While the southern boundary is

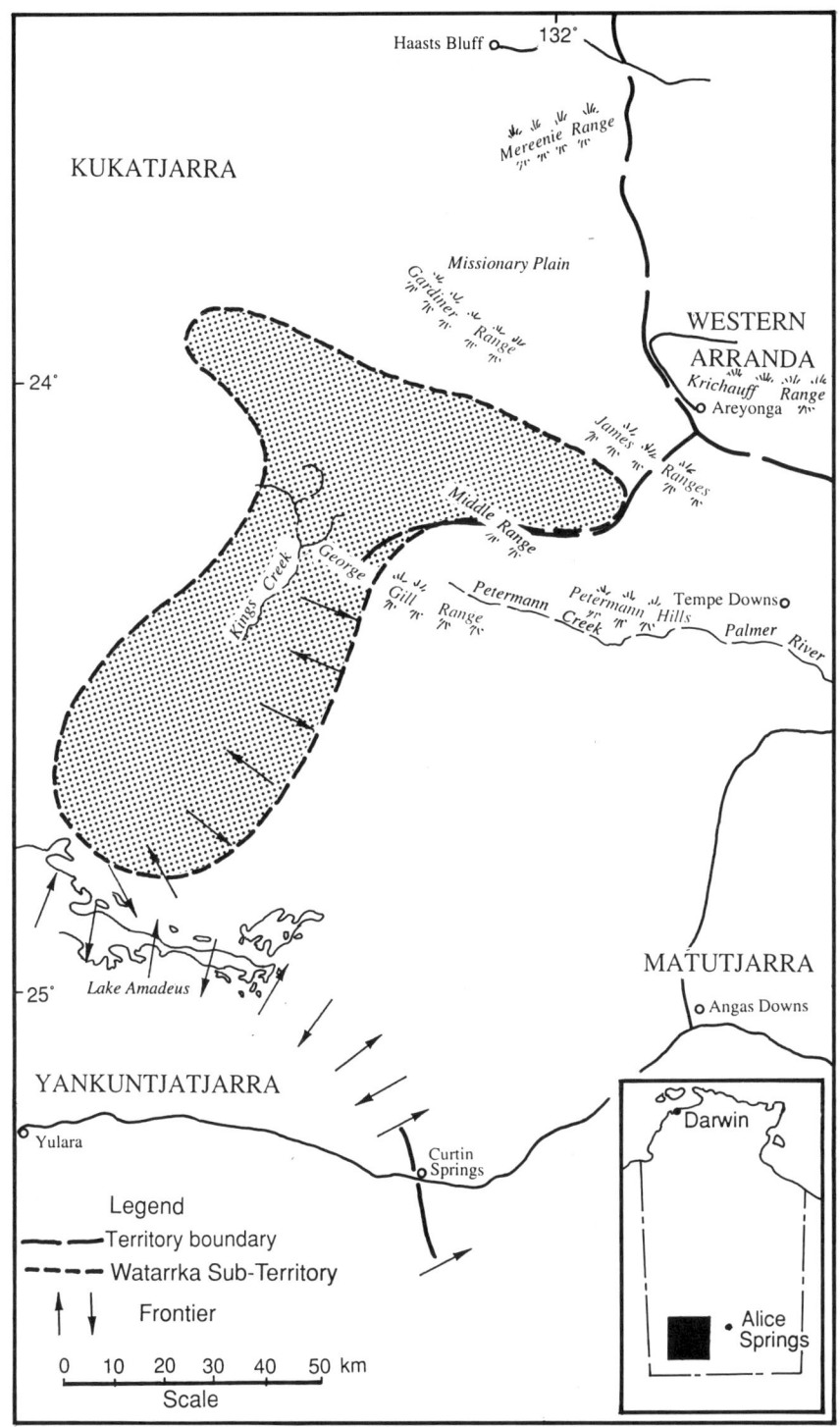

Map 12   Watarrka Sub-Territory, Lake Amadeus, Luritja Land Claim

evidenced, it may not be as clearly defined geographically by a physical feature which accords with a narrow line such as characterizes the boundaries to the north of the claim area.

The strong Arrandic influence of precision in boundary delineation and of exclusive territories serves to negate to a considerable degree the non-bounded overlapping model characteristic of the Western Desert. The clear distinction between the Kukatjarra and Matutjarra territories immediately north of the claim area is unexpected by researchers with a Western Desert bias. However the concept of an exclusive Watarrka sub-territory is not inconsistent with the Arrandic influence.

The symbolism of the Kuningga native cat identity, which is synonymous with the Watarrka sub-territory, is found in a number of locations along the dreaming track and pervades various parts of the life of the Watarrka group.

Traditional Proofs of Territorial Rights

The Kuningga native cat *tjurrungga* under the care of Helmut Parerultja, as displayed to Mr Justice Maurice at Kulpitjara, evidences the Watarrka waterhole design as the central motif surrounded by the symbolism of Wantuparri (the ceremonial leader) and the Maliyarra (young native cats). This design of the Watarrka is also found at the site known as Minytjukuna, a cave in an outcrop of rocks southwest of Kings Canyon (Map 11), and as a ground painting surrounding the central hole on the ceremonial or Nangurru ground during the performance of the Kuningga ceremony. It was Wantuparri and his sons, the travelling native cat *tjukurrpa* (ancestral beings) who built a camp at Watarrka on the ceremonial ground, hunted across the landscape (transcript: 3, 27 August 1987) and performed ceremonies with Tjatjiti, the resident native cat (*ngurra kutata*) (transcript: 3–4, 27 August 1987) who created the Watarrka waterhole (transcript: 7, 27 August 1987).

Helmut Parerultja explained that the travelling cat design of Wantuparri and the Maliyarra are not depicted in Kings Canyon as they are not resident native cats (transcript, p.506). This is consistent with Bagshaw (1983, pp. 62–3) who found that there are 'two kinds of supernatural being' recognised by the Luritja: a 'localised' being and a 'travelling' being. It is the resident being (*tjukurrpa ngurrakutu*) who was transformed into features of the localised landscape and is thus depicted. The extent of the travels of the local native cat, then, are limited in the north and south by the boundaries of the Watarrka sub-territory.

The design used on both the canvas painting and sacred *tjurrungga* stone to depict Wantuparri and the Maliyarra was painted on Helmut

Parerultja in the course of the performance of the Kuningga native cat ceremony at Kulpitjara on 26 August 1987. In the ceremony itself the sacred pole was painted with a similar design. The painting on the forehead of the young novices in the ceremony symbolises their affiliation with Wantuparri and the Kuningga ceremony. The Kuningga song cycle describes in detail the geography of the area through which Wantuparri and the young native cats pass on their travels.

In the performance of their daily activities, Wantuparri and the other *tjukurrpa* named and gave meaning to each locality in which any function was performed, whether it was a camp site, hunting area or ceremonial site. Each type of site is subject to specific access restrictions with accompanying degrees of punishments for violation of the site (Davis 1984).

Within the territory, the named localities generally are used to denote areas such as camp sites—being, more precisely, living spaces as they include more than the space needed to camp and sleep for the night. Immediately adjacent areas where firewood may be gathered and foraging may take place are generally included. Several locality names may be grouped together and subsumed under a more generic name, which may be used at a more inclusive level. Such a place will be identified particularly with the act of one ancestral being. People of a group charged with responsibilties for custodianship of the territory in which the site occurs may themselves be referred to by the site name. When a name is so used, the site is generally more restricted than the adjacent *ngurra* localities. Such a site generally posesses focal elements of the ritual cycle, being in particular ritual paraphernalia or embodiments of the ancestral beings themselves. The ritual emblems may be deposited there between performance of rituals. It may also be the site at which the ancestral beings, upon fulfilment of their services on the estate, voluntarily metamorphose into a feature of the landscape such as a rock outcrop, waterhole, species of fauna or flora. It will be focal to the identity of the estate and feature prominently in song cycles of the area. Song cycles, ritual emblems and paraphernalia focusing on such sites confirm the identification of the area with those who hold primary spiritual responsibility.

There are four sites at which the Kuningga ceremony can be performed within the area over which the Watarrka family exhibits primary responsibility. At the first site the ceremonial pole is used. At the second site the young native cats are healed in the smoking ceremony; the ceremonial pole may not be used. At the third site the ceremony may be performed in part as a teaching ceremony, but again the ceremonial pole may not be used. At both the second and third sites Watarrka men say that 'little ceremonies' are made in between (in between the two main sites, being the first and fourth). At the fourth site the ceremonial pole is used. Hence it is significant that the senior custodian has the *tjurrungga* in his care, stored not only on the Kuningga track at the fourth site but also at one of the two main sites for performance of the Kuningga ceremony.

The senior custodian explained two ways in which 'Watarrka' is used. Firstly, it is the name for a sub-territory which subsumes a considerable number of sites over an area of approximately 6300 square kilometres. Secondly, it refers specifically to the locality at which the statement is being made, i.e. Watarrka Waterhole. There is a third sense in which 'Watarrka' is used. The Native Cat ancestral being made a camp with the young native cats near the Watarrka Waterhole. The waterhole itself became the ceremony ground. During the day the old Native Cat man sat motionless on Puli Wima (Bald Hill) watching for the young native cats to return from the day's hunting. At the conclusion of each day the old man and the young native cats returned to the camp. Later they performed ceremonies at Watarrka Waterhole. The old Native Cat man and the young native cats were camped at Watarrka for many days or possibly weeks. The individual sites where they camped, hunted and performed ceremonies form a complex of sites (Davis 1984) known as Watarrka. 'Watarrka', then, is a term used on at least three levels to describe the individual site, the complex of sites and the sub-territory.

'Watarrka' is further used to denote both an individual and a group with primary spiritual responsibility for the Watarrka sub-territory in general but more specifically for the Watarrka complex of sites and the associated Kuningga dreaming. When referring to Multupanga, also known as Mirini Jack, a brother of Wapiti, Mick Wagu states (Davis 1989):

> Multupanga . . .
> He was Luritja,
> Watarrka man . . .
> Kuningga.

Similarly in reference to Billy Lang and his brother Waluta, he says:

> Billy Lang teach me Watarrka,
> Kuningga, songs . . .
> Waluta, Billy Lang's oldest brother,
> He was Watarrka man too.

A number of men commonly referred to as 'Watarrka men' are the forebears of living Watarrka men. Together they are referred to as the 'Watarrka family'. In both quotations above, Kuningga, the *tjukurrpa*, is synonymous with Watarrka, the site, the complex, the sub-territory.

Watarrka is the identity of the person and the unifying identity of the 'Watarrka family'.

In respect of any site such as Watarrka there may be a wide range of people with some limited knowledge of it. They may know its name and location and possibly be able to offer a first-hand description from personal experience of having visited or resided at or in the vicinity of the site. Possessing such information does not constitute 'ownership' of the site, although it may constitute subsidiary rights or secondary affiliation. Helmut Parerultja made a clear distinction between primary and secondary affiliation in respect of the Watarrka sub-territory when he said, 'I take a primary role and my Kutungurlu [ceremonial manager] take a secondary role' (transcript, p. 507).

Ownership is seen in terms of primary spiritual responsibilities. Bagshaw (1983, p. 50) confirms that 'qualitative status distinctions are made between those who "own" or "hold" (*kanyininpa*) a site and those who simply identify with it'. Bagshaw notes that Mick Wagu stated the criterion of ownership to be that 'proper owners' could 'sing and tell stories for a place'. Parerultja, Bagshaw continues (p. 56), 'emphatically stated that the site ownership depended on "knowing stories and tjurrungga numbers [sacred designs]"'. The detailed knowledge of men such as Jim Impu, Mick Wagu, Brawn Raggett, Gideon Jack and Aba Morris still does not, in Helmut Parerultja's view, give them primary responsibility for Watarrka 'country'. In the transcript of evidence, Parerultja confirms (p. 510) that he is 'the boss for that ceremony' related to Watarrka. Gideon Jack (p. 510) confirms that Parerultja's position is that of *kirta* (owner) of the Watarrka ceremony while he (Gideon) is Parerultja's *kutungurlu* (manager).

Subsidiary rights in a territory or part thereof may be accorded to particular persons not directly descended from the generation generally acknowledged as having primary spiritual responsibility for that territory. Through secondary or subsidiary rights may flow rights of occupation and use of the economic resources in the territory.

The bosses control the dissemination of knowledge and thus maintain power (Bagshaw 1983, pp. 56, 58):

> By controlling the transmission of knowledge, site 'bosses' effectively actualize or circumscribe the claims of others to identification with a site. In short, they determine the qualitative status of claims made by the less knowledgeable.
>
> Transmission of knowledge from one generation to another is largely predicated upon relational proximity to site 'bosses'. 'Bosses' are conceptualized either as incarnations of the site tjukurrpa or as descendants of an individual believed to be consubstantial with the site (via conception or death). Because

site-related knowledge confers significant rights and ritual status upon the holder, there is a marked tendency for 'bosses' to convey such esoterica to those with whom they are most closely associated, namely male members of their 'close family' (walytja).

Such transmission of rights is confirmed by Myers (1976, pp. 413–14) who notes that although there may be, as we have seen, a large and extended group of people who claim an affiliation to a particular tract of country, it is the men 'who control the related ritual . . . who "know" the ritual and esoterica, who must decide whether to teach an individual about it or not. It is they who decide on the status of claims'.

Transmission of knowledge about the Watarrka sub-territory was evidenced in the presence of the young men brought into the ceremony at Kulpitjara on 26 September 1987 and who were present at Watarrka next day. Clearly, none of the Central Land Council's claimants had been taught the knowledge relevant to the Watarrka native cat ceremony or the Watarrka sub-territory. Bagshaw's assessment (p. 58) of the transmission of ritual and site knowledge is born out in the present Watarrka group:

> Luritja site 'bosses' regard sons, sisters' sons and co-residents reclassified into either category as their closest kinsmen in the first descending generation. It is these men to whom knowledge of sites is generally transmitted.

Some of the Central Land Council's claimants contended that through their place of conception they assumed rights in a site, territory or ritual. Such rights may be actualised only through the acquisition of knowledge which obviously necessitates not only the consent of 'bosses' but also the active participation of both parties in the transmission of such knowledge. While the traditional mechanisms are available for negotiating such an acquisition of knowledge and status, bosses are not compelled to accede to such requests. In the context of this land claim the Watarrka people made it obvious that there was to be no transmission of any such knowledge to either the claimants or other Aboriginal people.

Bagshaw (p. 60) summarises the thrust of the ownership argument when he states:

> Traditional site 'ownership' as expressed in the concept of 'holding a country' appears to be achieved in a variety of ways. Foremost among these is bilateral filiation to 'bosses' in the senior generation. While actual connections to such men are emphasized, the prevailing ideology of co-residence as constituitive of 'close family' status is sufficiently strong to incorporate genealogically remote individuals within this framework of 'descent'. Finally, the negotiability of individual claims to identification with a site means that men who are genea-

logically unrelated to 'bosses' and do not regularly co-reside with them may also have the opportunity to acquire site-related esoteric knowledge.

The boundary between the Watarrka sub-territory and the adjacent territories is evidenced in the Kuningga song cycle which details the travels of the native cats. Kuningga left Wiputa and travelled along a water course in a northerly direction (Map 11). As he passed Black Hill he stayed on his track not deviating to the hill but continuing north to Watarrka where he is identified with the waterhole. Not only is his track to Watarrka synonymous with the water course (transcript 12, 27 August 1987), the water course *is* the Kuningga track. As Kuningga travelled north from Watarrka he again followed the valley through Kings Canyon (transcript 8 September 1987), crossing plains and identifying with water courses. After reaching the second ceremony site, Kuningga again travelled north through a gap in the range. As the Kuningga dreaming track weaves its way steadily in the northerly direction, the song cycle describes the particular geography of that landscape and the natural resources therein. The song cycle then is, in one sense, an oral map of the country.

In areas north of the claim area, especially those associated with the Arranda, the land holding group controls the dreaming track within their territory. This holds true for the Watarrka sub-territory. The group does not assert rights to the dreaming track beyond the limits of their own territory. The ancestral being is specifically identified with the particular territory. One indication, commonly cited by Aboriginal people, of such a changing identification is the way in which the ancestral being may change his name and his language as he crosses the border into a new territory or linguistic area. On this same point Bagshaw cites (p. 64) the '"changing voice" (i.e. language) at specific sites which now mark the border of contemporary linguistic and cultural domains'. This is similar to the situation alluded to by Helmut Parerultja where he states that 'in old time tjukurrpa handed over at each territory. Now claim for whole track through every territory'. He was adamant that he cannot speak for the Kuningga track beyond the bounds of his own territory. His responsibility for the track from which he derives his authority is subsumed by other Kuningga men at the border of his territory.

However, not all men of the Watarrka family will speak for the same section of the Kuningga track. Bagshaw (p. 66) similarly found a strict demarcation of that portion of a track. Gideon Tjupurrula (Gideon Jack) is cited in relation to a Kuningga dreaming track as saying, 'I can only speak for Mitukatjirri and up to Ngulinya—after that I pass the story on to a different mob. I can't tell it then'.

Among groups with territories displaying high relief landform such as the Arranda, the Kukatjarra and northern regions of Matutjarra one could reasonably expect that along with a firm definition of a boundary there is also a firm delineation of the extent of responsibilities along dreaming tracks. While the landforms of the Walpiri area in the north are not nearly as high, there are sufficient geographic features to define handover points on dreaming tracks, as noted by Mr Justice Toohey in the report on the Uluru Land Claim (para. 64):

> [Among the Walpiri] there was evidence of the handing over of dreamings at various places along dreaming tracks.

In the Western Desert area, however, it would appear that there are extended rights along a dreaming track to sites, if not territories, which are identified with the continuance of the track through the territory for which one has primary spiritual responsibility. Myers cites (1986, p. 53) the case of a Pintubi group who visited the Balgo area of Western Australia. The Pintubi men discovered that there seemed to be a continuance of a dreaming track with which they were familiar in their own territory many hundreds of kilometres away. 'We thought that story ended, went into the ground at Pinari. But, we found that it goes underground all the way to Balgo'. The act of the ancestral being in going 'into the ground' signifies the end of its activities in that vicinity. The Pintubi men's discovery thus signified that the ancestral being did not trespass upon the territory of intervening groups but travelled underground so as to bypass them. His emergence at Balgo gave a significance to a site and possibly the surrounding area which links the Pintubi men to Balgo and thus enables them to claim a particular right in that area. 'Places where exceptionally significant events took place, where power was left behind, or where the ancestors went into the ground and still remained are special sites (Yarta Yarta) because ancestral potency is near' (Myers p. 50). Thus for the Pintubi men the site at which the ancestral being entered the ground is extremely significant, as is the place at which he emerged. For Western Desert people such a link enables one to claim an affiliation with far flung sites and territories through the continuance of a dreaming track. This is not an invention of sites or claims but rather an assimilation to the 'pre-existing forms' (Myers, p. 53). Aboriginal people see these new discoveries or new links as revelations of a pre-existing situation as yet unrealised by them. But this does not give them primary rights in the territory over which the tjukurrpa passes. This is quite the converse of what would appear to be the situation among the groups of the Arranda and their near neighbours such as the Kukatjarra and Matutjarra.

The activities of Tjatjiti, the resident native cat (*tjukurrpa ngurrakutu*), in transforming the landscape and becoming part of the landscape by entering the ground as he sank down into the waterhole ensured for all time the focal importance of Watarrka. This is a site complex 'where power was left behind ... where the ancestor went into the ground' (Myers 1986, p. 50). These events give the site outstanding significance and ensure its ongoing potency. Watarrka thus assumes great significance not only along the Kuningga track but also as a focal site of the surrounding region, so much so that the local sub-territory takes its name from the Watarrka site.

The Luritja Frontier

The occurrence of handover points on dreaming tracks where primary responsibility is vested in an adjacent group signifies the existence of a boundary between the territories of the adjacent groups. In landscapes with a rich variety of features and readily available water sources, boundaries are generally well established and clearly delineated, as among Tiwi and Yolngu groups of Arnhem Land. In such areas sites subject to a high degree of restriction on access are generally small and localised (Davis 1984). Conversely, in arid areas the geography evidences a sparseness of outstanding geographic features, and sites and estates do not display the same precision of boundary delineation.

The area immediately north of the Luritja frontier displays a varied landscape from the George Gill Range through the James Range to the Mereenie Range. There are a number of vegetative zones, water courses and watersheds. The geography of the area confirms evidence given in the Lake Amadeus, Luritja Land Claim which indicates existing boundaries between adjacent groups (Map 13). Strehlow is uncompromising in stating the boundary between the Western Arranda and the adjacent Kukatjarra to the west and Matutjarra to the southwest to be clear cut and precise. Evidence in the Land Claim strongly suggests a firm boundary in the James Range between the Kukatjarra in the north and the Matutjarra to the south of the Middle and James ranges.

Relationships between the Western Arranda and the Kukatjarra were, at times, hostile and characterised by bloodshed and revenge killings (Strehlow 1947). In such circumstances one would fully expect boundaries to be precisely delineated and enforced. While the boundary between the Kukatjarra and the Matutjarra was not characterised by revenge parties and killings, it may not have been any less clearly defined.

The Arranda have a high density population with an intensive and complex land tenure system characterised by definite and precise

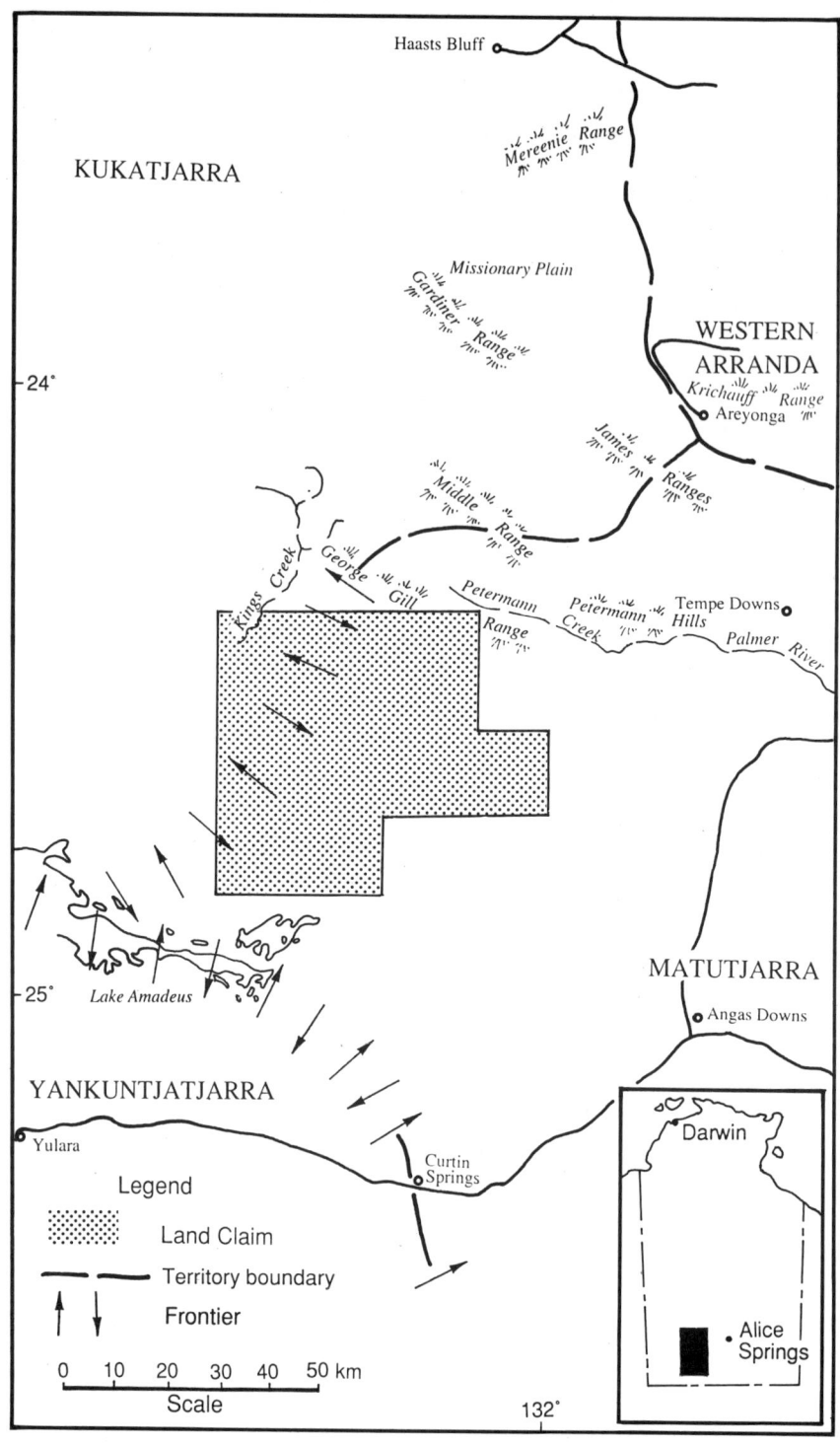

Map 13   Lake Amadeus Land Claim Boundaries and Frontier

boundary delineation with tenure secured by defended boundaries. In contrast the Western Desert groups to the southwest of the claim area display a more extended land use system with undefended and often ill-defined transit from one territory to another across frontiers.

A frontier is not a line but a transition zone evidencing cultural patterns. Changes in language, kinship and tenure system are all frontier 'markers' and in this sense the concept or identity of Luritja is a frontier of cultural homogeneity—linguistically, socially and culturally—between Western Desert and Arranda groups. As Bagshaw warned (1983, p. 1):

> Accordingly, when speaking of the 'Luritja' we would do well to bear in mind that we are employing an extremely flexible ideological construct formulated in recent times.

Thus we see many of the claimants identifying themselves as Luritja in an effort to assert the most inclusive identity which they hope will embrace their own position. In this sense 'Luritja' may at one moment refer to those people who are able to speak the Luritja language, at another to the extent of the combined Kukatjarra and Matutjarra territories, or again to the area over which the transition from the Western Desert to Arranda takes place. In all cases, as Williams indicates (1983, p. 100), it is the unity within the boundary upon which the identity is based:

> As long as focusing on a unity is the intention, he will use names that indicate that common boundary of the grouping rather than what might set its components apart.

Consistent with the heartland proposition put forward by Stanner (1965) is the idea of a lower density of population as one reaches the outer regions of a territory which is characterised by a frontier rather than a boundary. In terms of boundaries, territories which exhibit strong boundary delineation invariably also exhibit internal subdivisions in which populations are traditionally fairly evenly distributed. However, evidence in this regard is as yet not forthcoming for the Western Desert area and such other regions as are characterised by frontiers rather than boundaries.

Frontiers are also displayed by aggressive expansionist groups. In north Australia where there is little evidence of changes to boundaries, a particular clan group may find that one lineage may occupy an adjacent or nearby deceased territory thus establishing a sub-territory of the total clan group. In such a case the boundaries are not changed and the identity of the deceased group will remain synonymous with the identity of the territory until the names of the last members of the now deceased group are no longer able to be recalled by living persons.

However, in the more arid regions of Central Australia expansionism appears to have been more the case, particularly among the Warlpiri and to a lesser extent the Pintupi and Pitjantjatjara. In the latter cases the frontier is pushed ever outwards, slowly changing over time and subsuming more area of the adjacent groups until gradually displacing them. Such has been the case in the area of the now deceased Jumu group as documented by Tindale in 1932. This group, which originally lay between the Kukatjarra and the Ngalia/Warlpiri, died out as the result of disease in the early 1930s (Tindale 1974). Their vacant territory was taken over by an expansion of Kukatjarra from the south and Pintupi from the west, who were attracted to the area to obtain food from the mission and ration depots. The attraction was heightened by sustained drought conditions in the Western Desert. The railheads became a further source of food and goods as troops were moved north through Central Australia during the 1940s (Leske cited in Bagshaw 1983, p. 10):

> ... hordes of Aboriginals surrounding troop-trains at sidings or other stopping-places south of Alice Springs. If chased from one place, they ... find a way to appear at the next.

The expansionist tendency of the Pitjantjatjara and Yangkunkatjarra groups southwest of Lake Amadeus brought pressure from the south on the Matutjarra and Kukatjarra. This was met by a move to the north by the Kukatjarra to take up the vacant Jumu territory and transfer the focus of Matutjarra activities north, over the George Gill Range to the James Range. This move may not have led to a semi-permanent settlement of Matutjarra people in the north had it not been for the pastoral interest and settlement in the Middle Range area—one basic intention of which was the removal of Aboriginal people from the areas of outstanding interest to pastoralists. The combined effect of the establishment of settlements such as Hermannsburg and the efforts by pastoral interests and police to remove Aboriginal people from the George Gill Range and James Range areas meant that the surviving people moved north to well-watered country close to settlements. This gave rise to a temporary vacancy or a remission in the use of natural resources on the southern side of the George Gill Range.

The enforced dislocation of Aborigines through police action to ensure unhindered pastoral development precipitated the loss of specific boundary information in the Lake Amadeus area. The development of a frontier with the expansion of the Western Desert people into the area has been met by Western Arranda and associated people with a concerted effort to reintroduce boundaries extending southwest to Lake Amadeus. The conflict between the Western Desert and Arranda groups has been precipitated by the Central Land Council which lodged a claim to the area on behalf of the Western Desert groups. This was perceived by the Arranda groups as a move to usurp their rights, resulting in vigorous moves to reinstate the former boundaries.

While a frontier may be postulated in proximity of Lake Amadeus between the Yangkunkatjarra and Matutjarra (Map 13), in another sense the whole of the Matutjarra/Kukatjarra area may be considered a social or cultural frontier or a people in transition. *Lake Amadeus, Luritja Land Claim* (Hamilton and Vachon 1985, p. 1) nominates the area between 'the western Desert culture bloc and the Arrente (Arranda)' as a 'boundary zone'. It states the 'forms of social organisation, traditional patterns of land tenure and the religious and ritual traditions of these two groups' as 'markedly different'. Within this zone Matutjarra and Kukatjarra are identified as a cultural entity with their own distinctive cultural patterns.

The focus of identity among the Luritja may oscillate from generation to generation between Western Desert and Arrandic systems with varying degrees of emphasis. Where there is heightened and growing support among Arrandic groups, the Luritja may, during that generation, appear more akin to the Arrandic system or express more Arrandic influences in group identity, boundary delineation and ritual affiliations.

Conclusion

In summary then, there are two major systems of land tenure which bear on the Luritja frontier, the Arrandic system to the northeast and the Western Desert system to the southwest. While the Arranda lie totally within the Arrandic system and the Yangkunkatjarra totally within the Western Desert system, the frontier area within which the Lake Amadeus, Luritja Land Claim fell is neither totally one nor the other. Rather, it is an interface and mixing of the two systems. This confluence is generally congruent with the distribution of 'Luritja'—a term or identity which has escaped precise definition by numerous anthropologists and linguists. 'Luritja' is composed primarily of the Kukatjarra and Matutjarra groups; hence the use of the terms 'Kukatjarra Luritja' and 'Matutjarra Luritja' by many Aborigines to describe their affiliation.

Luritja is thus an identity which is a transition from the Western Desert social system with territoriality characterised by frontiers, to the Arranda social system with territoriality characterised by boundaries. The Luritja are at the margins of two social systems and thus have become a cultural and social frontier in themselves. Their case shows that not only can frontiers give way to boundaries but that the process can be reversed with Aboriginal culture having the potential to generate the information to support either proposition as the need may be.

5

Torres Strait

The people of Torres Strait identify themselves as distinctly different from the indigenous populations of the Australian mainland and Papua New Guinea. The shallow tropical waters, punctuated by numerous coral reefs, abound with marine life which forms the preferred diet of the local Torres Strait Islanders who permanently inhabit at least seventeen of the islands. To the south there was constant interaction between the Kaurareg people, principally of Muralag (Prince of Wales Island), Nurupai (Horn Island) and Waiben (Thursday Island), and Aboriginal groups of Cape York. It fluctuated between amicable trading enterprises and hostile head-hunting revenge parties. The people in the central and western islands were the interface between mainland Papua and Cape York (Moore 1972) speaking Mabuiag, a language related to the Aboriginal languages of Cape York, while the eastern Torres Strait Islanders spoke Miriam Mer, a language related to a Papuan language spoken around the mouth of the Fly River (Ray 1907).

Environment

Mabuiag (Jervis Island) is located in the western Torres Strait islands about midway between the Australian mainland and Papua New Guinea (Map 14) at latitude 9 degrees 57 minutes south and longitude 142 degrees 11 minutes east. It is a small tropical island of 6.2 square kilometres encircled by coral reefs and sandbanks studded with no less than twenty-two smaller islands ranging in size from 0.002 square kilometres Marrte (Marle Islet) to 0.42 square kilometres Wedul (Widul Island), all of which lie within 5 kilometres of Mabuiag (Map 15). Strong tidal streams of up to 7 knots which set between the islands may, in concert with the complex marine topography, generate whirlpools and outfalls with falls of water of up to 1 metre as the rush of the tide pushes over obstructions in its path (Johannes and McFarlane, in press, p. 182).

The island is incised by steep valleys between hills of up to 145 metres in height which dominate the landscape. The highest hill, Mount Jervis, has been incorrectly cited by Nietschmann (1989, p. 63) as 263 metres. The coastline is fringed by low gradient sandy beaches on the southeast side and mangroves on the southwest, whilst the north and northeast coast are indented by shallow bays in front of steep hills rising to almost 100 metres. Several springs of fresh water flow from the hills to the foreshore. Traditionally each clan was resident within its own territory with the more permanent of these streams providing a focus for settlement, as fresh water was required not only for drinking but also for cultivation of crops (Haddon 1935). The annual northwest monsoon ensured the replenishment of ground water and reliability for cultivation of crops.

The fringing and platform reefs yield more than 90 per cent of the marine resources obtained by the Maluigal (Nietschmann 1989, p. 70). Apart from the macro marine molluscs gleaned from the reefs, Islanders hunt dugongs and turtles across the seagrass beds which grow on the reefs. Like the Yolngu of northeast Arnhem Land, modern outboard motors and dinghies are used to ferry the hunters to and from the hunting grounds. During the hunt the outboard motor is retired in favour of a sail, so as not to frighten the prey. The harpoon, ancillary equipment and technique are still traditional as is the necessary knowledge of turtle and dugong habits.

European Contact and Exploration

The passage of vessels through Torres Strait must have been apparent to the local inhabitants for a considerable time between the first recorded European passage through the strait by Torres in September 1606 and the first recording of the customs of Torres Strait Islanders during a surveying expedition by the vessels *Bramble* and *Fly* in 1844.

Transits of Torres Strait by Cook (1770), Bligh (1789), Flinders (1802), P. P. King (1819), Wickham (1839) and Stokes (1841) had all but ignored the existence of the indigenous population on the islands. In August 1843 the crew of the *Fly* landed on Murray Island (Mer) as part of

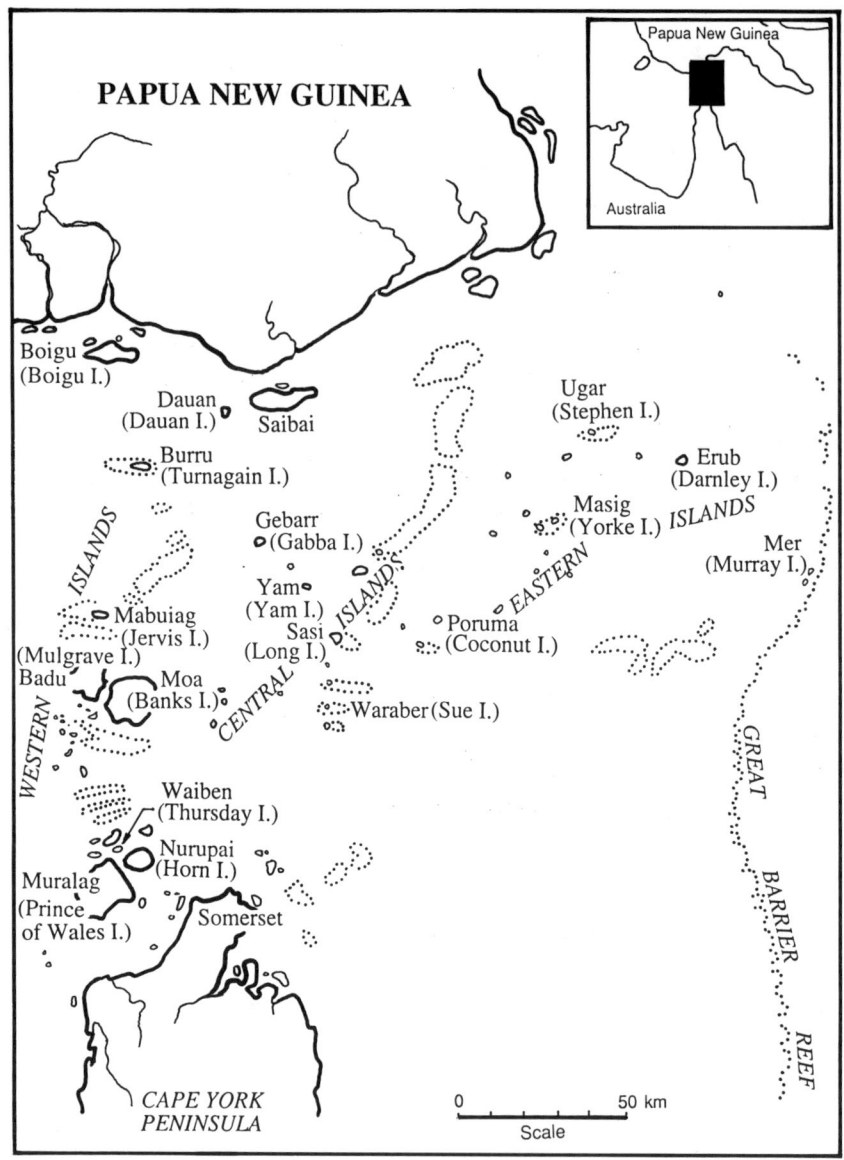

Map 14   Torres Strait

their extensive hydrographic surveys of the Coral Sea from 1842 to 1946. The survey continued in company with the *Bramble*, returning to Torres Strait in 1844 at which time a number of islands which had been neglected on former surveys were examined (Feeken *et al.* 1970, p. 138). During this voyage the first detailed observations of Torres Strait Islander customs were recorded.

In September 1792 Bligh entered the waters of Torres Strait with the vessels *Providence* and *Assistant* as part of an expedition promoted by Sir Joseph Banks to attempt to transplant breadfruit from Tahiti to the West Indies. During the three weeks that Bligh spent transiting and taking possession of Torres Strait and its islands his party met a mixed reaction from various encounters with Torres Strait Islanders. Several of Bligh's crew were wounded and one died as a result of one encounter which Bligh records as an unprovoked attack on his vessels by large boats manned with one hundred warriors. During the anxious hours of 12 September 1792, while probing a narrow passage between Badu (Mulgrave Island) and Kuik Pad (Jervis Reef) immediately south of Mabuiag, Bligh gave Mabuiag its English name of Jervis Island (Feekin *et al.* 1970, p. 51).

European contact with Islanders continued sporadically until the 1860s when the discovery of pearl shell in Torres Strait resulted in an influx of non-Islanders. In 1872 all the men on Mabuiag were engaged in the pearling industry (Haddon 1904) with ten pearling vessels operating out of a pearling base at Mabuiag in 1880 (Singe 1979).

In 1871 the London Missionary Society established a base at Erub (Darnley Island). Extending their work from the western Pacific the Society worked initially at Somerset on Cape York before moving to Erub and Mer (Murray Island). Accompanying Revds S. MacFarlane and A. W. Murray from the Society were a number of South Sea Island teachers from Raratonga, Lifu and Samoa (Done 1987, p. vi) who subsequently intermarried with Torres Strait Islanders. The Society selected Mabuiag as a base and settled there in 1913 after trying various other islands (Done 1987, p. vii). Many of the cultural practices of the Torres Strait Islanders were banned by the Society and were never revived.

With the diminution of cultural traditions primarily through the presence of the London Missionary Society, two contacts with Torres Strait Islanders provide the most detailed record of Islander cultural practices. The first is that of Barbara Thompson, a Scots girl who had been shipwrecked in Endeavour Strait in 1844 and subsequently adopted by the Kaurareg people on Muralag (Prince of Wales Island) until her rescue by the *Rattlesnake* in October 1849. Oswald Brierley, the ship's artist for the *Rattlesnake*'s surveying voyage of 1848–49, recorded detailed interviews

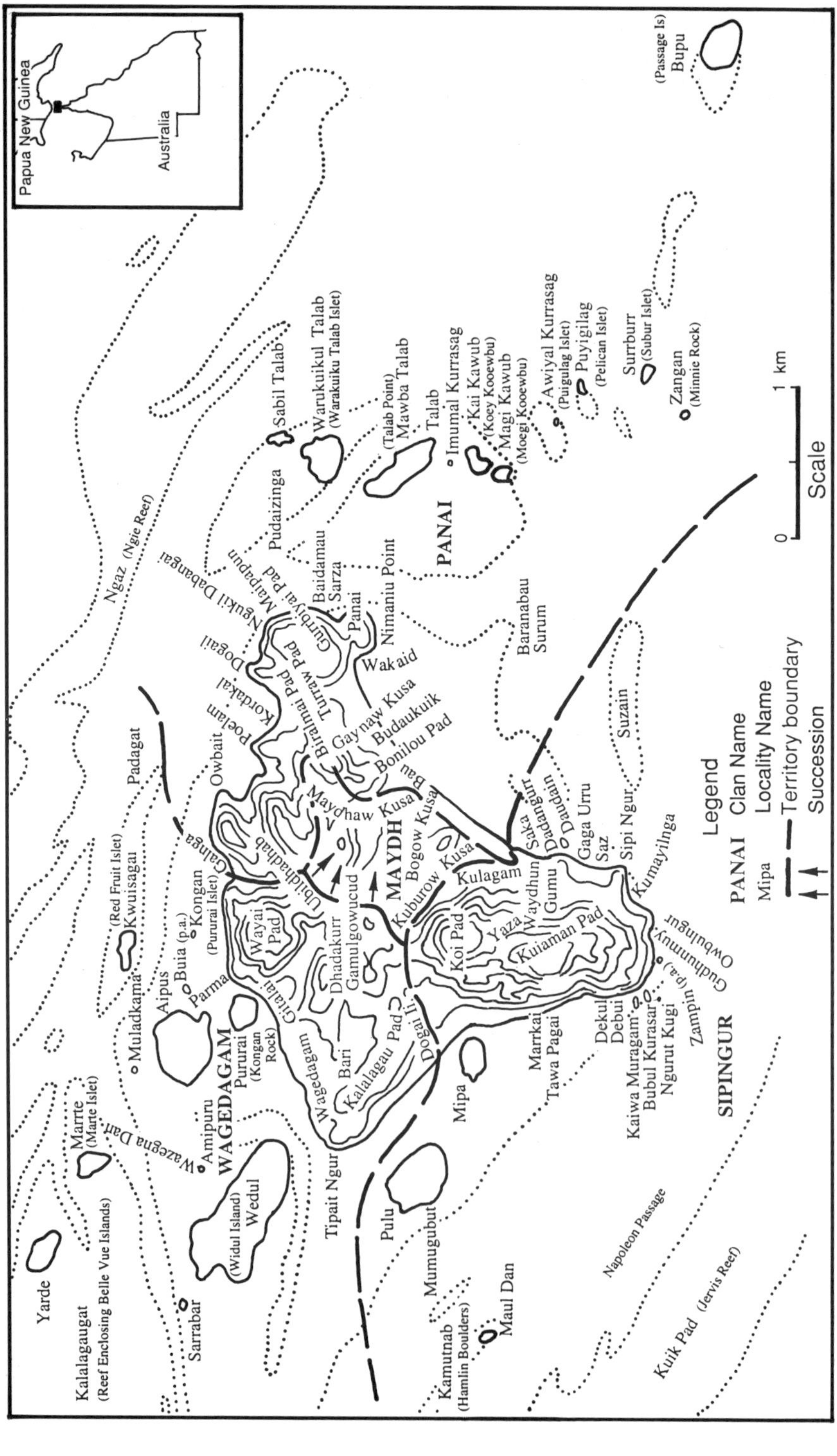

Map 15 Territories and Localities on Mabuiag Island

with Thompson who proved to be an observant and intelligent person attaining a complete fluency in the language of the Kaurareg people. Brierley's interviews continued daily for the duration of the two month voyage to England and provide an invaluable first-hand account of daily life of Torres Strait Islanders. The second outstanding contact is that of A. C. Haddon who initially visited Torres Strait to study the marine biology of the reef systems in 1888–89. So fascinated was he with the Islanders that he spent much of his time recording ethnographic data. Upon his return to Britain, Haddon directed his interests more to ethnography and began to plan a major expedition to Torres Strait which became the Cambridge Anthropological Expedition to Torres Strait 1898–99. Haddon led the multi-disciplinary team and edited the resultant six volumes of reports which were published between 1902 and 1935.

In 1915 the Society relinquished its work in Torres Strait in favour of the Anglican Church's Australian Board of Missions which also selected Mabuiag as its headquarters. Life for Torres Strait Islanders changed significantly. The Board was keen to integrate the local culture rather than oppress it as the Society had done. The use of indigenous languages was encouraged and many parts of Islander culture found their way into church services.

Concurrently Torres Strait Islanders lived under the policies of the Queensland Government which many regarded as overly repressive. Travel between islands was discouraged and Islander travel to the Australian mainland required permission. The *Torres Strait Islander Act* 1939 was a significant step in breaking down the direct control of the Queensland Government administration. The Act provided for the election of Islander councillors, devolving a greater degree of direct responsibility for domestic affairs to Islanders.

Many Islanders enlisted in the armed forces during the Second World War and experienced access to money, food, clothing, travel and goods previously unavailable to them. Their return from war service saw the onset of a migration of Islanders to the Australian mainland, primarily to the larger towns of Cairns and Townsville. Smaller but significant Islander populations have become established at other north Queensland coastal towns with the mainland Islander population now almost double that of Islanders living in Torres Strait (Department of Aboriginal Affairs 1988).

Maluigal Territory

Maluigal is an overarching sociopolitical identity for the Panai, Maydh, Sipi Ngur and Wagedagam clans whose traditional territories encompass Mabuiag and adjacent islands in Western Torres Strait (Map 16).

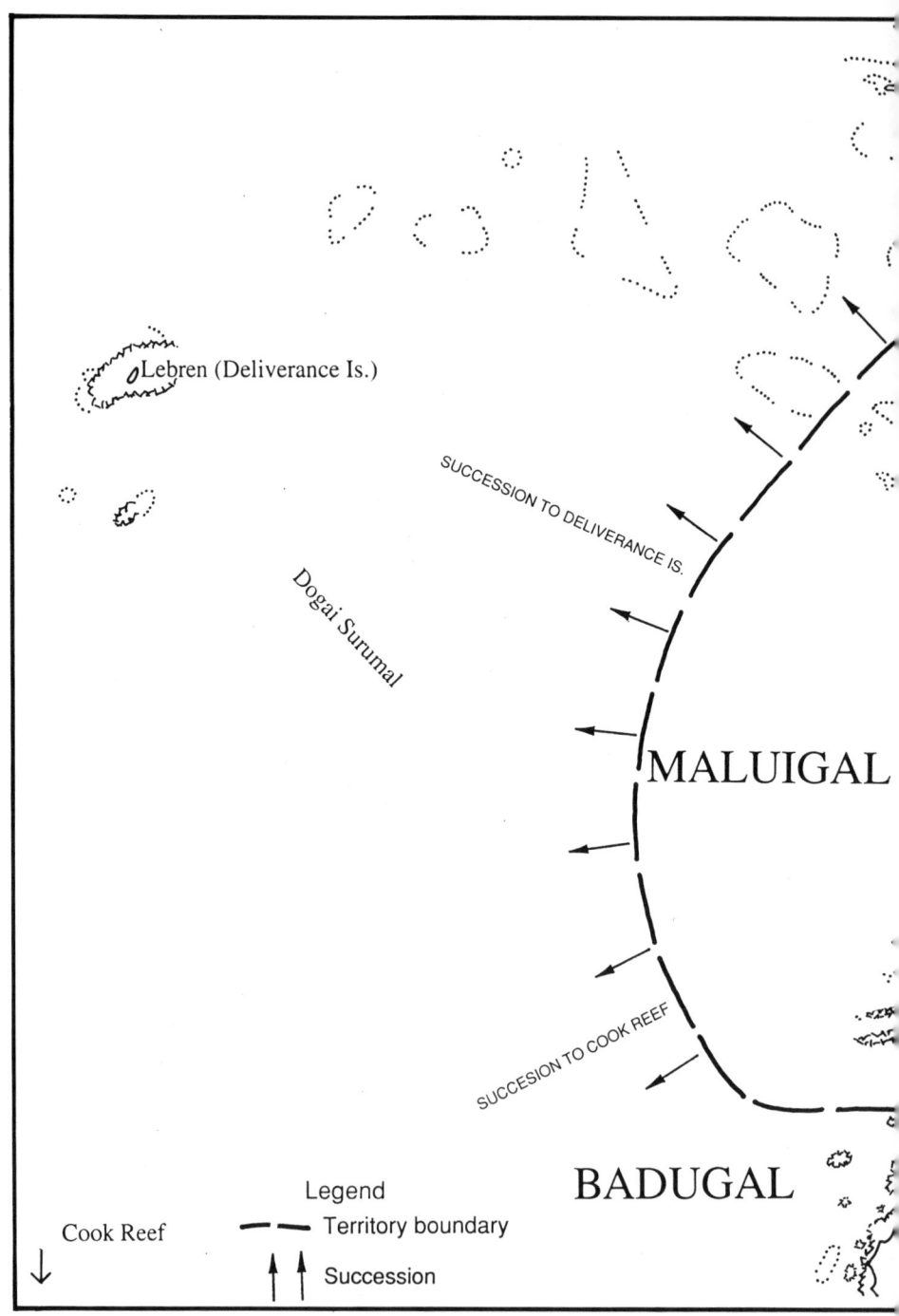

Map 16 Territories and Localities in Western Torres Strait

5 Torres Strait

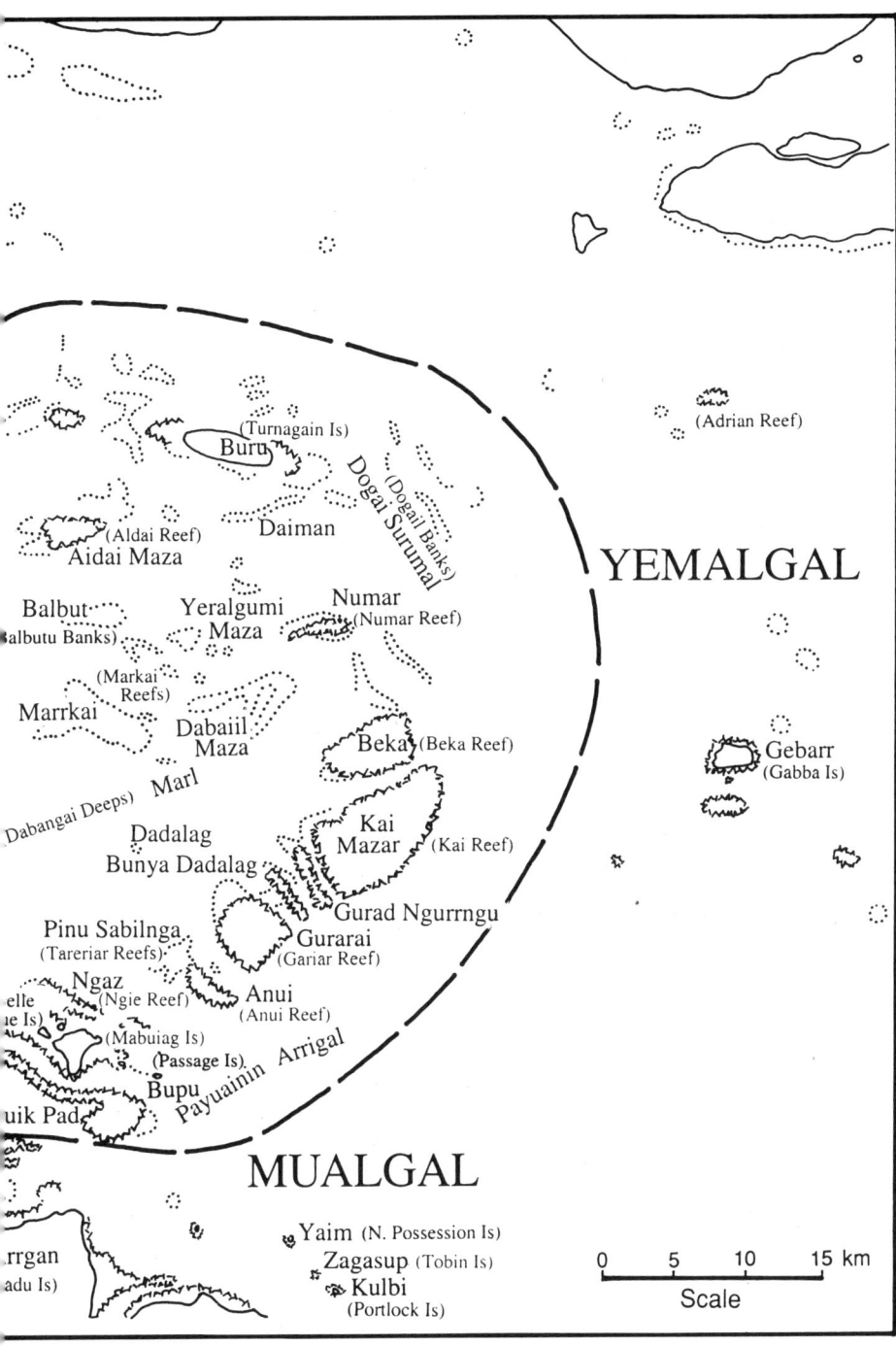

When describing the extent of Maluigal territory Gib Gaulai, a senior man, pointed out that the Dauan Island people lying to the north of Mabuiag Island were called Gudamaluigal, but the meaning of that term was unknown to the Mabuiag people. Not knowing its meaning was intended to confirm that the Mabuiag people had no territorial claim to that locality. Similarly Adrian Reef, lying east of Turnagain Island, was specifically denoted as lying outside Maluigal territory by stating 'Adrian Reef . . . that not for us. We got no name for that'. The absence of a name was a marker of lack of territorial rights. Conversely, naming localities is a marker of territoriality. Turnagain Island was cited by its Maluigal name Burru denoting its affiliation as Maluigal territory, and Deliverance Island was cited as Lebren similarly asserting it Maluigal affiliation. However, both islands appear to be more the subject of the current extension of Maluigal territorial claims. It is not clear whether these claims are based on recent knowledge obtained by Maluigal men who visited the islands whilst employed on European luggers this century, or on knowledge which preceded European settlement of the area and was gained by visits using the large traditional canoes documented by the Cambridge expedition.

There are at least 50 named localities on the main island of Mabuiag. Each rock, reef and passage within the home reef area of Mabuiag similarly has a specific name, adding a further 57 named localities to the total. Beyond the home reef the Maluigal specifically name at least another 20 reefs and banks (Map 16) making a total of at least 127 named localities within Maluigal territory.

We cannot be sure that every named locality recorded by the Cambridge Expedition has been transcribed on to the maps in the published volumes, but Wilkin did make some very specific statements in regard to the ownership of localities and territories: 'Every foot of land was owned by somebody. Even the small rocky islands around the coast had definite proprietors' (Wilkin 1904, p. 289). Through the identity of the proprietor each island was encompassed within the territory of one of the clans (*buai*). Pulu, an island now subsumed within the Sipi Ngur clan (Map 15), belonged specifically to the family of one man named Yamakuni. Wilkin (p. 289) noted that ownership was detailed and precise to the extent that:

> It has been said that every rock had an owner. Not only were rocks thus excluded from the possibility of becoming common land, but even waterholes were privately owned (though freely used by all) while adjacent reefs might be subject to some clan or buai.

The naming of the specific localities which compose the territory is a marker of territoriality. In former times such a marker would also have required specific knowledge of the meaning of each name. However, the meaning of place names is not being transmitted to the next generation.

The Maluigal territory extends beyond the sum of the territories of the four tribes which compose the Maluigal corporate group. The marine boundaries exclusive to each clan extend only to the inshore side of the home reef. Ngaz (Ngie Reef) and Kuik Pad (Jervis Reef) are available for access by all Maluigal (Map 15). They are not exclusive to any one clan. 'Ngaz . . . that reef for everybody. Not just one tribe.' Beyond the inshore reef the density of named localities diminishes significantly.

The tribes of Mabuiag identify themselves as an homogenous group. One of the attributes of the identity of the people is the boundary of the total Maluigal territory. When explaining the identity of the people on Mabuiag, a senior custodian said they were:

Murra Mabuiagiu *dagam*.
All people who belong to Mabuiag boundary.

The senior men gave a description of the extent of Maluigal territory. An examination of this description is of assistance in understanding Maluigal territoriality (see Map 16):

[*Eastern Boundary*]
Gebarr [Gabba Island] . . . That belongs to Yam people [people who live in the central community on Yam Island]. We call them Yemalgal. Kai Passage is the boundary for Mabuigilgal. East is Yemalgal.

Kai Passage is the eastern extent of the primary responsibility of Mabuiag people. East of Kai Passage control passes to the people from Yam Island.

[*Northern Boundary*]
Burru [Turnagain Island] . . . that's our boundary. That Adrian Reef [east of Turnagain Island, south of Saibai Island] that not for us. We got no name for that.

[*Western Boundary*]
Mabuigilgal go all the way to Lebren [Deliverance Island].

[*Southern and Southeastern Boundaries*]
[*Southern*] Kuik Pad [Jervis/Mabuiag Reef] is our home reef. After that, south side, is for Badu people . . . Badugal.

The reef itself does not belong to a specific clan but is part of the wider Maluigal territory.

[*Southeastern*] Mabuigilgal finishes at Payuainin Arrigal [Basilisk Banks]. Then steer southwest to Yaim [Possession Island], Zagasup [Tobin Island], Kulbi [Portlock Island]. All those three islanders are Mualgal [belong to the people from Moa] . . . not for Mabuigilgal. When people ask who we are we say 'Maluigal marl' . . . our country is Maluigal marl. We are all people who belong to Mabuiag boundary.

Clan Boundaries

The Cambridge Anthropological Expedition to Torres Strait noted that a number of clans had died out or the male line of a clan had died out prior to its work at Mabuiag in 1898. The use of the word 'clan' seems to refer to a lineage or descent group which 'resided in its own district before segregation induced by the missionary and other influences' (Haddon 1935, p. 57). Haddon refers to at least twelve such clans grouped into two moieties which the expedition denoted as 'L' (land animals) and 'M' (marine animals). The totems of the former included *kodal* (crocodile), *tabu* (snake), *umai* (dog) and *sam* (cassowary), whilst those of the later included *dangal* (dugong), *surlal* (turtle) and *kaigas* (shovel-nosed stingray).

Today these clans have, to a large degree, lost their specific identity. Their identity has subsequently become synonymous with the four districts which Rivers documented for Mabuiag (in Haddon 1935, p. 56):

(1) Panai in the northeast includes Panai and Dabungai and that corner of the island.
(2) Maydh (Maidi) on the east coast includes Bau, Maydn and Mui.
(3) Gumu in the southeast includes Gumu, Sipi Ngur, Kwoiam antra and the southern end of the island.
(4) Wagedagam, on the north coast towards the west, includes Wagedagam and probably one or two small villages. It probably also includes Aubait.

These districts have remained substantially the same and become the territories of the dominant clans. Each clan now identifies with one principal totem and, in the case of Gumu district which included Sipi Ngur, Sipi Ngur now dominates Gumu and has become the generic name for the territory. Thus the contemporary groups (tribes), territories and principal totems for Mabuiag as shown in Map 15 are:
(1) Panai of *dangal* (dugong) totem in the northeast
(2) Maydh of *tabu* (snake) totem in the east but not on the coast
(3) Sipi Ngur of *kaigas* (shovel-nosed stingray) totem in the south including Pulu
(4) Wagedagam of *kodal* (crocodile) totem in the northwest

The most obvious differences between River's mapping and Map 15 is that Owbait (Aubait) was assigned by Rivers to the Wagedagam (Wagedugam) district whereas it is now included in the Panai territory.

Rivers obviously was unsure of Owbait's affiliation for he thought that Owbait was 'probably' included in Wagedagam. The major change to have occurred this century as shown on Map 15 is that the portion of the eastern foreshore which Rivers noted to be included in the Maydh (Maidi) district has since been excised and is now included in the Panai territory.

The dominance of the Panai group in absorbing Owbait and excising the foreshore area of the Maydh territory is not unexpected in view of Haddon's comment (1935, p. 56) that 'Of the chief men of these four districts those of Panai appear to have been always predominant'. The location of the main community on what is now Panai territory has served to solidify, if not increase, the dominance of the Panai group who also assert their territoriality over the adjacent islands.

> All those Florence Islands from Sabil Talab right down to Surrburr belong to Panai tribe and Bupu [Passage Island] too . . . all Panai . . . Panaigal [belonging to Panai].

The locality of Bau is now used in a generic sense to refer to the foreshore area of the Panai territory which was excised from the Maydh district. This area formerly included the localities of Bau, Maydh and Mui (Haddon 1935, p. 56). Reference to the locality of Maydh is now rarely if ever made for to do so may renew claims to the foreshore from descendants of the Maydh group.

Maydh territory is now coupled with Wagedagam territory, which is to be expected when one considers that they both belong to the moiety 'L' (land animals) as opposed to Panai and Sipi Ngur which both belong to the moiety 'M' (marine animal totems). The excision of the former Maydh foreshore area by Panai has been made possible by the considerable decline in the Maydh population. There are no senior men of the Maydh group and hence Maydh territory is being overseen by the Wagedagam group whose territory adjoins the northwest Maydh boundary. Thus the interests of the Maydh group which remain strongest are those closest to the Wagedagam territory. The Maydh territory has thus become landlocked which has not posed a difficulty for there are no Maydh men to launch major maritime hunting expeditions. Significantly then, the Maydh territory no longer contains any marine area. The Maydh territory of the moiety of land totems has indeed become a land based group.

The fact that each tribe has distinct seaward boundaries that lie well within the horizon is quite unlike the situation among Australian Aboriginal groups. The seaward extent of Aboriginal marine territories seems to fade or dissipate as one approaches the limit of visual contact with the land. Aboriginal marine territories thus do not extend more than 12 to 15 kilometres from the mainland except where a large island or reef may occur in the intervening area which will serve to extend the territory. In the case of a large island the marine territory may be extended by a further 12 to 15 kilometres. If the island is small, or in the case of a reef or rock, the extension of the marine territory may be considerably less than 12 kilometres. The critical determinant of territorial extent is the seaward distance to which one may travel and maintain visual contact with the territorial component of the territory. Tidal and weather conditions may have a significant effect on the extent of a territory from day to day. Thus seaward boundaries are often vague. However, among the Maluigal the seaward boundaries of each territory terminate within 5 kilometres of Mabuiag, in every case with a distinct boundary.

A shift in the seaward boundary of individual clans becomes apparent with a comparison of comments by Wilkin (1904) and those of contemporary senior Maluigal men. Wilkin made reference to the Kaigas clan and their rights over Jervis Reef (Kuik Pad). We may assume this clan to be the Sipi Ngur group for several reasons. Firstly, the principal totem of the Sipi Ngur group is *kaigas*, the shovel-nosed stingray, and the Sipi Ngur group is referred to as Kaigas. Secondly, Jervis Reef (Kuik Pad) forms the southern and southwestern boundary of the Sipi Ngur territory, and no other group's territory is contiguous to Jervis Reef. Wilkin noted (1904, p. 298) that:

> The Kaigas clan exercised a sufficiently real authority over Jervis Reef to appropriate to their own use a wreck which occurred there some thirty years ago.

This would imply that the exclusive territory of the Kaigas or Sipi Ngur group included the home reef. Today the territory of each individual group extends only to the inshore side of the home reef. Sipi Ngur territory does not, at this time, include the home reef known as Jervis Reef or Kuik Pad.

A possible explanation for this withdrawal of the seaward extent of each group's territory may be that home reef stock was depleted in one or more territories and thus groups needed access to marine resources lying within other territories. More likely, the forced relocation of the Maluigal population to the main settlement at Bau meant that an accommodation of the hunting and foraging needs of people from tribes who did not own the area to which they were relocated had to be found. The simple solution was that the inshore resources were reserved to the tribes that owned the territory whilst the home reef was made common property to all Maluigal for hunting and foraging.

As discussed earlier, the outer boundary of each tribe is reasonably distinct in that each tribe's territory extends to the inshore edge of the home reef. Inshore from the home reef each reef and sandbank falls wholly within a territory. The boundaries weave their way from the home reef to the foreshore; in every case they follow a water course across the foreshore and thence up a valley to the watershed (Map 15). Sipi Ngur is divided from the other tribes by a boundary which follows water courses on the east and west of Mabuiag as so described. The boundary between Wagedagam and Maydh follows a ridge line, a criterion which also accords with the northern boundary between Maydh and Panai. The southeastern boundary of Maydh generally follows a line excluding the beach and foreshore area which has become the focal residential area for the Mabuiag population.

The name of the Wagedagam tribe itself means 'belonging to the Wage boundary'. Thus we see that not only is the concept of bounded territory well-founded and denoted by linguistic labels among the people of Mabuiag, but that the concept of a bounded territory is an integral part of the Maluigal identity.

Territorial Rights

In Torres Strait, rights within territories vary considerably. On Mer (Murray Island) bamboo fences were erected to distinguish between the properties of brothers. Ownership of specific gardens and fish-traps was distinct and clear as noted by Wilkin (1904). In comparison, land on Mabuiag was unimportant 'as a means of subsistence among a people so much addicted to fighting, fishing and trading' (Wilkin 1904, p. 289). Wilkin noted the cultivation of sweet potatoes, taro, yams, bananas, sugar-cane, water-melons and tobacco at the time of his research but could not determine whether any of these crops had been introduced by South Sea visitors. The Maluigal assured him that they had always cultivated these particular crops. It appears that the gardens on Mabuiag had probably not been as important as those on Mer, and formerly provided a food source secondary to that derived from the sea. However, by the time of the Cambridge Expedition in 1898 personal and family ownership of gardens had almost disappeared due to the breakdown of the land tenure system through the relocation of the various clans to a central community by the London Missionary Society. Ownership of territory had devolved to the level of the clan which was a corporate body with a recognised head, and the distinction between the land of a family and the land of such a clan was no longer clear (Wilkin 1904a, p. 286). This situation has continued to the present time wherein fishing rights associated with stone fish-traps on Mer are still strictly observed (Johannes 1984, p. 259). When a man leaves Mer to work on the Australian mainland, even for several years, others will be delegated to ensure his rights in a fish-trap are not infringed.

On Mabuiag, territorial rights continued at the clan level as Wilkin observed, and have since been solidified at that level. Individual affiliation is now given at the territory level. The relocation of the Maluigal people as a residential population to a single focal settlement under mission control accelerated the breakdown between the individual or family and any specific site or sub-territory. The strongest contemporary corporate identity is at the clan level through affiliation with the clan territory. The devolution of ownership of territory from the individual and family to the clan observed by Wilkin in 1898 have continued and are now complete.

The contemporary knowledge of clan territories on Mabuiag is detailed but now known to only a few older people. Similarly, the specific clan affiliation of each person is known only to these older people, with younger people being almost totally unaware even of the names of the four clans. This is a trend which the older people are keen to reverse, and in doing so they have begun to reassert territorial rights on behalf of the Maluigal people as a whole. Restrictions imposed on Torres Strait Islanders by the application of various state and federal Acts for the past one hundred years have seen an almost complete cessation of the exercise of traditional territorial rights by the Maluigal.

Historical records show Torres Strait Islanders to display a consistent ferocity in asserting their territorial rights prior to 1871. Wilkin noted that any stranger or uninvited arrival of whatever colour, condition or circumstance was killed (Haddon 1904, p. 278). John Macgillivray, a zoologist with the *Rattlesnake* survey of 1848–49, records the apparently unprovoked murder in June 1846 of four Europeans bartering for tortoise shell with the Badugal (Haddon 1904, p. 278). Barbara Thompson related to Brierley details of several hostilities, not only to Europeans but also to other Islander groups, which resulted in the taking of several heads (Moore 1972, pp. 338–9).

At approximately the same time that Barbara Thompson was living among the Kaurareg on Muralag (Prince of Wales Island), a European male named Wini (Weenie) was living with the Badugal on Badu. The Badu people travelled to Muralag to persuade Thompson to return with them to Badu, apparently to marry Wini. She refused but it wasn't long before sixteen canoes carrying two hundred men returned to make a more determined bid for her company. She evaded the party and stayed with the Kaurareg until her rescue (Moore 1972, p. 337). Wini remained with the Badugal for the rest of his life acquiring several wives, a canoe and gardens which he spent a considerable time cultivating (Haddon 1904, p. 278).

The cases of Thompson and Wini are the exception in what often appears to have been a ruthless exercise of territoriality which Haddon suggests to have been a precaution against danger to the community from the intruder or his allies should he return to his home. There appears to have been an abrupt cessation of such violent enforcement of territorial rights upon settlement by the London Missionary Society and the engagement of all the Maluigal men in pearling in the early 1870s (Haddon 1904).

A recent change in sentiment by the Australian Government towards the rights of the indigenous inhabitants of Australia including Torres Strait, and the need to negotiate a treaty with Papua New Guinea over the Torres Strait, have been a catalyst to an emerging widespread desire among Torres Strait Islanders to reassert their traditional territorial rights. The 1985 Torres Strait Treaty dealing with maritime boundaries between Australia and Papua New Guinea created a Protected Zone. It was created to acknowledge and protect the traditional way of life and the livelihoods of the traditional inhabitants (Department of Foreign Affairs 1978, pp. 15–26). The main provisions of the treaty include free movement and the unrestricted performance of lawful traditional activities such as fishing. These traditional rights will be maintained even if the rights of Papuans lie in areas under the jurisdiction of Australia or the rights of Australian Torres Strait Islanders lie in areas under the jurisdiction of Papua New Guinea. Mining or drilling in the Protected Zone is prohibited for a decade after the treaty took effect in 1985. Liaison and advisory arrangements were instituted to resolve local problems that might arise from time to time.

Conclusion

The Maluigal have strong affiliations with other Torres Strait Islanders but maintain their individual clan affiliations. The terrestrial boundaries of each clan group's territory follow ridge lines, water courses and other features of the landscape to their intersection with the foreshore. The boundaries then extend seaward to the inshore boundary of the home reef. Rights in the seas, reefs and marine resources of the seas beyond the home reef are held by the four Maluigal clans as a corporate group (Map 16). It is clear that this wider area in which corporate rights are held has been extended to the northwest since Maluigal began travelling to such distant localities on large vessels whilst employed as divers. The first hand knowledge thus gained of these islands, reefs and intervening seas has formed the basis for the Maluigal claims beyond what would almost certainly have been a significantly smaller corporate marine territory in pre-contact times.

The earliest documented accounts of contact with the Torres Strait Islands provides clear evidence that the Islanders exercised strong territorial rights in respect of fishing grounds. The Cambridge University Expedition led by A. C. Haddon in 1898 documented numerous examples of Islanders asserting and exercising territoriality through exclusive rights of access to fishing grounds (Haddon 1904, 1935). The Islanders assert that these rights have not been extinguished by European contact and occupation. To this end the Murray Island group have pursued legal action in the High Court of Australia to challenge the sovereign right of the Queensland and Commonwealth Governments to Murray Island and the adjacent seas. Other groups in the Torres Strait await the outcome of the Murray Island case and in the meantime are preparing their own cases.

The Maluigal are actively pursuing the preparation of their case, not only to gain recognition of their traditional territories and their rights therein but also to protect their marine resources from depredation by fishermen from Papua New Guinea. The governments of Papua New Guinea and Australia have entered into a treaty which allows fishermen from Papua New Guinea to fish in Australian waters. These fishermen often take crayfish from the home reef surrounding Mabuiag Island, in clear view of the Maluigal who live on the foreshore. The Maluigal view this not only as a gross violation of their traditional rights but as a violation which is endorsed by both the Australian and Papua New Guinea governments. The Maluigal both wish to defend their traditional territorial rights and are moving to protect a major source of cash income second only to social security payments from the Australian Government.

The exercise of exclusive access rights by Torres Strait Islanders over the inshore component of their traditional territories presents a daily opportunity for the people to impart the details of their traditions to their children. As the marine resources in the Torres Strait are depleted, so too are the opportunities for the Maluigal to move towards a degree of financial independence, and to practise and teach their traditions to their children.

6

Conclusions

Traditional Aboriginal Boundaries

> Territoriality has been an unexamined concept in most writing about hunters and gatherers, especially in discussions concerning land tenure.
> Myers 1986, p. 127

It might have been this neglect of territoriality that induced the members of the Resource Assessment Commission involved in the Kakadu Conservation Zone Inquiry to dismiss the concept in respect of the Jawoyn (Resource Assessment Commission 1991, vol. 1, p. 164 and vol. 2, pp. 293–4).

The two quotations cited by the Commission to justify their view were taken from the useful book on human territoriality by Sack (1986). This was the main book relied on by Davis in his evidence on territoriality to the Commission. No exception can be taken to the quotation dealing with the Chippewa. It notes that this hunting and gathering group on the western shores of Lake Superior often asserted control only in an imprecise, seasonal and strategic manner (Resource Assessment Commission 1991, vol. 2, p. 293; Sack 1986, p. 8). The second quotation appears as follows:

> We can surmise that . . . not all of [these peoples] may have made use of territoriality and many may have done so only intermittently.
> Resource Assessment Commission 1991, vol. 2, p. 294

In presenting Sack's opinion it is more useful to give the whole sentence and the one that follows (p. 52):

> By observing contemporary pre-literate hunting-gathering societies and reflecting upon the reason why such groups have been territorial in the past, we can surmise that, although each of these pre-historic peoples occupied geographic area, not all of them may have made use of territoriality and many may have done so intermittently. Still there were enough to place the number of territorial autonomous units at tens of thousands.

Tens of thousands is a big number and our earlier literature survey demonstrates that some of the boundaries of hunting and gathering communities have been identified in the Americas and some islands in the South Pacific.

We can refine concepts of territoriality by establishing whether or not the areas occupied by groups were precisely defined. The aim of this book is to establish that territories over which Aboriginal people exercise primary political influence within Aboriginal tradition are defined either by frontiers or precise boundaries. We do not know the origin of these frontiers and boundaries for they are lost in antiquity, nor do we know if they evolved as in other parts of the world from no-man's lands to frontiers, then by encroachment to boundaries.

Aboriginal people generally believe that each sociopolitical group variously described in the literature as a clan or tribe was made corporate by its birth from ancestral beings upon an area which became identifiable as a territory at the moment of birth of the group with whom the territory is identified. The acts of ancestral beings in conferring territories and giving birth to each group established for all time the identity of those groups and the boundaries of the territories with which they are identified. Evidence of the corporateness of the group and their affiliation and responsibilities for their territory are found in the ritual emblems and paraphernalia made, painted and revealed to initiates in the course of the performance of ceremonies. These symbols, together with songs, dances, ground designs, body markings and paintings serve as the markers of territoriality.

The ancestral being primarily identified with the group physically travelled over the territory in the creative epoch conducting all those daily activities necessary for the continuance of life, such as hunting, fishing, sleeping, singing songs and performing ceremonies. In so doing the ancestral being gave form to the land and seascape and named each locality at which any act was performed. The extent of his activities thus defines the parameters of the group's territory. Before repeating the cycle of events in other areas the ancestral being often changed his name and his language. Thus not only does the sum of all named localities constitute a full description of the group's territory but the language in which the names are given confirms the identity of the group which holds primary rights in the territory. The group is linked to other groups through song lines and ceremonies which recount the activities of the ancestral being. The point on the song line or dreaming track at which the ancestral being changed his name and language denotes the boundary or frontier between contiguous territories.

The principles of boundary definition which operate as clearly on land as they do on sea have been used to develop a technique for identifying Aboriginal boundaries and frontiers wherever they may occur in Australia. The applications of this technique throughout most of Australia runs contrary to the history of mapping of Aboriginal groups in Australia. Early in our contact history, writers ignored the existence of frontiers between Aboriginal groups and chose to show only boundaries on maps. More recently, some have completely refuted the existence of boundaries during the presentation of Aboriginal claims to land under the terms of the *Aboriginal Land Rights (Northern Territory) Act* 1976.

It is now clear that not only has precise boundary information been maintained by many Aboriginal groups in the period since contact, but that frontiers are certainly in evidence between many groups, particularly in the arid areas. Unfortunately, in much of the southern areas of Australia such information appears to be no longer held within current Aboriginal traditions. Recent publications of the Aboriginal and Torres Strait Islander Commission (ATSIC) confirm this loss of information. A pamphlet on Aboriginal peoples of New South Wales produces a map but records that 'It is impossible to establish precise territories' (ATSIC 1990). A similar pamphlet for Victoria notes that 'The boundaries are only approximate and the spelling of Aboriginal names varies' (ATSIC 1990a). There is a pattern evident in the occurrence of the remaining traditional frontiers and boundaries between Aboriginal groups throughout Australia which reflects a strong match between the physical characteristics of a region and the boundaries and frontiers.

Three points flow from this conclusion. Firstly, Aboriginal territories increase in size with increasing latitude from the humid zone in the north to the arid zone in Central and Western Australia. This trend is broken only in areas of high relief landform around Tennant Creek in the semi-arid zone and Alice Springs in the arid zone, where territories are small. These areas in the arid and semi-arid zones generally have a higher carrying capacity than surrounding areas of low relief landform, which is directly related to the types of vegetation and availability of surface water. Secondly, boundaries prevail throughout the humid zone, in the coastal areas of the tropical north of Australia and in the isolated areas of high relief landforms. In the semi-arid and arid areas, where carrying capacities are lower, both boundaries and frontiers are encountered in defining Aboriginal territories. It is not simply the carrying capacity in an average year which is important. Those humid areas with high carrying capacities are also the areas where annual fluctuations in food supply rarely cause serious food deficiencies. In contrast, there is a much higher chance that in the arid areas, where carrying capacity is low, the fluctuations in food supplies will cause serious problems several times in each generation. Thirdly, boundaries are most often coincident with geographical features such as watersheds, creeks and rivers or the perimeters of distinct vegetative zones. Frontiers occur most commonly in arid areas and are generally coincident with natural barriers such as salt lakes and the perimeters or disjunctions between natural regions such as the edge of a desert. In the sea, extensive tidal channels are the feature most commonly used to define boundaries, particularly in areas of high tidal amplitude.

The boundaries between Aboriginal territories are not delimited in treaties or demarcated on the ground as are the international and internal boundaries of most countries. Rather, they are defined in oral traditions, through songs, ceremonies, and non-permanent symbolism such as body painting, bark painting and ground designs. However, this does not detract from the precision with which Aboriginal people define territorial boundaries or the consistent accuracy of definition that is maintained from generation to generation. Each Aboriginal group which is a labelled sociopolitical entity is synonymous with a territory to which the group's claim may not necessarily be exclusive of the access and rights of all other groups. Each group may control or regulate access across its boundaries which define the extent of the group's territory.

Primary rights in territories accorded to Aboriginal groups by the ancestral beings are contingent upon the Aboriginal custodians continuing to care for the territory by singing the songs and performing the ceremonies associated with the territory as well as by caring for the sacred objects and places. Subsidiary rights may be held by other people who, among the Yolngu for example, most often claim affiliation to the territory through uterine relatives of the patrilineal descent group. Among the Tiwi, subsidiary rights of access may be claimed through, among other things, associations with particular places such as one's paternal grandfather's (*amini*) burial site or one's totemic site (*imunga*).

Holders of subsidiary rights may be considered to have a standing invitation to enter and use the resources of that territory. However, even where such an invitation exists, a prospective user of the territory will ensure wherever possible that the senior custodians are aware of his intentions and, upon his return from their territory, will share with them the foods or goods collected or make other appropriate acknowledgment of their primary rights. There are, then, established rules and procedures within Aboriginal tradition, primarily through kin relationships, which will afford access across the boundaries of contiguous territories.

Although we have no information on the status of frontiers or boundaries between Aboriginal groups in the pre-contact period, Tindale's map (1974) tries to show boundaries at the time of European contact, and Tindale was aware of the concept of frontiers. We do know that it is highly likely that some frontiers have developed from boundaries in the post-contact period primarily through a prolonged absence of both the adjacent groups from the area in the immediate vicinity of the boundary. In the pre-contact period it is unlikely that such a situation would have occurred, as the traditional Aboriginal mechanism of succession would have ensured that the integrity of the boundaries of a deceased territory was maintained by a group who succeeded to that territory through kinship and ceremonial relationships with the deceased group. The successors would have possessed skills and knowledge developed in a similar environment to the deceased territory in order for them to be able to sustain themselves on this new territory. If the deceased territory and the successor's original territory were contiguous then it is highly likely that the intervening boundary would have disappeared leaving one larger territory. In such cases, the deceased territory would be identified as a sub-territory within the larger territory and have at least one lineage or family group of the successor group identified with it. Alternatively, if other territories lay between the deceased territory and the successors' original territory then the deceased territory would have become a regional territory of the successor group. These are the primary ways in which changes in the extent of territories take place and traditionally these changes took place over the course of a generation or more.

Administrative Aboriginal Boundaries

On 10 December 1987 the Minister for Aboriginal Affairs announced proposals for the creation of a national commission to administer Aboriginal affairs. The original proposal involved the creation of 28 regions to cover the whole of the Australian mainland and Tasmania. In May 1988 this number was doubled and it was noted that some regions would straddle state boundaries. When the Aboriginal and Torres Strait Islander Commission (ATSIC) came into being in 1990 the number of administrative regions was 60 (Map 17).

In each region there is a regional council and the members of these councils were elected in November 1990. The function of the regional councils is to discover what the electors want to do to improve their economic, social and cultural life; to make proposals to the Commission to achieve those improvements, and to implement the plans agreed to and funded by the Commission. The 60 regions are grouped into 17 zones and the councillors in each zone select one member to serve as a commissioner to represent the zone. Another two commissioners and the chairperson of the Commission are appointed by the Minister for Aboriginal Affairs.

The boundaries of the regions were determined after an extensive consultative process over a period of two years. The consultations were undertaken by Gerry Hand, then Minister for Aboriginal Affairs, senior officers of the Department of Aboriginal Affairs and members of the ATSIC task force. Every incorporated Aboriginal body and organisation was invited to attend the meetings that were held throughout Australia. The geographic area of a regional council is based on:

- Aboriginal and Torres Strait Islander opinion on the commonality of cultural, traditional, social and economic factors effecting (sic) a specific area, and
- the viability of the area in terms of decisions relating to priorities, policies and the need for services.

Personal communication, Michael Stewart 1991

The boundaries of the regions were described in drafts prepared by the Australian Surveying and Land Information Group (AUSLIG) and presented to the ATSIC Board of Commissioners in March 1990. The Board agreed to the proposed boundaries in April 1990 and the Minister of Aboriginal Affairs, then Robert Tickner, approved them in May 1990. The Minister's notice defining the boundaries was published in Gazette GN 22 on 6 June 1990. The boundary descriptions are based on the 1986 population and housing census collection districts and the 1984 pastoral maps of the Northern Territory and Western Australia. The only exception to this pattern is the regional council of Launceston which occupies the whole of Tasmania. The three methods of boundary definition are illustrated in the following extract (pp. 17–18):

Regional Council Area: Wyalcatchem Zone: Western Australia (South)
- Census collection districts 023501 to 023602 inclusive;
- Census collection districts 022601 to 022604 inclusive;
- Census collection districts 030101 to 030109 inclusive;
- Census collection districts 040101 to 042406 inclusive.

6 Conclusions

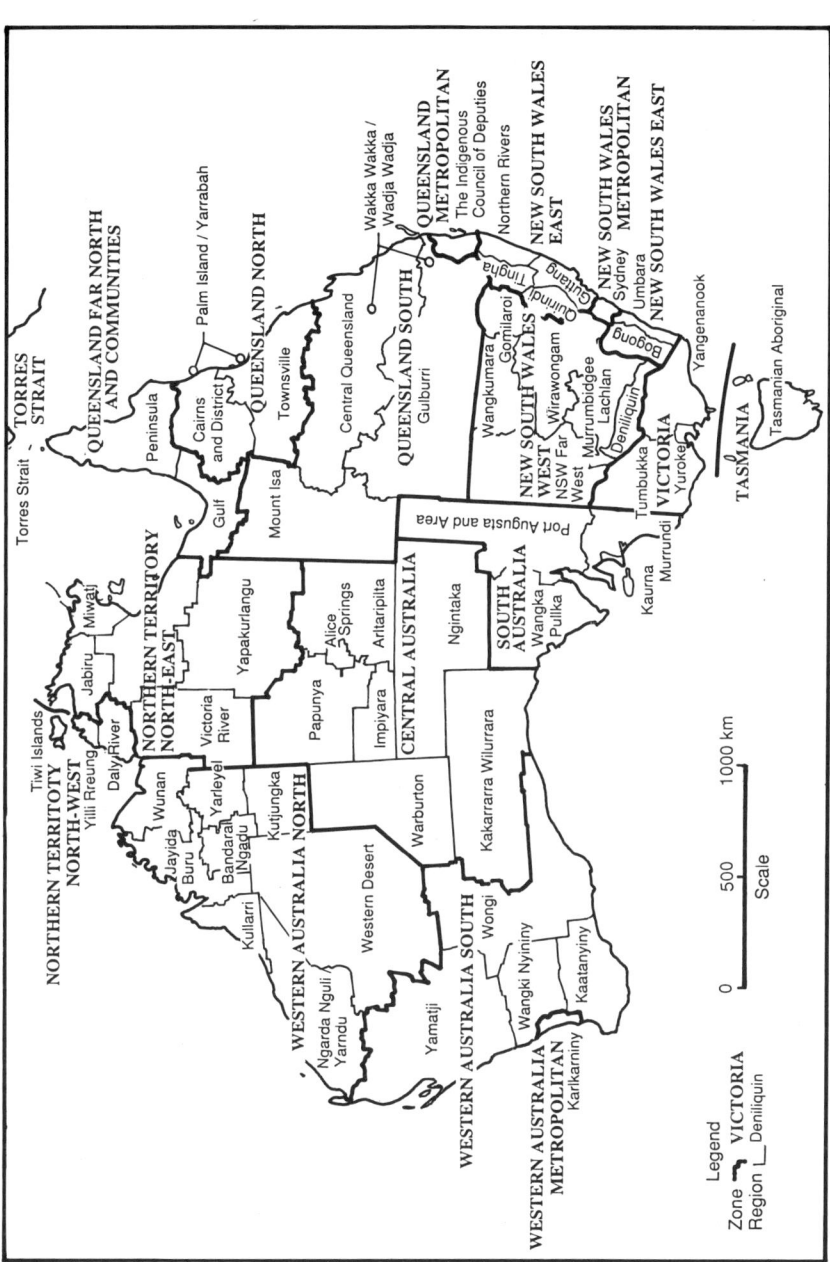

Map 17 Boundaries of Regions and Zones Created by the *Aboriginal and Torres Strait Islander Commission Act 1989*

State: Tasmania

Regional Council: Launceston Zone: Tasmania
- The state of Tasmania

State: Northern Territory

Regional Council Area: Alice Springs Zone: Central Australia
- The eastern, northern and western boundaries of Yambah Station;
- The western boundary of Hamilton Downs Station and the western and southern boundaries of Owen Springs Station;
- The southern and eastern boundaries of Undoolya Station and the northern boundary of Santa Teresa Reserve;
- The western boundary of Todd River Station between Santa Teresa Reserve and Loves Creek Station and the western boundary of Loves Creek Station to the intersection of The Garden and Undoolya Stations boundary;
- The southern and western boundaries of The Garden Station from Loves Creek Station to the southern boundary of Bushy Park Station.

It is apparent that the types of traditional Aboriginal boundaries that we have described and analysed in this study have not provided the basis for the boundaries of the ATSIC regions. It would be stretching credulity to imagine that traditional Aboriginal boundaries coincided with the limits of pastoral leases or census districts. There is no evident distinction between the regional boundaries where traditional knowledge still enables the traditional boundaries to be identified and those areas where that traditional knowledge is no longer available. It can be shown that in the Northern Territory there are at least 16 traditionally based Aboriginal groups whose territories lie in more than one region. These groups are Kungarakany, Wulnaminitja, Jawoyn, Wandarang, Wardaman, Yangman, Mudburra, Gurdandji, Garawa, Waanyi, Kartangarurru, Walpiri, Alyawarra, Anmatjarra, Kukatjarra and Matutjarra.

This division of territories between regions will not be a serious problem in those cases where all members of the group live in one of the regions and the detached area has no economic significance. Problems might arise if the population of the group is divided between two regions or if the detached part is economically important. For example, the Jawoyn might prefer to have Katherine Gorge and Coronation Hill in a single region.

The Anmatjarra of the area centred 60 kilometres north of Alice Springs complained to the Minister for Aboriginal Affairs about the way their territory had been divided into three parts in Tennant Creek, Papunya and Harts Range Regions (letter dated 14 October 1988; cited in

Report to Senate Select Committee on the Administration of Aboriginal Affairs 1989, p. 37):

> You can't split our country up. You can't put us with those other people from different country. That mob from south haven't got skin groups like us. You can't put us with them.

Three regions extend across state boundaries. Kununurra is mainly in Western Australia and includes a narrow strip of the northwest of the Northern Territory. It measures about 55 kilometres by 300 kilometres, and it appears to divide at least three traditional territories. Doomadgee is mainly in Queensland along the southern coast of the Gulf of Carpentaria but it includes a pedicle extending into the Northern Territory. This area of about 4000 square kilometres straddles the traditional boundary of the Garawa and Waanyi groups. Deakin is a very large region that occupies the southeast corner of Western Australia and the southwest corner of South Australia. One area where it would have been appropriate to cross state boundaries involves the Wangkungurru. They mainly live near Birdsville in western Queensland but parts of their territory are in the Northern Territory and South Australia, which means that their territory lies within Mount Isa, Harts Range and Indulkana regions.

The 1989 Act that created ATSIC appears to have recognised the potential problem that the lack of correspondence between regional and traditional boundaries might present. Division 9 of the Act allows the Minister of Aboriginal Affairs to convene a panel to review either the boundaries of a region or the groupings of regions into zones. One of the triggers for convening a review panel is a valid petition calling for a review of a region's boundaries. A valid petition must be signed by more than 25 per cent of the region's voters within six months of its being presented to the Minister, and must include the date on which it was signed and the address of each signatory.

Any review panel will consist of at least three people. They are a commissioner who will act as chairman, someone nominated by the Australian Electoral Commissioner and an Aboriginal or Torres Strait Islander who is not an ATSIC commissioner. If the Minister deems it appropriate a member of AUSLIG can be added to the panel in accordance with Division 9 of the Act. It was reported in November 1991 that a boundary review panel would be set up to examine existing boundaries.

One of the early decisions of many regional councils was to change the region's name in accordance with powers granted in Article 93 of the Act. Only 13 regional councils kept their original name. In most cases a regional name, such as Mount Barnett, was changed to an Aboriginal name, Jayida Buru. In one case an Aboriginal name, Jigalong, in central Western Australia was given the regional title of Western Desert. In another case one regional name was exchanged for another; thus Casino in northeast New South Wales became Northern Rivers, and Wilcannia in the State's west was changed to NSW Far West. Brisbane and Launceston were changed to indicate the new administrative order, Brisbane being renamed the Indigenous Council of Deputies [Region]. In some cases one Aboriginal name was displaced by another; Yulara became Implyara.

The ATSIC regional boundaries are the latest set of administrative Aboriginal boundaries and they are comprehensive in the sense that they apply to the whole of the Australian mainland and Tasmania. For many years Aboriginal groups in different parts of Australia have secured land under various forms of tenure. Some land is held as freehold or leasehold by Aboriginal land trust, ATSIC or incorporated Aboriginal groups. Other areas, called reserves, consist of Crown Land reserved for Aborigines. Finally, there are areas in Western Australia and the Northern Territory that are held by churches on a freehold or leasehold basis for Aboriginal missions. This last classification is usually styled mission land.

Additions to Aboriginal freehold and leasehold land are made somewhere in Australia each year. In 1987 those categories accounted for 79 per cent of all land held by Aboriginal groups. Land held privately by Aborigines was not considered in this description. In 1987 reserves accounted for 20.9 per cent of Aboriginal land and mission land accounted for 0.1 per cent. The location and extent of each parcel of land in the various categories is shown on excellent maps produced by the Division of National Mapping and its successor AUSLIG. Both maps entitled *Aboriginal Land and Population* are drawn at a scale of 1:5 000 000. The first edition published in 1982 shows the situation in late 1980; the second edition published in 1988 shows the position in mid-1987. The major changes in the period 1980 to 1987 are summarised in Table 1.

The area of Aboriginal land increased by 26 per cent in the seven years to 1987. In the period 1980 to 1986 the Aboriginal population had increased by 24.6 per cent. Thus in 1987 the Aborigines, who formed about 1.5 per cent of the Australian population, held about 12 per cent of the States and Territories. There is an uneven distribution of Aboriginal land throughout Australia. Slightly over half of all Aboriginal land is in the Northern Territory where 15 per cent of Aborigines lived in 1986. The Northern Territory, South Australia and Western Australia with 38 per cent of Aborigines contained 96 per cent of Aboriginal land. Victoria, New South Wales and Tasmania with 35 per cent of Aboriginals contained only 0.1 per cent of Aboriginal land.

6 Conclusions

Table 1 Aboriginal Land by Area in mid-1987 ('000 hectares)

State or Territory	Freehold	Leasehold	Reserve	Mission	TOTAL
Northern Territory	44 863(26)	2 483(15)	*(0)	4(0)	47 350(26)
Western Australia		3(200)	4 260(58) 18 443(-4)	76(17)	22 782(4)
South Australia	18 315(72)	51(-2)			18 366(53)
Queensland	*(0)	2 747(214)	663(-68)		3 410(16)
New South Wales†	19(58)	83(822)			102(385)
Victoria	3(60)				3(60)
Tasmania	*(0)				*(0)
Australia	63 203(37)	9 624(66)	19 106(-10)	80(16)	92 013(26)

(-5) percentage change since 1980
* less than 1000 hectares
† includes Australian Capital Territory and Jervis Bay Territory
Source: AUSLIG 1988, *Australian Land and Population* (2nd edition)

The extent of individual holdings of Aboriginal land shows wide variations. In the desert and semi-desert country straddling meridian 130° east there are huge blocks of Aboriginal land between the trans-Nullabor railway and Newcastle Waters. In South Australia Pitjantjatjara land occupies 10.1 million hectares, in Western Australia the Central Australia (Warburton) area covers 8 million hectares, and in the Northern Territory the Central Desert zone measures 8.4 million hectares. There are also large blocks in the humid coastal strip of the Northern Territory with Arnhem Land accounting for 9 million hectares and Daly River for 1.3 million hectares. Blocks of between 480 000 and 1.1 million hectares are found along Western Australia's tropical coast while the largest single area in Queensland's Cape York is Aurukun with 750 000 hectares.

These large units of Aboriginal land are in sharp contrast to the small holdings in Tasmania, New South Wales and Victoria. In Tasmania holdings are less than 1000 hectares, in Victoria less than 10 000 hectares and in New South Wales less than 50 000 hectares. The major change between 1980 and 1987 has been in New South Wales where most of the additional 81 000 hectares are made up of holdings less than 1000 hectares in extent, some along the northern coast. For example, between the Queensland border and Sydney ten new holdings were created after 1980. They are Yelgun, Broken Head and Goanna Headland near Lismore; Lanitza near Grafton; Greenhill and Ngaku near Kempsey; Wauchope and Doyles River near Port Macquarie; and Kulnura and Narara at Gosford. New leasehold areas of up to 30 000 hectares were created at Winbar and Weinteriga Station northeast and southwest of Wilcannia respectively.

As the name Weinteriga Station suggests, the boundaries of these freehold and leasehold areas and of the reserves and mission lands are real estate limits, not traditional Aboriginal boundaries. In the Northern Territory land claims have been won by demonstrating strong and continuing spiritual and material relationships with areas of land, but the claimed land has been unalienated Crown Land bounded by surveyed lines recorded in land registers. This situation is shown clearly in the attempts by the Victorian Government to transfer an urban area to the Wurundjeri Tribe Land and Compensation Heritage Council Incorporated in 1991. The land is called Richmond Circus and it is bounded by Yarra Boulevard, Swan Street and the railway between Burnley and Hawthorn.

Aboriginal Boundaries in the 1990s

In 1991 it was reported that there would be a review of the ATSIC regional boundaries (personal communication, J. Kelly October 1991). It can be expected that any reviews conducted under the terms of Division 9 of the 1989 Act will refine the original boundaries so that they correspond more closely with the aspirations of Aboriginal communities. In most States and the Northern Territory new areas are likely to be granted to Aboriginal groups under freehold or leasehold arrangements. It can be expected that large blocks are more likely to be granted in the Northern Territory and in Western Australia. In Queensland, New South Wales, Victoria and Tasmania it is probable that grants will be in sections of less than 1000 hectares. Such developments would follow patterns established in the 1980s. The boundaries of these new areas will be fixed in almost all cases by existing real estate limits of farms, stations and Crown Land.

When the future of traditional Aboriginal boundaries in the 1990s is considered the following developments are either probable or possible.

1. Traditional knowledge that allows territories to be precisely defined will continue to be lost. Fewer traditional ceremonies will be performed, songs will no longer by sung in some communities, ritual paraphernalia will be destroyed or stolen, and old men will die before passing information to the next generation. Already more than 75 per cent of the senior Aboriginal custodians who have been our main source of traditional boundary information are now deceased.

2. Land claims under Northern Territory legislation will continue to face rigorous standards of proof of spiritual affiliation with the land which new claimants will find harder and harder to meet.

3. The standards of proof needed for Aboriginals to be involved in government decisions about resource development projects will remain much lower than the standards set by the Northern Territory land rights legislation. This was made clear in the Resource Assessment Commission's Inquiry into the Kakadu Conservation Zone (Resource Assessment Commission, 1991 vol. 2, p. 291). This conclusion is also supported by Section 10.4 of the *Aboriginal and Torres Strait Islander Heritage Protection Act 1984*, which allows the Minister for Aboriginal Affairs to protect a significant Aboriginal area that is under threat of desecration or injury. Such action would follow a request received from an Aborigine or Aboriginal group and a report received in accordance with Section 10.4 (Stewart 1991, pp. 1 and 3). The report by the appointed person must deal with the following matters (Stewart 1991, p. 5):

(a) the particular significance of the area to Aboriginals;
(b) the nature and extent of the threat of injury to, or desecration of, the area;
(c) the extent of the area that should be protected;
(d) the prohibitions and restrictions to be made with respect to the area;
(e) the effects the making of a declaration may have on the proprietary or pecuniary interests of persons other than the Aboriginals by or on whose behalf the application for a declaration was made [i.e. the Aboriginals referred to in s.10(1)(a)];
(f) the duration of any declaration;
(g) the extent to which the areas are or may be protected by or under a law of a State or Territory, and the effectiveness of any remedies available under any such law; and
(h) such other matters [if any] as are prescribed.

The Act provides some help in interpreting the phrase 'particular significance' (Stewart, p. 19):

3.02   In the interpretations section of the Act (s.3) the following definitions appear:
'significant Aboriginal area' means
(a)   an area of land in Australia or in or beneath Australian waters;
(b)   an area of water in Australia; or
(c)   an area of Australian waters,
being an area of particular significance to Aboriginals in accordance with Aboriginal tradition.

'Aboriginal tradition' means the body of traditions, observances, customs and beliefs of Aboriginals generally or of a particular community or group of Aboriginals, and includes any such traditions, observances, customs or beliefs relating to particular persons, areas, objects or relationships.

Stewart (p. 19) regarded attempts to define the phrase on the basis of the legislation as somewhat circular, and after canvassing the legal precedents he declined to develop a definition of 'particular significance'. He then examined the diverse views on the issue received during the hearings and concluded that the Minister could be satisfied that the Conservation Zone is of particular significance to Aborigines in accordance with Aboriginal tradition (p. 24). The evidence relied upon does not appear to match the rigour demanded in successful land claims in the Northern Territory.

Apart from the apparently lower standard of proof required for involvement of Aborigines in resource development decisions there is also the issue of elaboration of religious thought. The Resource Assessment Commission (1991, vol. 2, pp. 307–10) noted that some evidence expressed concern at the malleability of some Aboriginal beliefs and the possibility that elaboration might be used to serve land ownership ambitions. One witness observed that the details of some traditions related to the Bula myth were only a decade old (p. 307). Another witness noted that pressures and opportunities helped Aboriginal groups to restore more specific form and content to traditions inherited from previous generations (p. 308). It was the Commission's view that elaboration, such as linking Bula to recently discovered gold at Coronation Hill, results from genuine Aboriginal processes (p. 309).

4. State governments will continue to wrestle with the design of legislation to establish land rights. The Victorian Government tried and failed in 1983–84. The Western Australian Government commissioned an inquiry into Aboriginal land rights in 1983 and received a detailed report from Commissioner Seaman (1984). No legislation resulted from this report. In 1991 Premier Goss announced proposals for land rights legislation in Queensland that were severely attacked by Aboriginal groups.

The difficulty for all such proposals is the level of proof that should be demanded for any claim to be successful. In Western Australia Seaman received a letter from the Minister for Aboriginal Affairs expressing the hope that the Northern Territory claim process should be avoided if possible. In fact for much of New South Wales, Victoria, Tasmania, southern Queensland, west and south Western Australia and eastern South Australia the Northern Territory standards are inappropriate. Those standards would prevent any successful claim.

There are at least three possible arrangements for awarding land to Aboriginal groups in those areas. First, while still requiring Aboriginal groups to demonstrate a relationship with a specific area the proofs of that relationship could be of a lower standard than required in the Northern

Territory. So historical proofs, for example, might play a more important role than the possession of traditional knowledge by present elders and their performance of ceremonies and enforcement of prohibitions. Or it might be considered sufficient for a long association by residence to justify land grants. Second, it could be decided that since it is impossible in certain areas to identify the traditional territories of some Aboriginal groups an agreed area should be awarded as compensation for past losses. The land would be granted not because the Aboriginal group had any special relationship with it, but because of previous acts of oppression and dispossession.

Seaman (1984, p. 42) suggested a third possibility: that land rights be granted on a basis of need. After noting that enquiries about traditional relationships had no relevance to the land aspirations of the majority of Aboriginal communities in Western Australia he made this suggestion:

> Need is so broad a concept as to be almost incapable of definition but I recommend to you that a local incorporated Aboriginal organisation should be entitled to claim the available land referred to in Chapter 4, if it can establish before the Tribunal the following matters:
> (a) that it has the consent in writing of the relevant regional Aboriginal organisation; and
> (b) that it has a specific proposal for the use of the land which is likely to provide social benefit to its members.

The land referred to in Chapter 4 of Seaman's report (p. 15) excluded the private property of any citizens or land in which people have the contractual right to acquire freehold title. So available land for Aborigines might include unallocated Crown Land, unused public lands and national parks, forests and conservation reserves.

While it is not possible to predict that any State government will devise land rights legislation which is satisfactory from the perspective of all parties, it is fairly safe to suggest that no federal government in the 1990s will attempt to impose national land rights arrangements on the States and Territories. It is probable that the concern of Aboriginal communities with land rights will rise through the decade of reconciliation that leads to centennial celebration of federation in 2001. This is already shown by proposals for a massive land claim by the Worora, Wunambul and Ngarinyin communities of the Kimberleys in northwest Australia (*Australian*, 2–3 February 1991, p. 33). The territory takes in an arc of the hinterland of the coast between King Sound and Kalumburu south of Cape Londonderry. The claimants are reported to intend an action in the High Court. The grounds apparently will include assertions that the claimed area was not *terra nullius* (land belonging to no state) and was not claimed either in 1788 by Captain Phillip or in 1829 when the Swan River colony was established. According to McLelland (1971, p. 676) the limits of Western Australia were defined formally in March 1831.

5. Aboriginal groups may begin to take a greater interest in making claims to coastal waters. Such claims can already be made in the Northern Territory to waters within 2 kilometres of the low-water line of Aboriginal lands. These claims permit the Administrator to close those seas to provide for their quiet enjoyment by Aboriginals who are entitled by Aboriginal tradition to enter them, and for the protection of marine sacred sites. There are exemptions for government employees in defence, police, customs and immigration and for persons holding an existing exploration permit.

Two claims near Milingimbi and at the mouth of the Woolen River have already been granted. The legislation that permits such claims is based on the unquestionable fact that Aboriginal communities regarded inshore waters as part of their territory. Further, the marine sections of the territory were also delimited by precise boundaries that often coincided with the deepest parts of tidal channels. Sometimes the waters between the mainland and offshore islands formed part of the territory and often there were reefs and rocks which were regarded as sites of special significance.

Our experience is that this integration of land and sea territories also occurred off the coast of northwest Australia, in parts of the Gulf of Carpentaria, on the Great Barrier Reef and in Torres Strait. Other areas where such integration would not be surprising are located near the Archipelago of the Recherche and on the southeast coast of Tasmania.

6. Traditional mechanisms of succession to deceased estates will be accelerated, especially in areas either subject to large-scale development or sensitive to public opinion and political policy in line with Coronation Hill developments. Such applications of succession processes will also become much more widespread, forcing government intervention and highlighting the inadequacies of existing legislation.

It has been our task in this book to set out clearly the concepts of frontiers and boundaries of Aboriginal territories at a time when government sentiment surrounding Australia's bicentennial has launched formal moves towards first a treaty between the Government and the Aboriginal people, and second a reconciliation between Aborigines and other Australians. The political and social climate surrounding the bicentennial brought many Aboriginal organisations to an awareness of the possibilities of compensation and concessions never available on such a scale to their people. Any resultant headlong rush into claims might serve to divide further the Aboriginal or the Australian communities. This will happen if information necessary to assess such claims and to formulate appropriate legislation is not quickly developed. Political geographers and scholars in other disciplines have a significant role to play in this process. This book has laid a firm foundation in respect of an important part of the solution. The remaining parts of that foundation dealing with topics such as economics, resource development and federal–state administration of Aboriginal affairs must be constructed by others, with as much skill, objectivity and accuracy as possible. Only then will it be possible to build a lasting solution.

Glossary of Aboriginal Words

bäparru	clan group (Gupapuyngu language, north east Arnhem Land)
inkura	ceremonial ground
matha	language (Gupapuyngu language)
ngurra	land/place (Pitjatjantjarra, Luritja and a number of other Western Desert languages)
njinanga/section	the patrilinear group or section which has the on-going residential rights
pmara kutata	*pmara*: land/place *kutata*: always
tjukurrpa	dreaming track (Arranda language, Central Australia)
tjurrungga	ritual objects such as boards and stones incised with sacred designs (Arranda language)
tnatantja	totem or ceremonial pole
wangarr	ancestral being (Gupapuyngu language)

References

1 Territorial Limits of Aboriginal Peoples

Bergin, A.
1991 'Aboriginal Sea Claims in the Northern Territory of Australia', *Ocean and Shoreline Management*, vol. 15, pp. 171–204.

Burrows, E. G.
1939 'Breed and Border in Polynesia', *American Anthropologist*, vol. 41, pp. 1–21.

Clark, I. D.
1991 'Mapping the Aboriginal Occupance of Central and Western Victoria', *The Globe*, no. 35, pp. 43–8.

Cooper, J. M.
1939 'Is the Algonquian Family Hunting Ground System Pre-Columbian?', *American Anthropologist*, vol. 41, pp. 66–90.
1963 'The Yaghan', in J. H. Steward (ed.), *Handbook of South American Indians*, vol. 1, *The Marginal Tribes*, pp. 81–106, Cooper Square, New York.
1963a 'The Ona', in J. H. Steward (ed.), *Handbook of South American Indians*, vol. 1, *The Marginal Tribes*, pp. 106–25, Cooper Square, New York.

Correll, T. C.
1976 'Language and Location in Traditional Inuit Societies', in M. M. R. Freeman (ed.), *Inuit Land-use and Occupancy Project*, vol. 2, pp. 173–9, State Ministry of Supply and Services, Ottawa.

Davidson, D. S.
1928 'The Family Hunting Territory in Australia', *American Anthropologist*, n.s., vol. 30, pp. 614–31.
1938 'An Ethnic Map of Australia', *Proceedings of the American Philosophical Society*, vol. 79, pp. 649–80.

Davis, S. L.
  1984 Aboriginal Tenure and Use of the Coast and Sea in Northern Arnhem Land, MA thesis, University of Melbourne.
  1989 *Man of All Seasons*, Angus and Robertson, Sydney.
  1991 Potential Maritime Conflicts with Australian Aboriginals, paper presented to Symposium on Regional Planning in Offshore Areas at the XVII Pacific Science Congress, Honolulu.
Dening, G.
  1980 *Islands and Beaches: Discourse on a Silent Land Marquesas 1774–1880*, Melbourne University Press, Melbourne.
East, W. G.
  1937 'The Nature of Political Geography', *Politica*, vol. 2, pp. 259–86.
Forde, C. D.
  1952 *Habitat, Economy and Society: a Geographical Introduction to Ethnology*, Methuen, London.
Grey, G.
  1841 Journals of Two Expeditions of Discovery in North-west and Western Australia during the Years 1837, 38 and 39, under the Authority of Her Majesty's Government, describing many newly discovered, important and fertile districts, with observations on the moral and physical condition of the Aboriginal inhabitants etc., etc., 2 volumes, T. and W. Boone, London.
Gyorgy, A.
  1944 *Geopoliticas: the New German Science*, University of California Publications in International Relations, vol. 3, pp. 141–304.
Hartshorne, R.
  1935 'Recent Developments in Political Geography', *American Political Science Review*, vol. 29, pp. 758–804, 943–66.
Haushofer, K.
  1927 *Grenzen im ihrer Geographischen und Politischen Bedeutung* [The Geographical and Political Significance of Boundaries], Vowinckel, Berlin.
Hiatt, L. R., Lee, R. and Pilling, A. R.
  1968 'Ownership and Use of Land Among the Australian Aborigines', in R. Lee and A. R. Pilling (eds), *Man the Hunter*, Aldine, Chicago.
Jenness, D.
  1935 *The Ojibwa Indians of Parry Island, their Social and Religious Life*, Bulletin 78, Anthropology Series No. 17, National Museum of Canada.
Jones, S. B.
  1945 *Boundary-making, a Handbook for Statemen, Treaty Editors and Boundary Commissioners*, Carnegie Endowment for International Peace, Washington DC.
Kelly, I. T.
  1934 Southern Paiute Bands, *American Anthropologist*, vol. 36, pp. 548–60.
Lapradelle, P. de
  1928 *La frontiére:étude de droit international* [The Boundary: a Study of International Law], Les Editions Internationales, Paris.
Lester, G. S.
  1981 *The Territorial Rights of the Inuit of the Canadian Northwest Territory: a Legal Argument*, Victoria Law Foundation, Melbourne.

Lowie, R. H.
   1963   'Property Among the Tropical Forest and Marginal Tribes', in J. H. Steward (ed.), *Handbook of South American Indians*, vol. 5, *The Comparative Ethnology of South American Indians*, pp. 35–82, Cooper Square, New York.

McGee, W. J.
   1898   'The Seri Indians', in P. W. Powell, *17th Annual Report of the Bureau of American Ethnology to the Secretary of the Smithsonian Institute 1895–6*, Part 1, Government Printing Office, Washington DC.

Memmott, P.
   1983   'Social Structure and the Use of Space Amongst the Lardil', *Aborigines, Land and Land Rights*, Australian Institute of Aboriginal Studies, Canberra.

Naval Intelligence Division
   1944   *The Belgian Congo*, HMSO, London.

Nicholson, N. L.
   1954   *The Boundaries of Canada its Provinces and Territories*, Memoir 2, Department of Mines and Technical Services, Geographical Branch, Ottawa.

O'Grady, G. N., Voegelin, C. F. and Voegelin, F. M.
   1966   'Languages of the World: Indo-Pacific Fascicle 6' (with appendix by K. L. Hale), *Anthropological Linguistics*, vol. 2.

Parker, L. S.
   1989   *Native American Estate: the Struggle Over Indian and Hawaiian Lands*, University of Hawaii Press, Honolulu.

Parkhouse, T. A.
   1895   'Native Tribes of Port Darwin and its Neighbourhood', *Australian Association for the Advancement of Science* (Section F), vol. 6, pp. 638–47.

Perry, T. M.
   1963   *Australia's First Frontier*, Melbourne University Press, Melbourne.

Peterson, N. (ed.)
   1976   *Tribes and Boundaries in Australia*, Australian Institute of Aboriginal Studies, Canberra.

Peterson, N. and Long, J.
   1986   *Australian Territorial Organisation: a Band Perspective*, University of Sydney, Sydney.

Post, L. van der
   1988   *The Lost World of the Kalahari*, Morrow, Bury St Edmunds.

Post, L. van der and Taylor, J.
   1984   *Testament to the Bushman*, Viking, New York.

Powell, A.
   1988   *Far Country: a Short History of the Northern Territory*, 2nd ed., Melbourne University Press, Melbourne.

Prescott, J. R. V.
   1986   *Maritime Political Boundaries of the World*, Methuen, London.
   1987   *Political Frontiers and Boundaries*, Allen and Unwin, London.
   1990   *I confini politici del mare: un panorama mondiale* [Maritime Political Boundaries: a World Survey], (revised edition of Prescott 1986), Mursia, Milano.

Ratzel, F.
  1897 *Politische Geographie* [Political Geography], Olderbourg, Berlin.

Ray, D. J.
  1967 'Land Tenure and Polity of the Bering Strait Eskimos', *Journal of the West*, vol. 6, pp. 371–94.

Resource Assessment Commission
  1991 *Kakadu Conservation Zone Inquiry, Final Report*, 2 vols, Australian Government Publishing Service, Canberra.

Reynolds, H.
  1987 *Frontier*, Allen and Unwin, Sydney.

Rowe, J. H.
  1963 Inca Culture at the Time of the Spanish Conquest, in J. H. Steward (ed.), *Handbook of South American Indians*, Vol. 2, The Andean Civilisations, pp. 183–330, Cooper Square, New York.

Rumley, D. and Minghi, J. V. (eds)
  1991 *The Geography of Border Landscapes*, Routledge, Guilford.

Schofield, R.
  1991 *Kuwait and Iraq: Historical Claims and Territorial Disputes*, The Royal Institute of International Affairs, London.

Snow, D. R.
  1968 'Wobanaki "Family Hunting Territories"', *American Anthropologist*, vol. 70, pp. 143–51.

Speck, F. G.
  1915 'Family Hunting Territories and Social Life of Various Algonkian Bands of the Ottawa Valley', *Canada Geological Survey Memoir 70*, Anthropological Series No. 70, Government Printing Service, Ottawa.

Spencer, W. B.
  1914 *Native Tribes of the Northern Territory of Australia*, Macmillan, London.

Stanner, W. E. H.
  1933 'The Daly River Tribes, a Report of Fieldwork in North Australia', *Oceania*, vol. 3, pp. 377–405 and vol. 4, pp. 10–20.
  1965 'Aboriginal Territorial Organisation: Estate, Range, Domain and Regime', *Oceania*, vol. 36, pp. 1–26.

Steenhoven, G. van den
  1962 *Leadership and Law Among the Eskimos of the Keewatin District, Northwest Territories*, Uitgeverij Excelsoir, Rijswijk.

Strehlow, T. G. H.
  1947 *Aranda Traditions*, Melbourne University Press, Melbourne.

Taylor, J. C.
  1976 'Mapping Techniques and the Reconstruction of Aspects of Traditional Aboriginal Culture', *Australian Institute of Aboriginal Studies Newsletter*, no. 5, pp. 34–43.

Tindale, N. B.
  1974 *Aboriginal Tribes of Australia*, University of California Press, Berkeley, California.

Turner, F. J.
  1953 *The Frontier in American History*, Holt, New York.

Wurm, S. A.
  1972 *Languages of Australia and Tasmania* [sic], Mouton, The Hague.

2 Tropical Coast

Berndt, R. M.
- 1951 *Kunapipi*, Cheshire, Melbourne.
- 1955 '"Murngin" (Wulamba) Social Organisation', *American Anthropologist*, vol. 57, pp. 84–106.
- 1976 'Territoriality and the Problem of Demarcating Socio-cultural Space', in N. Peterson (ed.), *Tribes and Boundaries in Australia*, Australian Institute of Aboriginal Studies, Canberra.

Berndt, R. M. and C. H.
- 1954 *The First Australians*, 2nd ed., Ure Smith, Sydney (rev. ed., 1974).
- 1977 *The World of the First Australians*, 2nd ed., Ure Smith, Sydney.

Bird, E.
- 1983 Personal communication (coastal geomorphologist, Department of Geography, University of Melbourne).

Davis, S. L.
- 1984 Aboriginal Tenure and Use of the Coast and Sea in Northern Arnhem Land, MA thesis, University of Melbourne.
- 1989 Tribes and Territories: Aspects of Political Geography of Aboriginal Tribes in the Northern Territory of Australia, Ph.D. thesis, University of Melbourne.

Hart, C. W. M.
- 1930 'The Tiwi of Melville and Bathurst Islands', *Oceania*, vol. 1, pp. 167–80.

Hiatt, L. R.
- 1967 'Authority and Reciprocity in Australian Aboriginal Marriage Arrangement', *Mankind*, vol. 6, pp. 468–75.
- 1982 'Traditional Attitudes to Land Resources', *Aboriginal Sites, Rights and Resource Development*, University of Western Australia Press, Perth.

Keen, I.
- 1978 One Ceremony, One Song, Ph.D. thesis, Australian National University, Canberra.

MacKnight, C. C.
- 1969 The Macassans: a Study of the Early Trepang Industry along the Northern Territory Coast, Ph.D. thesis, Australian National University, Canberra.
- 1976 *The Voyage to Marege*, Melbourne University Press, Melbourne.

Messel, H., Wells, A. G. and Green, W. J.
- 1980 *Surveys of Tidal River Systems in the Northern Territory of Australia and their Crocodile Populations*, Monograph 6, Pergamon Press, Sydney.

Mountford, C. P.
- 1958 *The Tiwi, Their Art, Myth and Ceremony*, Phoenix, London.

Peterson, N.
- 1972 'Totemism Yesterday: Sentiment and Local Organisation Among Australian Aborigines', *Man*, vol. 7, no.1, pp. 12–31.
- 1975 'Sacred Sites and the Aboriginal', in R. Edwards (ed), *The Preservation of Australia's Aboriginal Heritage*, Australian Institute of Aboriginal Studies, Canberra.

Prescott, J. R. V.
- 1975 *The Political Geography of the Oceans*, David and Charles, Exeter.

Rosengren, N.
: 1984 Personal communication (geomorphologist, Department of Geography, University of Melbourne).

Ross, J. and Walker, A. T.
: 1983 *Gumatj Wordlist: Part One*, Northern Territory University Planning Authority, Darwin.

Schebeck, B.
: 1968 Dialect and Social Groupings in North East Arnhem Land, unpublished MS, copy held in Australian Institute of Aboriginal Studies, Canberra.

Warner, W. L.
: 1937 *A Black Civilization*, Harper, New York (new ed., 1958).

Williams, N. M.
: 1983 'Yolngu Concepts of Land Ownership', *Aborigines, Land and Land Rights*, Australian Institute of Aboriginal Studies, Canberra.

Wood, R. K.
: 1978 'Some Yuulngu Phonological Patterns', *Pacific Linguistics: Papers in Australian Linguistics*, no. 11.

Zorc, R. D. P.
: 1979 *Functor Analysis of Yolngu*, School of Australian Linguistics, Darwin.

3 Southwest Arnhem Land

Arndt, W.
: 1962 'The Nargorkan-Narlinji Cult', *Oceania*, vol. 32, pp. 298–319.

Bauer, F. H.
: 1964 *Historical Geography of White Settlement in Part of Northern Australia*, Part 2: The Katherine-Darwin Region, CSIRO, Canberra.

Berndt, R. M. and C. H.
: 1954 *The First Australians*, Ure Smith, Sydney (rev. ed., 1974).
: 1970 *Man, Land and Myth in North Australia: The Gunwinggu People*, Ure Smith, Sydney.

Cole, K.
: 1975 *A History of Oenpelli*, Nungalinya Publications, Darwin.

Davis, S.
: 1989 Tribes and Territories: Aspects of Political Geography of Aboriginal Tribes in the Northern Territory of Australia, Ph.D. thesis, University of Melbourne.

Elkin, A. P.
: 1938 *The Australian Aborigines*, Angus and Robertson, Sydney.

Feeken, E. H. J., Feeken, G. E. E. and Spate, O. H. K.
: 1970 *The Discovery and Exploration of Australia*, Nelson, Melbourne.

Jones, T. G.
: 1987 *Pegging the Northern Territory*, Northern Territory Government Printer, Darwin.

Kearney, W. J.
: 1987 *Jawoyn (Katherine Area) Land Claim*, Report by the Aboriginal Land Commissioner, Australian Government Publishing Service, Canberra.

Merlan, F.
: 1986 *Mataranka Land Claim*, Northern Land Council, Darwin.

Merlan, F. and Rumsey, A.
: 1982 *The Jawoyn (Katherine Area) Land Claim*, Darwin, Northern Land Council.

Mollah, W. S.
  1986 'Rainfall Variability in the Katherine-Darwin Region of the Northern Territory and Some Implications for Cropping', *Journal, Australian Institute of Agricultural Science*, vol. 52, pp. 28–36.
Northern Territory Department of Mines and Energy
  1984 *Catalogue of Surface Hydrological Records of the Northern Territory to 1984*, Report no. 19, 1986, Water Resources Division.
Resource Assessment Commission
  1991 *Kakadu Conservation Zone Inquiry Final Report*, vols I and II, Australian Government Publishing Service, Canberra.
Spencer, W. B.
  1914 *Native Tribes of the Northern Territory of Australia*, Macmillan, London.
Stuart, J. McDouall
  1865 *The Journals of John McDouall Stuart*, edited by W. Hardman, Saunders, Otley, London.
Sutton, P. and Palmer, A.
  1981 *Malak Malak (Daly River) Land Claim*, Northern Land Council, Darwin.
Thonemann, H. E.
  1949 *Tell the White Man*, Collins, Sydney.
Tindale, N. B.
  1974 *The Aboriginal Tribes of Australia*, University of California Press, Berkley, California.
Toohey, J.
  1981 *Finniss River Land Claim*, Report by the Aboriginal Land Commissioner, Australian Government Printing Service, Canberra.

4 Central Australia

Bagshaw, G.
  1983 *Aspects of Traditional Land Tenure in the Luritja Region of Haasts Bluff Land Trust*, Central Land Council, Alice Springs.
Davis, S. L.
  1984 Aboriginal Tenure and Use of the Coast and Sea in Northern Arnhem Land, MA thesis, University of Melbourne.
  1989 Tribes and Territories: Aspects of Political Geography of Aboriginal Tribes in the Northern Territory of Australia, Ph.D. thesis, University of Melbourne.
Duncan, R.
  1967 *The Northern Territory Pastoral Industry 1863–1910*, Melbourne University Press, Melbourne.
Feeken, E. H. J., Feeken, G. E. E. and Spate, O. H. K.
  1970 *The Discovery and Exploration of Australia*, Nelson, Melbourne.
Hamilton, W. and Vachon, D.
  1985 *Lake Amadeus, Luritja Land Claim*, Central Land Council, Alice Springs.
Hartwig, M. C.
  1965 The Progress of White Settlement in the Alice Springs District and its Effects upon the Aboriginal Inhabitants, 1860–1894, Ph.D. thesis, University of Adelaide.

Myers, F. R.
- 1976 To Have and to Hold: a Study of Persistence and Change in Pintupi Social Life, Ph.D. thesis, Bryn Mawr College.
- 1986 *Pintupi Country, Pintupi Self*, Australian Institute of Aboriginal Studies, Canberra.

Pearce, H.
- 1987 'Bowson's Hole Homestead', *National Trust (N.T.) Newsletter*.

Rose, F. G. G.
- 1965 *The Wind of Change in Central Australia*, Akademie Verlag, Berlin.

Spencer, W. B. and Gillen, F. J.
- 1899 *The Native Tribes of Central Australia*, Macmillan, London.

Stanner, W. E. H.
- 1965 'Aboriginal Territorial Organisation Estate, Range, Domain and Regime', *Oceania*, vol. 36, pp. 1–26.

Strehlow, T. G. H.
- 1947 *Aranda Traditions*, University of Melbourne Press, Melbourne.
- 1969 *Journey to Horseshoe Bend*, Angus and Robertson, Sydney.
- 1971 *Songs of Central Australia*, Angus and Robertson, Sydney.

Tindale, N. B.
- 1974 *The Aboriginal Tribes of Australia*, University of California Press, Berkley, California.

Toohey, J.
- 1980 *Uluru (Ayers Rock) Land Claim*, Report on the Uluru (Ayers Rock) Land Claim, Australian Government Publishing Service, Canberra.

Williams, N. M.
- 1983 'Yolngu Concepts of Land Ownership', *Aborigines, Land and Land Rights*, Australian Institute of Aboriginal Studies, Canberra.

Willshire, W. H.
- 1896 *Land of the Dawning*, Adelaide.

5 Torres Strait

Brierley, Oswald
- 1849 Interviews with Barbara Thompson, Brierley Papers, Torres Strait *Rattlesnake* Voyage, MS. A509: 19, Sept.–Nov. 1849, Microfilm PM 4/2560, State Library of New South Wales.

Department of Foreign Affairs
- 1978 Treaty between Australia and the Independent State of Papua New Guinea concerning sovereignty and maritime boundaries in the area between the two countries including the area known as Torres Strait including related matters, Government Printing Office, Canberra. [The treaty was signed on 18 December 1978 in Sydney and ratified on 15 February 1985.]

Done, J. E.
- 1987 *Wings Across the Sea*, Boolarong Publications, Brisbane.

Feeken, E. H. J., Feeken, G. E. E. and Spate, O. H. K.
- 1970 *The Discovery and Exploration of Australia*, Nelson, Melbourne.

Haddon, A. C.
- 1904 *Reports of the Cambridge Anthropological Expedition to Torres Straits*, vol. 5, Cambridge University Press, Cambridge, pp. 9–121.
- 1935 *Reports of the Cambridge Anthropological Expedition to the Torres Straits*, vol. 1, Cambridge University Press, Cambridge.

Johannes, R. E. and McFarlane, J. W.
  1984   'Traditional Sea Rights in the Torres Strait Islands, with Emphasis on Murray Island', in K. Ruddle and T. Akimichi (eds.), *Maritime Institutions in the Western Pacific, Senri Ethnological Studies*, no. 17, National Museum of Ethnology, Osaka.
  (in press)   *Traditional Fishing in the Torres Strait Islands*, Department of Primary Industry and Energy, Canberra.

Moore, D. R.
  1972   'Cape York Aborigines and Islanders of Western Torres Strait', in D. Walker (ed.), *Bridge and Barrier: the Natural and Cultural History of Torres Strait*, Australian National University, Canberra.

Nietschmann, B.
  1989   'Traditional Sea Territories, Resources and Rights in Torres Strait', in J. C. Cordell (ed.), *A Sea of Small Boats*, Cultural Survival Inc., Cambridge, Mass.

Ray, S. H.
  1907   'Linguistics' in A. C. Haddon (ed.), *Reports of the Cambridge Anthropological Expedition to Torres Strait*, vol. 3, Cambridge University Press, Cambridge.

Rivers, W. H. R.
  1908   'Social Organisation' in A. C. Haddon (ed.), *Reports of the Cambridge Anthropological Expedition to Torres Straits*, vol. 6, Cambridge University Press, Cambridge, pp. 169–84.

Singe, J.
  1979   *The Torres Strait*, University of Queensland Press, St. Lucia.

Wilkin, A.
  1904   'Land Tenure and Inheritance at Mabuiag', in A. C. Haddon (ed.), *Reports of the Cambridge Anthropological Expedition to Torres Straits*, vol. 5, Cambridge University Press, Cambridge, pp. 284–92.
  1904a   'Chieftainship in Mabuiag and Badu', in A. C. Haddon (ed.), *Reports of the Cambridge Anthropological Expedition to Torres Straits*, vol. 5, Cambridge University Press, Cambridge, pp. 266–7.
  1908   'Property and Inheritance', in A. C. Haddon (ed.), *Reports of the Cambridge Anthropological Expedition to Torres Straits*, vol. 6, Cambridge University Press, Cambridge, pp. 163–8.

6 Conclusions

Aboriginal and Torres Strait Islander Commission
  1990   *Aboriginal People of New South Wales*, Australian Government Publishing Service, Canberra.
  1990a   *Aboriginal People of Victoria*, Australian Government Publishing Service, Canberra.

Australian InFo International
  1989   *Australian Aboriginal Culture*, Australian Government Publishing Service, Canberra.

McClelland, M. H.
  1971   Colonial and State Boundaries in Australia, *Australian Law Journal*, vol. 45, pp. 671–9.

Myers, F. R.
  1986   *Pintupi Country Pintupi Self*, Smithsonian Institution Press, Washington DC.

Report to Senate Select Committee on the Administration of Aboriginal Affairs
    1989   Australian Parliament, Canberra.

Resource Assessment Commission
    1991   *Kakadu Conservation Zone Inquiry Final Report*, 2 volumes, Australian Government Publishing Service, Canberra.

Sack, R. D.
    1986   *Human Territoriality, its Theory and History*, Cambridge University Press, Cambridge.

Seaman, P.
    1984   *The Aboriginal Land Inquiry*, Government Printer, Perth.

Stewart, D. G.
    1991   *Report to the Minister for Aboriginal Affairs on the Kakadu Conservation Zone*, Australian Government Publishing Service, Canberra.

Index

compiled by Dorothy F. Prescott

f figure   m map   t table

Aboriginal Affairs, Department of, 119, 136
Aboriginal Affairs, Minister for, 2-3, 24, 135, 136, 139, 143
Aboriginal and Torres Strait Islander Commission (ATSIC), 3, 24, 133, 135, 137m, 139; administrative regions, 135-8, 139; (boundaries); 136-8, 137m, 139, 140, 142; (comparison of regions with traditional Aboriginal territories, 138); regions, (names of, 139-40); (review of, 139, 142)
Aboriginal and Torres Strait Islander Heritage Protection Act 1984, 143-4
aboriginal boundaries and frontiers, 4, 11, 15, 18-20, 22, 23; in Africa, 13-15; in Australia, 2-3, 15-24, 133-46; in North America, 4-9; in South America, 9-11; in the Pacific, 11-13; *see also* Australian Aboriginal boundaries; Australian Aboriginal frontiers
Aboriginal group unity, 1
Aboriginal Land Act 1978, 12
Aboriginal Land and Population (map), 140
Aboriginal Land Rights (Northern Territory) Act 1976, 61, 73, 77, 79, 83, 133
Aboriginal languages, 2, 7, 10, 35, 71, 133; maps of, 18-19, 20, 36
Aboriginal massacres by pastoralists, 65
Aboriginal Sacred Sites Authority, 73, 76–7

The Aboriginal Tribes of Australia, 78
Aboriginal women, sexual exploitation of, 68
Adrian Reef, 120-1m, 122, 123
alcohol, 68
Aleut, *see* Eskimo
Algonquian, 5-6
Alice Springs, N.T., 85m, 88m; mounted police, 87; size of Aboriginal territories, 133; telegraph station, 86
Alligator Rivers, N.T., land claim, 74-5m; mineral activity, 66-7m
Alyawarra people, 138
Amadeus Basin–Darwin gas pipeline, 76
Amadeus frontier, 95-9, 100, 110m, 113
Amata, N.T., 88m, 94
ancestral being, 2, 40, 41, 46, 48, 52, 102, 103, 107, 108, 132-3
Andiraningoo Creek, Melville Island, 50
Angas Downs Station, N.T., 92, 93, 94, 101m, 110m
Anmatjarra (Unmatjera) territory, 97, 99, 138-9
Apsley Strait, 48-9
Areyonga, N.T., 85m, 94, 101m, 110m
Arnhem Land, 28-59; Aboriginal groups, 28, 35, (territory size, 28); north coast, (environment, 30-3); northeast, 28-59; southwest, 60-82
Arnhem Land, northeast, 28-59;

159

Aboriginal groups, 35; boundary delineation, 46-8; boundary evolution, 44; clan territories, 38-41; environment, 31-3; evolution of boundaries, 43, 45; non-Aboriginal contact, 37-8; people, 35-6; seasonal use of resources, 33-5; succession, 45, 51

Arnhem Land, southwest, 60-82; boundaries in the modern period, 78-9; dislocation of Aboriginal tribes, 61, 68, 69, 70, 78; environment, 61, 64; exploration, 64-70; effects of European contact, 60, 65, 68, 78; land claims, 70-8; non-Aboriginal settlement, 64-70; pastoral ventures, 64-5; population movement, 69; railway construction, 65, 68, 69

Arranda people, 19, 83, 94; boundary with Western Desert people, 94, 96, 102, 112-13; dreaming tracks, 107-8; land claim, 99; maps of, 19; nature of boundaries, 100, 108; movement north to escape pastoralists, 92; social system, 96; warfare with Matutjarra people, 89; sub-territories, 96, 98, 99-102; territoriality, 113; *see also* Western Arranda people

ATSIC boundaries, *see* Aboriginal and Torres Strait Islander Commission

Aubit (Owbait), 124, 125

Aurukun, Qld, 141

Australia: Aboriginal land holdings, 141t

Australia, Division of National Mapping, 140

Australian, 145

Australian Aboriginal boundaries: administrative, 135-42; ATSIC, 135-42; cartographic evidence for, 16-24; coincidence with certain geographical features, 134; definition of, 45-50, 109, 133, 134; future, 142-6; in semi-arid and arid areas, 101m, 110m, 134; loss of information about, 133; maps of, 18-19, 20, 36, 101m, 110m, 133; maritime, 134; past research on, 133; prevalence in humid zone, 133-4; regulation of access over, 134, 135; relationship to physical geography, 133

Australian Aboriginal frontiers: Arranda-Western Desert, 94, 101m, 110m, 111; displayed by expansionist groups, 111-12; evidence of, 133; in arid areas, 101m, 109, 110m, 133, 134; in post-contact era, 135; in pre-contact era, 135; loss of information on, 133; movement of Amadeus, 95-9; occurrence, 134; past research on, 133; relationship to physical geography of the region, 133

Australian Board of Missions, 119

Australian Electoral Commissioner, 139

Australian Surveying and Land Information Group (AUSLIG), 135, 139; maps of Aboriginal land, 140

Badu Island, *see* Mulgrave Island
Badu people, 37
Badugal people, 101m, 110m, 128
Bagshaw, G., 102, 105-7, 111, 112
Balgo, W. A., 108
Balmawuy territory, 42, 43, 44m, 47m; sub-territory, 44m
Banyan Island, N.T.: ancestral being's site, 52; Macassan sites, 37; territory boundary, 47m
bark painting, 134
Barotse Kingdom, 23
Barrow Creek, N.T., 86-7, 88m; Mounted Police, 87
Basilisk Banks (Payuainin Arrigal), 120-1m, 123
Bathurst Island, N.T.: Aboriginal territories, 28; boundary delineation, 43; changes in boundary location, 50; environment, 29-30, 32; mission, 38; non-Aboriginal contact, 38; people, 36
Batjimurrungu people, 40, 54
Bau, 125, 126
Bauer, F. H., 65, 68
Baydjini people, 37
Bennett, George, 90

Index

Bergin, A., 12
Berndt, R. M., 35, 37
Berndt, R. M. and C. H., 37, 70
Bickerton Island Aboriginal people, 2
Binalolombo people, 16-17,
Bininyuwuy people, 42-4
Bird, E., 45
Birdie Creek, N.T., 78
Birrkili people, 36, 37, 58
Bligh, William, 115, 117
body painting, 134
Boggy Hole, N.T., 87, 88m, 90
Botocudo, 10
boundaries, see also Australian Aboriginal boundaries
boundaries in political geography, 20-4; of hunter gatherer groups, 23, 80-lm, 109, 125, 132, 133
boundary definition, 45-50; in arid areas, 109; principles of, 133
boundary evolution, 43-4
boundary location, changes in, 50-1
boundary studies: by anthropologists, 16-20; by political geographers, 20-4
boundary violations, 54, 57
Bradshaw, Joseph, 65
Bramble (ship), 115, 117
Brierley, Oswald, 117, 119, 128
Browne, W. J., 64-5
Brtaua-Lung people, 17
Buchanan, Nat, 65
Buckingham Bay, N.T., 58
Bula myth, 73, 77, 144
Bula Sickness Country, 63-4m, 76-7
Bupu, see Passage Island
Burrows, E. G., 11
Burru, see Turnagain Island
Burrumngur Yolngu people, 58
Bushmen, see San
Buwa 'nandhu, 40

Callanan, Mt, N.T., 78
Cambridge Anthropological Expedition to Torres Straits, 119, 124, 127, 130
Campbell, Duncan, 65
Cape York Aboriginal people, 114
cartographic evidence for the existence of Aboriginal boundaries, 16-24, 133; in Gippsland, Victoria, 17-18; in New South Wales, 133; in Northern Territory, 16-17, 19; in Torres Strait, 124; in Victoria, 133
Cashinawa, 10
Castlereagh Bay area, N.T.: boundary maintenance, 45; clan territories in, 35, 47m; environment, 29, 31, 32, 33; islands, 29; language, 35; Macassan sites, 37; population, 37-8; resource use, 33-5
cattle spearing, 87, 89, 90, 92, 96, 97
Central Australia: effect of disease on Aborigines, 92-3; environment, 84, 86; exploration of, 86-7; pastoral settlement, 87-94; territoriality, 94, 96; tribal frontiers, 111-12
Central Land Council: and Aboriginal territories, 2; and the Lake Amadeus Luritja Land Claim, 83-4, 98, 112; claimants to Watarrka sub-territory, 106
Central Reserve, N.T., 93
Charlotte Waters, N.T., 86, 88m; Mounted Police, 87
Chemehuevi, 4-5
Chewings, Charles, 89
Chinese goldminers, 68
Chippewa, 131
clans: as social units, 18; as sociopolitical groups, 38-9; boundaries of, 132; identity of, 1, 40, 132, 133; links with other groups, 133; limits of territory, 1, 18, 24, 33; territories, 38-44; sub-territories, 57-8
Clark, I. D., 17, 18
closure of seas, 12
coastal waters: claims in, 146
Cole, K., 70
Confalonieri, Father Angelo, 16-17
Cook, James, 115
Cooper, J. M., 5, 9, 10, 23
Coronation Hill, N.T., 73, 74-5m, 77, 79
Correll, T. C., 6-7
Coulthard, Bob and Bill, 90, 92
Coulthard, Jack, 97
Cowboy Alec (Wagaman), 78

Cowle, Constable, 96, 97
Crocodile Islands, N. T., 29; boundary maintenance, 45; clan territories in, 35; dugong hunting, 34; environment, 31-3; language, 35; resource use, 33-5; succession, 51-2; turtle hunting, 34
Curtin Springs Station, N.T., 93

Dakawarr, 42-4
Daly River coppermine, 69
Dare's Plain, N.T., 96
Darnley Island (Erub), 116m, 117
Dauan Island, 116m, 122
Davidson, D. S., 17-18, 19-20, 23-4
Davis, S. L., 3, 12, 30, 54, 97, 99-100, 103, 104, 109, 131
Daygurrkurr (Gupapuyngu) people, 37
deceased estates, 60, 77, 79, 82, 135
Deliverance Island (Lebren), 120-1m, 122, 123
Dening, G., 11-12
Dhabitjin people, 51, 52, 54
Dhuwa people, 35, 41, 51
dislocation, 61, 66, 67, 112
Djab wurrung language area, 18
Djambarrpuyngu people, 42
Docker River, N.T., 94
doggers, 93
Done, J. E., 117
dreaming tracks, 94-6, 97, 99, 102, 104, 107, 108, 109, 133
dugong hunting, 34, 50, 115
Duncan, R., 89, 93

East, W. G., 21
East Mereenie, N.T., 86
Eastern and African Cold Storage Company, 65
Edith River, N.T., 73, 74-5m, 76, 78
Edward River area, Cape York, 20
Elkin, A. P., 17, 70
Elsey Station, N.T., 62-3m, 65, 69, 70, 88m
Ernabella Mission, N.T., 88m, 93
Erub, *see* Darnley Island
Eskimo, 6-7

Falanruw, M. C., 13
Fanny Creek, N.T., 78

Feeken, E. H. J. and G. E. E., 64, 87, 117
Finniss River Land Claim, 70
fishing, 34, 35
Flinders, Matthew, 115
Florence Islands, 125
Fly (ship), 115-16
Forde, C. D., 3-4, 14, 15
Foreign Affairs, Department of, 129
Forrest, John, 87
Fort Dundas, Melville Island, 38
Francis, C. F., 67, 78
frontiers, 2, 22, 23, 83; *see also* Australian Aboriginal frontiers

Gaba Island (Gebarr), 116m, 120-1m, 123
Gamalangga people, 41, 47m, 51-2, 54, 57
Garawa people, 138, 139
Gebarr, *see* Gaba Island
Geopolitik, 21
George Gill Range, N.T., 84, 85m, 86, 92, 93, 94, 95-6, 98, 110m, 112
Gibson Desert, 19
Giles, Archie, 92
Giles, Ernest, 87
Gillen Frank, 90
Gillen F. J., 97
Gimbat Pastoral Lease, 62-3m, 77
Gippsland, Victoria, 17-18
Glencoe Station, N.T., 65, 69, 88m
Goodparla Pastoral Lease, 62-3m, 77
Gorryindi people, 51-2, 54
Gosse, W. C., 87
Goulburn Island, N.T., 70
Great Sandy Desert, 19
Great Victoria Desert, 19
Gregory, A. C., 64
Grey, G., 16
Groote Eylandt Aboriginal people, 2
ground designs, 134
Gudamaluigal people, 122
Gunwinggu people, 70, 80-1m
Gupapuyngu people, 35, 36, 58
Gurdandji people, 138
Gyorgy, A., 21

Haast's Bluff, N.T., 94
Haddon, A. C., 115, 117, 119, 124,

125, 128, 129, 130
Hamilton, G., 16
Hamilton, W., 113
Hand, Gerry, 2-3, 136
The Handbook of South American Indians, 10
Hardy Island, Buckingham Bay, N.T., 58
Hart, C. W. M., 36
Hartshorne, R., 21
Hartwig, M. C., 87, 89, 90, 93
Haushofer, K., 21
Hawaii, 12
Henbury Station, N.T., 88m, 89
Hermannsburg, N.T., 80m, 96, 97, 112
Hermannsburg Land Trust boundary, 100
Hermannsburg Mission, N.T., 88m, 90-1, 92
Hiatt, L. R., 19
Horn Island, 114, 116m
Horn Scientific Expedition, 87
Hviding, E., 13

Ilanos, 10
Illamurta Springs, N.T., 88m; Mounted Police, 87, 90
Impu, Jim, 105
Inindia Bore, Lake Amadeus, N.T., 86
International Boundaries Research Unit, 22
intertribal warfare, 89
Inuit, *see* Eskimo
Iwadja people, 38

Jack, Gideon, 105, 107
James Range, N.T., 93, 97, 98, 101m, 110m, 112
Jawoyn (Djauan) people: boundary knowledge, 69, 76; dislocation, 61, 68, 69; knowledge of sites, 76; land claims, 60, 62-3m, 70-9, 74-5m; spiritual affiliations of, 72, 73; succession by, 77-8, 79; territory, 61, 76-7, 78, 80-1m, 131, 138, (size, 61); use of legislation, 26
Jawoyn (Katherine Area) Land Claim, 70, 74-5m, 77
The Jawoyn (Katherine Area) Land Claim, 70-1
Jenness, D., 5
Jervis Island (Mabuiag), Qld, 27, 114, 116; clan affiliation, 128; districts, 124; environment, 114-15; European contact, 115, 117, 119; London Missionary Society, 117, 129; name, 117; named localities, 118m, 120-1m, 122-3; pearling, 117, 129; territorial claims, 130; territorial knowledge, 128; territorial rights, 128, 129; territories, 118m
Jervis Reef (Kuik Pad), 117, 118m, 120-1m, 123, 126
Johannes, R. E., 115, 127
Jones, S. B., 21
Jones, T. G., 67, 78
Jumu people, 93, 98, 112

Kai Passage, 123
Kaigas people, 126
Kakadu (Alligator Rivers) Stage 3 Land Claim, 77-8, 79
Kakadu (Gagadju) people, 70
Kakadu Conservation Zone Inquiry, 131, 143
Kakadu National Park, 77; land claim, 74-5m, 77
Karadjeri people, 17
Kartangarurru people, 138
Katherine, N.T., 60, 88m; land claims, 74-5m; mining, 60, 63m
Katherine River, N.T., 64, 73, 78; Aboriginal interests, 62-3m; pastoral interests, 62-3m; lands claims, 74-5m
Kaurareg people, 26, 114, 117, 119
Kearney, W. J., 71-2, 77
Kearney line, 62-3m, 71, 72, 73, 77-8
Keen, I., 37, 38, 39
Kelly, Isabel, 4-5, 23
Kelly, J., 142
killing of Aboriginal people: by pastoralists, 65, 88-9, 92; by police, 90, 97
Kimberleys, W. A., 145-6
King, Phillip Parker, 64, 115
Krichauff Range, N.T., 92, 93
Kuik Pad, *see* Jervis Reef
Kulbi, *see* Portlock Island

Kulpitjara, N.T., 103
Kungarakany people, 17, 70, 138
Kuningga native cat ritual cycle, 94-6, 97, 99, 102, 103, 104, 107
Kurauatunga-Lung people, 17
Kutjinti, 99, 101m
Kutkatjarra people, 84, 89, 90, 93, 94, 95, 98, 99, 138
Kutkatjarra territory, 99, 100, 102, 107, 108, 110m, 112

Lake Amadeus, N.T., 84, 85m; absence of Aboriginal people, 94; loss of boundary information, 112; movement of Aborigines in, 94, 112
Lake Amadeus, Luritja Land Claim, 113
Lake Amadeus, Luritja Land Claim, 83-4, 92, 101m, 110m; area, 84, 85m, 113; boundary evidence, 109; environment, 84; Kuningga native cat dreaming track, 94-6, 97, 99; map, 101m; Watarrka territorial claim, 99-102; text on, 113
land, Aboriginal: distribution of, 140, 141t; extent of holdings, 141; future grants, 142; relationship with, 1; tenure of, 140, 141t
land claims: Arnhem Land, 70-8; Arranda, 99; Finniss River, 70; in the Northern Territory, 142; Jawoyn (Katherine area), 60, 70-9; Jervis Island, Qld, 130; Kakadu (Alligator Rivers) Stage 3, 77-8, 79; Katherine River, 74-5; Lake Amadeus, Luritja, 83-4, 85m, 92, 110m; Maluigal, 129-30; Murray Island, Qld, 130; South Alligator River, 71, 73, 74-5m; Uluru, 100, 108; Yirrkala, 53
land rights, Aboriginal: acceptance of, 1, 2; granting of, 23, 24; legislation (state), 144-6
Lang, J. D., 16
Lapradelle, P. de, 21
Lardil, 20
Larrakeya people, 17
Lebren, *see* Deliverance Island
Lee, R., 19
Leichhardt, L., 64

leprosy, 60
Lester, G. S., 6
Liberal Party: and Aboriginal land rights, 1
Liddle, William, 92
Liyagawumirr people, 54
London Missionary Society, 117, 127
Loritja (Kutkatjarra) territory, 99
Lowie, R. H., 9, 10
Lunggutja people, 58
Luritja frontier, 109-13; boundaries north, 109; land tenure systems on, 113
Luritja people, 26, 27, 83-113; affiliations, 98, 113; ancestral beings, 102; at Angas Downs Station, 92; boundaries of territory, 100; definition of, 111; distribution of, 113
Lyndavale Station, N.T., 93

Macassans, 28, 37
McGee, W. J., 7-9
Macgillivray, John, 128
McKinlay, J., 64
MacKnight, C. C., 37
McLelland, M. H., 146
McNamara, William, 92
Madarrpa ritual group, 41
Maidi district (Maydh), 125
Mälarra people, 51-2, 54, 57
Malbangka, Tralgett, 97
Maliyarra (young native cats), 102
Maluigal people, 27, 115, 118m; affiliations, 129; claims, 129-30; clan boundaries, 118m, 124-7, 129; clans, 124; fishing rights, 130; identity, 123-4; relocation, 126, 127; rights in the seas, 129; territorial rights, 127-9; totems, 118m, 124
Maluigal territory, 119-24; boundaries, 120-1m, 123; clan territories, 124; description of, 120-1m, 123; marine boundaries, 123, 125, 126
Malunga, 99, 101m
Mamakun, 58
Mandjikay people, 40
Mangala people, 17
Mangarray (Mangari) people, 70-1

Mangarray territory, 61, 64, 80-1m
Manharrngu territory boundary, 46-8
Mantiyupwi people: clan boundary, 45; territory boundary, 48-9
Manupula people, 36
Maori, 11
Maranboy tin field, N.T., 66-7
maritime boundaries: Aboriginal, 12-13, 55, 125-6; Torres Strait Islander, 123, 125
Marle Islet (Marrte), 115, 118m
Marquesas, 11-12
Marrte, *see* Marle Islet
Matutjarra people, 84, 89, 90, 94, 98, 99, 100, 101m, 102, 107, 108, 110m, 112, 113
Maurice, M., 177
Maydh people, 119-21, 125; boundary, 118m, 127; moiety, 125; territory, 118m, 125
Melville Island, N.T., 30; Aboriginal territories, 28, 56m; boundary delineation, 43, 46, 48-9, 56m; buffalo shooters, 38; environment, 30, 32; marine areas held in common, 55, 56m; non-Aboriginal contact, 38; pearl shell, 38; people, 36
Memmot, P., 20
Mer, *see* Murray Island
Merlan, F., 69, 71
Messel, H., 29
Mgangele people, 17
Middle Range, N.T., 86
Middleton Ponds Station, N.T., 85m, 88m, 93
Mildjingi territory boundary, 46-8
Milingimbi Island, N.T.: deceased estate, 54, 58; Macassan sites, 37; rights of access, 54, 57; ritual cycles, 40; shared access routes, 57; Yolngu focus, 37
Milirrpum people, 53
Minghi, J., 22
Minytjukuna (cave), N.T., 95m, 102
Miriam Mer language, 114
Mitukatjirra, 107
Mollah, W. S., 61, 64
Moore, D. R., 114, 128
Morris, Aba, 105

Mount Cavenagh Station, N.T., 93
Mount Quinn Station, N.T., 93
Mounted Police, 87
Mountford, C. P., 36, 48
Mualgal people, 120-1m, 123-4
mud crab gathering, 34
Mudburra people, 138
Mulgrave Island (Badu), 116m, 117
Multupanga (Mirini Jack), 104
Mulwala, Vic., 18; cartographic evidence of Aboriginal boundary, 18
Munupi territory boundary, 48-9, 56m
Munupula people, 55, 56m
Muralag, *see* Prince of Wales Island
Muralag Tribal Torres Strait Islander Corporation, 26
Murngin, 35
Murray Island (Mer), 115-16, 117, 127; fishing rights, 127-8; territorial claim, 130
Murrungga Island, N.T., 52, 57
Myers, F. R., 100, 106, 108, 109, 131

named localities, 41-2, 44m, 73, 97, 103
Nanga, 99, 101m
New South Wales: Aboriginal land holdings, 141t
New Zealand: aboriginal territories in, 11
Ngalakan people, 71
Ngalia people, 98
Ngalkbon people, 71
Ngarinyin people, 145
Ngaz, *see* Ngie Reef
Ngie Reef (Ngaz), 118m, 123
Ngulinya, 107
Ngurruwulu people, 57
Nicholson, N. L., 23
Nietschmann, B, 115
Norman Ross Mandjal-walkwalk (Wadjak), 78
Northern Land Council, 2-3, 70, 77
Northern Territory: Aboriginal land holdings, 141t; claims to coastal waters, 146; cartographic evidence of Aboriginal boundaries, 16-17, 19; heritage legislation, 24, 142, 144; land claims, 142, 144; land rights legislation, 24;

pastoral stations, 88m, 89-90, 93; political control of, 86; settlements, 88m
Northern Territory Department of Mines and Energy, 64
Nurupai, 114, 116m
Nygina people, 17

Oenpelli, N.T., 70
O'Grady, G. N., 19
Ona, 9-10
opium, 60, 68, 69
Overland Telegraph Line: as a base for exploration, 87; construction of, 60, 86; impact on Aborigines, 69, 70, 86-7; stations, 86
Owbait, see Aubait

Paatlirmiut, 6-7
Palmer, A., 71
Palmerston, N.T., 64, 88m
Palpirrwarra, 99, 101m
Panai people, 119-21, 124, 125; boundary, 118m, 127; totem, 126
Pantu (Lake Amadeus), 99, 100, 101m
Parerultja, Helmut, 99, 100, 102; and Watarrka ceremony, 105; body painting, 102-3; on ownership of sites, 105
Parker, L. S., 6, 7, 12, 23
Parkhouse, T. A., 17
Passage Island (Bupu), 118m, 125
pastoral stations in N.T., 65, 69, 70, 77, 88m, 89-90, 93
patrilineage, 35, 51
Payuainin Arrigal, see Basilisk Banks
Pearce, H., 92
Perry, T. M., 23
Peterson, N., 16, 19-20, 39, 53
Phillip, Arthur, 146
Piki, 99, 101m
Pilling, A. R., 19
Pine Creek, N.T., 60, 88m; gold discovery, 65, 68; land claims, 74-5m; mining, 60, 63m, 65, 66-7, 68, 69; pastoral leases, 62-3m; 'Wulwulam territory, 78
Pintubi people, 84, 100, 108, 112
Pitjantjatjara people: and doggers, 93; eastward movement, 94; expansionism, 112; extent of land, 141; Lake Amadeus Luritja Land Claim, 83-4; numbers in Central Reserve (1936), 93
political geographers: boundary research methods, 25-7
Portlock Island (Kubli), 120-1m, 123
Possession Island (Yaim), 120-1m, 123
Post, L. van der, 14, 15
Powell, A., 16
pre-European contacts, 37-8
Prescott, J. R. V., 21, 22, 49
Prince of Wales Island (Muralag), 114, 116m, 117; Australian Board of Missions on, 119; Barbara Thompson on, 128; London Missionary Society on, 117
Puli Wima (Bald Hill), N.T., 104
Puyulutu, see Tent Hill

Quecha language, 10
Queensland: Aboriginal land holdings, 141t
Queensland Government, 119

Raggett, Brown, 105
railway construction, 68, 69
Rattlesnake (ship), 117, 119, 128
Ratzel, F., 20-1
Ray, D. J., 6, 114
Rembarrnga people, 71
Report to Senate Select Committee on the Administration of Aboriginal Affairs 1989, 139
Resource Assessment Commission, 3, 60, 77, 79, 82, 131, 143
resource development decisions, Aboriginal involvement, 143-4
Reynolds, H., 23
rights in common, 55, 57
rights of access, 53-8
ritual cycles, 40, 98, 103, 132, 134; see also Kuningga native cat ritual cycle
ritual emblems and paraphernalia, 1, 102, 104, 105, 132, 142
ritual groups, 39; Ma<u>d</u>arrpa, 41; Mandjikay, 40
Rivers, W. H. R., 124-5
Robinson, George, 18
Roper River, N.T., 64, 70
Roper River Aborigines, 2

Rose, F. G. G., 92
Rosengren, N., 45
Ross, J., 35
Rowe, J. H., 10, 11
Rumley, D., 22
Rumsey, A., 71
Running Waters, N.T., 88m, 90

Sack, R. D., 131-2
San, 14-15
Schebeck, B., 35
Schofield, R., 22
sea rights, 12, 24; in Northern Territory, 12
Seaman, P., 144, 145
Seri Indians, 7-9, 8m
Shark Bay, Melville Island, 55-7
shellfish gathering, 33, 35, 50
Sims, N. A., 13
Singe, J., 117
Sipi Ngur people, 118m, 119-121, 122, 125, 126; boundaries, 118m, 127; territory, 126
Snake Bay, Melville Island, 48
Snow, D. R., 5, 6
song cycles, 73, 97, 99, 103, 134, song line, *see* dreaming tracks
South Alligator River, 60, 64, 74-5m; Jawoyn presence, 62-3m, 79; land claims in, 71, 73, 74-5m; mineral discoveries, 61, 69; pastoral interests in, 62-3m; sacred sites, 76
South Australia: Aboriginal land holdings, 141t
South Sea Islanders, 117
Southern Paiute, 4-5
Speck, F. G., 6
Spencer, W. B., 17, 97
Springvale Station, N.T., 65, 69
Stanner, W. E. H., 17, 19, 69, 70, 111
Steenhoven, G. van den, 6
Stewart, D. G., 77, 82, 143, 144
Stokes, J. Lort, 115
Strehlow, T. G. H., 18, 19, 89, 90, 93, 97, 98, 109
Stuart, J. McD., 64, 86
succession, 45, 51-2, 61, 73, 77-8, 79, 146
Sutton, P., 71
Swan River Colony, 146

Tasmania: Aboriginal land holdings, 141t
Tatunma, 99, 101m
Taylor, J., 14, 15
Taylor, J. C., 20
Tehuelche, 10
Tempe Downs Station, N.T., 88m, 89-90, 101m, 110m
Tennant Creek, N.T., 88m, 133
Tent Hill (Puyulutu), 99
terra nullius, 146
territoriality, 71, 73, 76, 113, 131-5; markers of, 132
territory: boundary definition, 2, 45-50, 134; changes in extent of, 135; demarcation of, 10, 56m; description of, 80-1m, 133; in the arid zone, 61; in the humid zone, 61; knowledge of, 58-9, 105-6, 142; limits of, 1-27, (in other countries, 3-16, 132); nature of boundaries, 100, 133-4; primary rights to, 134; proof of rights to, 102-9; size of, 133; sub-territory, 135; subsidiary rights to, 105, 134-5
Thompson, Barbara, 117, 119, 128, 129
Thonemann, H. E., 69
Thursday Island, 114, 116m
Tickner, Robert, 136
Tikalaru clan boundary, 45
Tiklauila people, 36
Tindale, N. B., 18-19, 73, 76, 78, 93, 98, 112, 135
Tiwi Land Council, 44, 50
Tiwi people: ancestral beings, 48; boundaries, 44-5, 46, 48, 109; British contact, 38; clans, 36; Macassan contact, 29, 38; marine boundary delineation, 26; seasonal movement, 33-5; territoriality, 30, 58-9; territories, 39; use of resources, 33-5
Tjatjiti (resident native cat), 102, 108-9
Tjungkuba, 99, 101m
Tobin Island (Zagasup), 120-1m, 123
Toohey, J., 68, 70, 100, 108
Torres, Luis Baez de, 115
Torres Strait: cultivation of crops,

127; environment, 114-15; European contact, 115, 117, 119; intermarriage with South Sea Islanders, 117; map of, 116m; missions, 117; pearling, 117; people, 114, (customs, 117, 119), (first recording of customs, 115, 117), (migration to Queensland, 119), (place names, 122); territorial rights, 127; western, 120-1m

Torres Strait Islander Act 1939, 119

Torres Strait Treaty, 129, 130

Travers and Sergison syndicate, 64

tribes: boundaries of, 132; identity, 132, 133; links with other groups, 133; maps of, 18-19

Turnagain Island (Burru), 116m, 122, 120-1m, 123

turtle hunting, 34, 50, 115

Ulpinyali, 99, 101m

Uluru Land Claim, 100, 108

Upper South Alliator Valley, 71, 73; Bula Complex, 76; registration of sacred sites, 77

Vachon, D., 113

Victoria: Aboriginal land holdings, 141t

Waanyi people, 138, 139

Wabanaki, 5-6

Wadaman territory, 71, 79

Wagaitj people, 17

Wagaman territory, 61, 71, 78, 79, 80-1m

Wagedagam people, 119-21, 124-5; boundary, 118m, 127; name, 127

Wagu, Mick, 104, 105

Waiben, 114, 116m

Walamangu people, 40, 57

Walker, A. T., 35

Walki Spring, George Gill Range, N.T., 97

Wallace, Abraham, 65

Walpiri people, 61, 138; Lake Amadeus Luritja Land Claim, 84

Walpiri territory, 61, 98, 108

Wandarang people, 138

Wangkungurru people, 139

Wangurri people, 36, 37, 40

Wanmarra, 99, 101m

Wantuparri (ceremonial leader), 102, 103

Warburton, P. E., 87

Wardaman people, 138

Warner, W. L., 35, 38-9, 43

Warrawarra people, 41

Warray, 17, 80-1m

Wat:a people, 73, 78, 79, 80-1m

Watarrka people, 96, 97, 98, 99, 104-5, 107

Watarrka site, 103, 104-5, 109; ownership, 105

Watarrka sub-territory, 94, 95, 97, 98, 104; boundaries, 99-102, 101m, 107; ceremonial ground, 102, 103-4; dreaming track, 94-6, 97, 99, 102-3, 104, 107; knowledge of, 106

Watarrka Waterhole, N.T., 100: and Kuningga, 107; creation of, 102; design, 102; name, 104

Wedul, *see* Widul Island

Weeni (Wini), 128, 129

Wellesley Islands, Gulf of Carpentaria, 20

Western Arranda people, 84, 96, 98; boundaries and relationship with adjacent peoples, 109, 110m, 112

Western Arranda territory, 99

Western Australia: Aboriginal land holdings, 141t

Western Desert, Central Australia: territoriality, 83

Western Desert people, 83; boundaries, 100, 102, 111; conflict with Arranda people, 112-13; dreaming tracks, 108; social system, 95, 113

Wickham, J. C., 115

Widul Island (Wedul), 115, 118m

Wilirangkuwila people, 55, 56m

Wilkin, A., 122, 126, 127, 128

Williams; N. M., 35, 42, 51, 58, 111

Willshire, W. H., 90

Wiputa, N.T., 96, 99, 107

Wood, R. K., 35

Woolen River, N.T., 47m; claim, 146

Woomera Rocket Range, N.T., 94

Worora people, 145

Wubulkarra people, 40
Wulanba cultural bloc, 35
Wulnaminitja people, 17, 80-1m, 138
'Wulwulam people, 73, 78, 80-1m
'Wulwulam territory, 71, 76, 78, 79, 80-1m
Wunambul people, 145
Wurm, S.A., 19
Wurundjeri Tribe Land and Compensation Heritage Council Incorporated, 142

Yaghan, 9
Yaim, *see* Possession Island
Yam Island, 116m
Yam people, 123
Yangkunkatjarra people: expansionist tendencies, 112; frontier with Matatjarra, 110m, 113; Lake Amadeus Luritja Land Claim, 83-4, 101m, 110m
Yangkunkatjarra territory, 100
Yangman territory, 61, 64, 71, 79, 138
Yanhangu language group, 51-2, 54, 57
Yankuntjatjarra, *see* Yangkunkatjarra
Yarringku, 99, 101m
Yaruro people, 10
Yauor people, 17
Yemalgal territory, 120-1m
Yirritja people, 35, 41, 57
Yirrkala land case, 53
Yolngu people, 35-6; boundaries, 27, 109; boundary dispute, 54, 57; dialects, 35; knowledge of territory, 58-9; Macassan contact, 28, 37; seasonal movement, 33-5; seasonal resource availability, 34f; succession, 45, 51; use of resources, 33-5
Yolngu territory, 39

Zagasup, *see* Tobin Island
Zorc, R. D. P., 35